THE COMPUTER GLOSSARY

iT'S NOT JUST A glossary!™

PRENTICE-HALL, INC., Englewood Cliffs, New Jersey 07632

THE COMPUTER GLOSSARY

it's not just a glossary!™

fOR EVERYONE   by Alan Freedman

Editorial/Production Supervision: *Lynn Frankel*
Cover Design: *Alan Freedman & Irma Morrison*
Manufacturing Buyer: *Gordon Osbourne*

THIRD EDITION

This third edition of THE COMPUTER GLOSSARY FOR EVERYONE:
IT'S NOT *JUST* A GLOSSARY! is published by Prentice-Hall, Inc.
Previous editions were published by The Computer Language
Company Inc. under the ISBN 0-941878-00-7

Printed in the United States of America

10 9 8 7 6 5 4 3 2

Library of Congress Catalog Card Number 82-62626

ISBN 0-13-164483-1

Prentice-Hall International, Inc., *London*
Prentice-Hall of Australia Pty. Limited, *Sydney*
Editora Prentice-Hall do Brasil, Ltda., *Rio de Janeiro*
Prentice-Hall Canada Inc., *Toronto*
Prentice-Hall of India Private Limited, *New Delhi*
Prentice-Hall of Japan, Inc., *Tokyo*
Prentice-Hall of Southeast Asia Pte. Ltd., *Singapore*
Whitehall Books Limited, *Wellington, New Zealand*

about the author

Alan Freedman is the President of THE COMPUTER LANGUAGE COMPANY INC., an organization devoted to computer education and training for non-technical people. His COMPUTER LITERACY® seminar has helped to raise the level of technical awareness for thousands of managers in organizations like AT&T, the New York Stock Exchange, New England Telephone Company, Hershey Foods, Knight-Ridder Newspapers, McGraw-Hill, Connecticut General Life Insurance Company and The New York Times.

With over 20 years experience in every aspect of the computer world, Alan Freedman has become well known for his special ability to present complex, abstract concepts in a simple and concrete manner. He puts the whole thing into a "meaningful perspective" for the non-technical person.

THE COMPUTER GLOSSARY's unique blend of reference work and instructional format reflects Alan Freedman's years as a hands-on technical person, as well as his experience in teaching and consulting.

a note from the author

I hope you find this Glossary a valuable companion as you wade through the mysterious world of COMPUTERS. The jargon will only get worse, and yet the basic concepts behind today's technology have not really changed at all. Many sophisticated state-of-the-art HARDWARE and SOFTWARE products now in use were conceived and developed many years ago. The COMPUTER industry is just beginning to mature. If mistakes have been made along the way, it's all part of the growing-up process in a "Future Shock" world.

Just because COMPUTERS are getting smaller in size, don't underestimate their capabilities or their complexity. In the near future, no area will be untouched by them. If you invest your time in learning about these amazing devices now, you'll be able to recognize all the potential APPLICATIONS for your personal and business use.

This Glossary represents the results of over ten years of work, reducing technical COMPUTER jargon into a perspective which can be understood by everyone.

The TEXT was created on a MICROCOMPUTER using WORD PROCESSING SOFTWARE and was ELECTRONICALLY manipulated to the stage you are reading. The Glossary, which contains over 500,000 CHARACTERS of TEXT and more than 1,000 definitions, was EDITED dozens of times and copied over and over again onto a FLOPPY DISK. In the three years between the creation of the First Edition and the printing of the Third Edition, over 300 million pulses were ELECTRONICALLY transferred into and out of the COMPUTER. The Glossary was transferred from the MICROCOMPUTER by direct cable connection to the PHOTOTYPESETTER which composed the pages you are reading (minus the handwriting).

Please write to me at The Computer Language Company, and let me know your reaction to this Glossary. The feedback I've received from thousands of managers in my seminars has helped me to develop it. Your help will continue to make it better.

Good Luck.

Alan Freedman

illustrated by

Eric Jon Nones

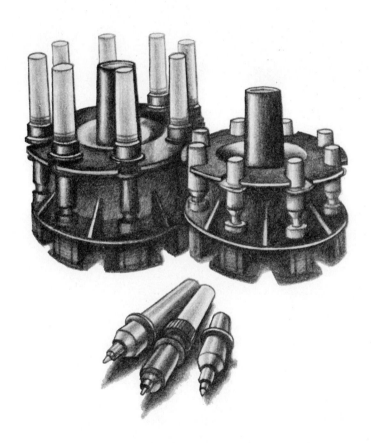

with special thanks to:

Irma Lee Morrison
Vice President
The Computer Language Company
New York, New York

acknowledgements

The author wishes to acknowledge the following professionals for their reviews, critiques and assistance with this Glossary:

EDWARD J. BIVIANO
Advisory Systems Engineer
IBM Corporation
Harrison, New York

JAGDISH R. DALAL
Director of Information Systems
Data General Corporation
Westboro, Massachusetts

HOLLY DE VAN
Division Manager
Information Systems & Technology Division
American Management Associations
New York, New York

EMILIO DEL BUSTO
Assistant Professor
Division of Business & Management
New York University
New York, New York

JAMES J. FARRELL III
Manager of Technical Communications
Motorola, Inc.
Austin, Texas

JERROLD M. GROCHOW
Vice President
American Management Systems, Inc.
Arlington, Virginia

DR. PHILIP HAYES
Research Computer Scientist
Department of Computer Science
Carnegie Mellon University
Pittsburgh, Pennsylvania

MARGARET A. HERRICK
Principal
Margann Associates
Cambridge, Massachusetts

HERBERT M. KLITZNER
Consultant
Forest Hills, New York

WALTER A. LEVY
President
Edgewood Computer Associates
New York, New York

DR. JOEL N. ORR
Chairman
Orr Associates, Inc.
Danbury, Connecticut

HOWARD J. POPOWITZ
Operations Research Analyst
CIT Financial Corporation
New York, New York

JOSEPH RUSSO
Director
Creative Quest Enterprises
New York, New York

STEPHEN SLADE
Assistant Director
Yale Artificial Intelligence Project
Yale University
New Haven, Connecticut

ELLEN W. SOKOL
Associate Director
The Diebold Group
New York, New York

IRVING L. WIESELMAN
Vice President
Dataproducts Corporation
Woodland Hills, California

ROBERT F. WILLIAMS
President
Cohasset Associates, Inc.
Chicago, Illinois

IT'S NOT JUST A GLOSSARY!
...it's a guide to "Computer Literacy"

Regular reading of this Glossary will help you keep up with the terminology, concepts and perspective necessary to get the most out of COMPUTERS and COMPUTER professionals. This Glossary has been cross-referenced as an additional help to non-technical people. Every time you see a term in capital letters (after the first sentence which is always capitalized), you know you can look up its definition elsewhere in the Glossary and expand your understanding of the subject.

If you hear a term that is not in the Glossary, it may be an acronym for a vendor's particular HARDWARE or SOFTWARE product. It may be the model name or number for a CPU, TERMINAL, OPERATING SYSTEM, PROGRAMMING LANGUAGE or DATA BASE MANAGEMENT SYSTEM. Find out what category it falls into and then look it up in the Glossary.

On the next six pages are overviews for the business manager, the student, and the first-time personal computer buyer. They will provide you with an outline to work your way through the Glossary depending on your immediate interest.

to the business manager

The MANAGEMENT SYSTEM is you and your associates setting objectives and ensuring that they are accomplished. INFORMATION SYSTEMS help you run and control your daily operation. DECISION SUPPORT SYSTEMS help you plan your operations and let you see the impact of your management decisions. COMPUTER SYSTEMS store, retrieve and PROCESS the INFORMATION you require.

Managers involved with vendors and SYSTEMS professionals should understand the SYSTEM DEVELOPMENT CYCLE, which is the series of steps that transforms INFORMATION requirements into working INFORMATION SYSTEMS. The SYSTEMS ANALYSIS & DESIGN phase must be performed slowly and carefully. The FUNCTIONAL SPECIFICATIONS, which are the design and blueprint of the INFORMATION SYSTEM, must be thoroughly understood by the USER. PROTOTYPING the new SYSTEM, if possible, can lead to a better definition of requirements. If PROTOTYPING is not possible, then once the USER has signed off on the design, the PROGRAMMING should be done as quickly as possible.

Be aware of the importance of well-designed PEOPLE/MACHINE INTERFACES, the advantages of DATA BASE MANAGEMENT SYSTEMS (for providing flexibility for future changes), and the problems with STANDARDS & COMPATIBILITY.

You ought to think about the kinds of ad hoc questions you want your SYSTEM to answer. The COMPUTER'S ability to quickly manipulate DATA into meaningful INFORMATION may provide the largest payback to management. DECISION SUPPORT tools should be considered and integrated into the INFORMATION SYSTEM design from the beginning. USER-FRIENDLY QUERY LANGUAGES, REPORT WRITERS and FINANCIAL PLANNING SYSTEMS give you hands-on capabilities.

COMPUTERS are invaluable for business, but they are not magic. Your thorough understanding of their application is essential.

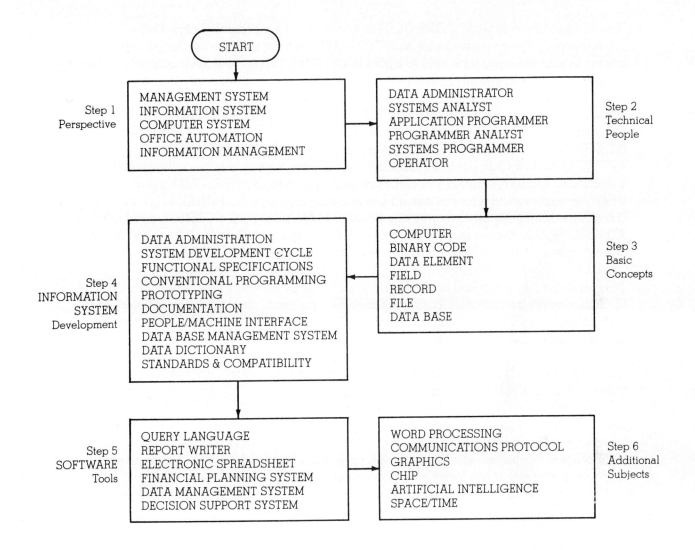

START

Step 1
Perspective

MANAGEMENT SYSTEM
INFORMATION SYSTEM
COMPUTER SYSTEM
OFFICE AUTOMATION
INFORMATION MANAGEMENT

DATA ADMINISTRATOR
SYSTEMS ANALYST
APPLICATION PROGRAMMER
PROGRAMMER ANALYST
SYSTEMS PROGRAMMER
OPERATOR

Step 2
Technical
People

Step 4
INFORMATION
SYSTEM
Development

DATA ADMINISTRATION
SYSTEM DEVELOPMENT CYCLE
FUNCTIONAL SPECIFICATIONS
CONVENTIONAL PROGRAMMING
PROTOTYPING
DOCUMENTATION
PEOPLE/MACHINE INTERFACE
DATA BASE MANAGEMENT SYSTEM
DATA DICTIONARY
STANDARDS & COMPATIBILITY

COMPUTER
BINARY CODE
DATA ELEMENT
FIELD
RECORD
FILE
DATA BASE

Step 3
Basic
Concepts

Step 5
SOFTWARE
Tools

QUERY LANGUAGE
REPORT WRITER
ELECTRONIC SPREADSHEET
FINANCIAL PLANNING SYSTEM
DATA MANAGEMENT SYSTEM
DECISION SUPPORT SYSTEM

WORD PROCESSING
COMMUNICATIONS PROTOCOL
GRAPHICS
CHIP
ARTIFICIAL INTELLIGENCE
SPACE/TIME

Step 6
Additional
Subjects

to the student

A solid foundation of basic COMPUTER concepts will be extremely helpful for understanding the myriads of new ELECTRONIC products that are coming in the future. In addition, you'll be able to apply the COMPUTER in your own unique way for solving problems in your profession.

If you're planning a career in the INFORMATION PROCESSING industry, you have many choices. You can be involved at the ELECTRONICS level as a COMPUTER DESIGNER, or as a FIELD SERVICE engineer. As a SYSTEMS ANALYST or APPLICATION PROGRAMMER you can work on problems in any kind of industry. As a SYSTEMS PROGRAMMER you can work as a technical CONSULTANT within a USER organization, or you can design and develop SYSTEM SOFTWARE for vendors. If business operations intrigue you, the fields of MANAGEMENT SCIENCE and DATA ADMINISTRATION are open to you. Sales and marketing of COMPUTER products also offer a wide variety of opportunities for people who enjoy COMPUTERS.

Take some time to learn and understand the differences between the COMPUTER SCIENCES and the INFORMATION SCIENCES. In theory, they are distinct fields, each with different objectives and disciplines. In practice, they are thoroughly intertwined and the casual observer often cannot perceive their differences.

Also, read the overview to the business manager (previous page). It will help you look at the world of COMPUTERS from a USER'S point of view.

Getting comfortable with COMPUTERS will give you an advantage in any field, whether you're a proprietor in a small business or an engineer in the most advanced technologies. No matter what your chosen profession, the COMPUTER can be used to help you perform that job faster and more accurately.

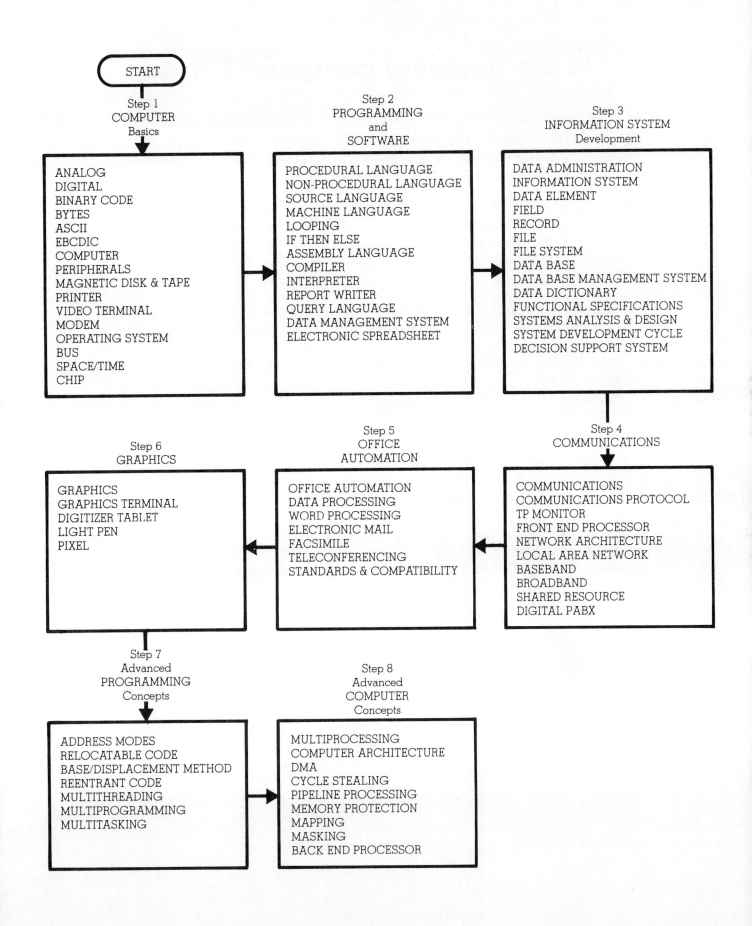

START

Step 1
COMPUTER
Basics

ANALOG
DIGITAL
BINARY CODE
BYTES
ASCII
EBCDIC
COMPUTER
PERIPHERALS
MAGNETIC DISK & TAPE
PRINTER
VIDEO TERMINAL
MODEM
OPERATING SYSTEM
BUS
SPACE/TIME
CHIP

Step 2
PROGRAMMING
and
SOFTWARE

PROCEDURAL LANGUAGE
NON-PROCEDURAL LANGUAGE
SOURCE LANGUAGE
MACHINE LANGUAGE
LOOPING
IF THEN ELSE
ASSEMBLY LANGUAGE
COMPILER
INTERPRETER
REPORT WRITER
QUERY LANGUAGE
DATA MANAGEMENT SYSTEM
ELECTRONIC SPREADSHEET

Step 3
INFORMATION SYSTEM
Development

DATA ADMINISTRATION
INFORMATION SYSTEM
DATA ELEMENT
FIELD
RECORD
FILE
FILE SYSTEM
DATA BASE
DATA BASE MANAGEMENT SYSTEM
DATA DICTIONARY
FUNCTIONAL SPECIFICATIONS
SYSTEMS ANALYSIS & DESIGN
SYSTEM DEVELOPMENT CYCLE
DECISION SUPPORT SYSTEM

Step 6
GRAPHICS

GRAPHICS
GRAPHICS TERMINAL
DIGITIZER TABLET
LIGHT PEN
PIXEL

Step 5
OFFICE
AUTOMATION

OFFICE AUTOMATION
DATA PROCESSING
WORD PROCESSING
ELECTRONIC MAIL
FACSIMILE
TELECONFERENCING
STANDARDS & COMPATIBILITY

Step 4
COMMUNICATIONS

COMMUNICATIONS
COMMUNICATIONS PROTOCOL
TP MONITOR
FRONT END PROCESSOR
NETWORK ARCHITECTURE
LOCAL AREA NETWORK
BASEBAND
BROADBAND
SHARED RESOURCE
DIGITAL PABX

Step 7
Advanced
PROGRAMMING
Concepts

ADDRESS MODES
RELOCATABLE CODE
BASE/DISPLACEMENT METHOD
REENTRANT CODE
MULTITHREADING
MULTIPROGRAMMING
MULTITASKING

Step 8
Advanced
COMPUTER
Concepts

MULTIPROCESSING
COMPUTER ARCHITECTURE
DMA
CYCLE STEALING
PIPELINE PROCESSING
MEMORY PROTECTION
MAPPING
MASKING
BACK END PROCESSOR

to the personal computer buyer

Before you purchase a PERSONAL COMPUTER you should define your needs carefully. The more specific your requirements, the better your choice will be. All COMPUTERS are not equal. A particular COMPUTER SYSTEM may be fantastic for GRAPHICS and terrible for WORD PROCESSING or vice versa.

COMPUTER SOFTWARE is not easy to evaluate, but it should be done before the HARDWARE selection is made. Every type of SOFTWARE PACKAGE has its own set of evaluation criteria. What makes one ELECTRONIC SPREADSHEET better than another has nothing to do with what makes one WORD PROCESSING PACKAGE better than another.

Once a particular COMPUTER vendor has been selected (based on the availability of SOFTWARE) the COMPUTER SYSTEM can be sized according to its DISK storage and MEMORY capacities. DISK capacity determines the maximum size of the FILES that can be stored. MEMORY capacity determines the size (and complexity) of the PROGRAMS it can run.

Remember, the moment you purchase a PERSONAL COMPUTER, you have set standards for the future. In time, your investment in SOFTWARE PACKAGES and/or your own custom-developed PROGRAMS, may be considerable. Moving your SOFTWARE to a different COMPUTER SYSTEM later on may not always be possible.

PERSONAL COMPUTER buyers should become familiar with COMPUTER fundamentals and have an understanding of the primary categories of SOFTWARE PACKAGES that are available. Most importantly, the first-time buyer should "test-drive" each prospective machine. Sit down at the TERMINAL and try your hand at a couple of SOFTWARE PACKAGES. It's not going to be any easier when you get it home.

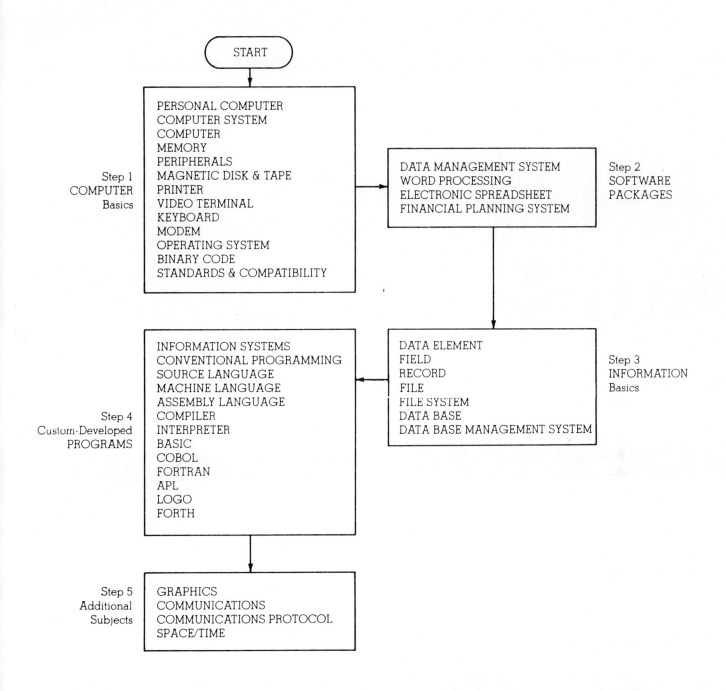

START

Step 1
COMPUTER
Basics

PERSONAL COMPUTER
COMPUTER SYSTEM
COMPUTER
MEMORY
PERIPHERALS
MAGNETIC DISK & TAPE
PRINTER
VIDEO TERMINAL
KEYBOARD
MODEM
OPERATING SYSTEM
BINARY CODE
STANDARDS & COMPATIBILITY

Step 2
SOFTWARE
PACKAGES

DATA MANAGEMENT SYSTEM
WORD PROCESSING
ELECTRONIC SPREADSHEET
FINANCIAL PLANNING SYSTEM

Step 4
Custom-Developed
PROGRAMS

INFORMATION SYSTEMS
CONVENTIONAL PROGRAMMING
SOURCE LANGUAGE
MACHINE LANGUAGE
ASSEMBLY LANGUAGE
COMPILER
INTERPRETER
BASIC
COBOL
FORTRAN
APL
LOGO
FORTH

Step 3
INFORMATION
Basics

DATA ELEMENT
FIELD
RECORD
FILE
FILE SYSTEM
DATA BASE
DATA BASE MANAGEMENT SYSTEM

Step 5
Additional
Subjects

GRAPHICS
COMMUNICATIONS
COMMUNICATIONS PROTOCOL
SPACE/TIME

abend

UNPLANNED PROGRAM TERMINATION; When the COMPUTER is directed to
EXECUTE an INSTRUCTION or PROCESS INFORMATION it cannot recognize, it
abnormally **ends** that particular PROGRAM. Small COMPUTERS, running a single
PROGRAM at a time, will often just stop; large COMPUTERS will attempt to abort just
the problem PROGRAM and keep on running the rest. This is determined by the
design of the COMPUTER and its OPERATING SYSTEM. An ABEND is also called a
CRASH or BOMB.

If you consider what goes on inside a COMPUTER, you might wonder why it doesn't
CRASH more often. Consider this: A large COMPUTER'S MEMORY can contain 288
million storage cells. Some of the cells are in a charged state, some are uncharged.
Within every second that passes, millions of these cells change their state from
uncharged to charged (and vice versa). If one of those cells is inadvertently set to the
wrong state— that's 1 out of 288 million, the entire COMPUTER could come
"crashing" to a halt! Makes you want to have another COMPUTER standing by, just in
case, doesn't it?

absolute address

PHYSICAL STORAGE ADDRESS; The ABSOLUTE ADDRESS is the actual physical
MEMORY location, storage TRACK or SECTOR, or specific PERIPHERAL device. The
COMPUTER requires an ABSOLUTE ADDRESS to reference its MEMORY or
PERIPHERAL resources. See BASE ADDRESS, RELATIVE ADDRESS and
RELOCATABLE CODE.

access

TO RETRIEVE; ACCESS usually refers to the retrieval of INFORMATION from a
DISK. However, DISKS must be ACCESSED in order to store INFORMATION, as
well. See ACCESS ARM and ACCESS METHOD.

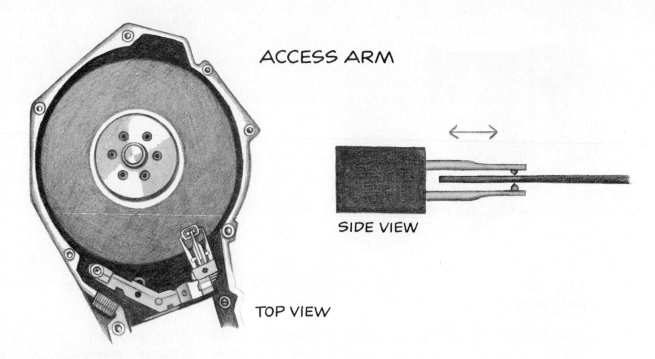

ACCESS ARM

SIDE VIEW

TOP VIEW

access arm

A MECHANICAL ARM THAT MOVES THE READ/WRITE HEAD ACROSS A DISK SURFACE; The ACCESS ARM is similar to the tone arm on a phonograph turntable. The ACCESS ARM allows DIRECT ACCESS to any TRACK on the DISK. The ACCESS ARM is directed by the INSTRUCTIONS in the PROGRAM.

access code

USER CODE FOR COMPUTER LOG-ON; An ACCESS CODE is any number or group of CHARACTERS which identifies a USER to the COMPUTER SYSTEM. The ACCESS CODE usually consists of a USER identification number and a password.

access method

AN INFORMATION STORAGE AND RETRIEVAL METHOD; ACCESS METHODS are INPUT/OUTPUT SOFTWARE for DISKS, TAPES, and COMMUNICATIONS. The ACCESS METHOD handles the transfer of INFORMATION between the PERIPHERAL device and the USER'S PROGRAM which requested the transfer. TAPE ACCESS METHODS store and retrieve INFORMATION SEQUENTIALLY on TAPE. DISK ACCESS METHODS often use INDEXES (like tables of contents) to keep track of RECORDS and FILES on the DISK (See ISAM).

COMMUNICATIONS ACCESS METHODS (such as IBM's TCAM and VTAM) transfer INFORMATION between local and remote TERMINALS and the USER'S PROGRAM. ACCESS METHODS for LOCAL AREA NETWORKS (like CSMA/CD and TOKEN PASSING) establish a PROTOCOL for connecting TERMINALS and COMPUTERS to the NETWORK.

ACCESS METHODS are part of the OPERATING SYSTEM and are called upon by the USER'S APPLICATION PROGRAM whenever INFORMATION must be transferred into or out of the COMPUTER. The ACCESS METHOD contains routines to detect and correct (if possible) any errors encountered in the transfer.

access time

MEMORY OR DISK RESPONSE TIME; MEMORY ACCESS TIME is based on the speed of MEMORY (how fast a CHARACTER in MEMORY can be transferred to or from the PROCESSOR). DISK ACCESS TIME is how fast the ACCESS ARM can position the READ/WRITE HEAD over the requested DISK surface.

ACK

COMMUNICATIONS CODE; The ACK is a specific CODE which **ack**nowledges the error-free receipt of a MESSAGE or **ack**nowledges the desire to transmit. Contrast with NAK, which is a **n**egative **ack**nowledgement.

ACM

ASSOCIATION FOR **C**OMPUTING **M**ACHINERY; Founded in 1947, over 57,000 COMPUTER professionals are members of the ACM. Their objective is to advance the arts and sciences of INFORMATION PROCESSING. In addition to special awards and publications, ACM also maintains 32 special interest groups in the COMPUTER field (called "SIGs").

ACS

ADVANCED **C**OMMUNICATION **S**ERVICE;
See AIS/NET 1000.

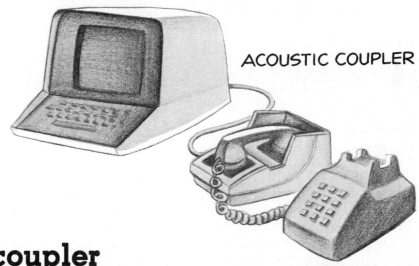

ACOUSTIC COUPLER

acoustic coupler

DEVICE THAT CONNECTS A TERMINAL TO A TELEPHONE; ACOUSTIC COUPLERS allow USERS at TERMINALS to dial-up and transfer INFORMATION to and from a COMPUTER using a standard telephone. One end of the ACOUSTIC COUPLER connects to the TERMINAL and the other end is a shaped foam bed in which the telephone HANDSET lies. The ACOUSTIC COUPLER generally contains the MODEM (necessary to convert DIGITAL pulses from the TERMINAL to AUDIO tones for telephone transmission).

A-D converter

See ANALOG TO DIGITAL CONVERTER.

Ada

HIGH-LEVEL PROGRAMMING LANGUAGE DEVELOPED AS A STANDARD FOR THE DEPARTMENT OF DEFENSE; ADA is a PASCAL-based language, but much more comprehensive than PASCAL, being designed for both commercial, SCIENTIFIC and EMBEDDED APPLICATIONS. ADA is a COMPILER language which can be COMPILED in separate segments and is noted for its MULTITASKING capabilties. ADA was named after Augusta Ada Byron (1815-1852), Countess of Lovelace and daughter of the English poet, Lord Byron.

ADABAS

DATA BASE MANAGEMENT SYSTEM; ADABAS is an example of the use of INVERTED FILE structures. INVERTED structures facilitate quick response to complex interrogations (QUERIES). ADABAS runs on IBM and DEC COMPUTERS and is a product of Software AG of North America.

ADAPSO

ASSOCIATION OF DATA PROCESSING SERVICE ORGANIZATIONS; ADAPSO members are primarily SERVICE BUREAUS which perform services such as TIME-SHARING. ADAPSO is involved in improving management methods and defining standards of performance for COMPUTER services. ADAPSO is also concerned with governmental regulations as they affect the COMPUTER services industry. ADAPSO was founded in 1960.

ADC

See ANALOG TO DIGITAL CONVERTER.

address

THE NUMBER OF A PARTICULAR MEMORY OR STORAGE LOCATION; Each MEMORY location (BYTE) has its own unique ADDRESS or number, just like a post office box. INSTRUCTIONS in a PROGRAM refer to actual MEMORY locations by their ADDRESS. An example of a MACHINE LANGUAGE INSTRUCTION: OUTPUT to the PRINTER the contents of MEMORY locations 1401 to 1532. TRACKS on a DISK are also referenced by a numeric TRACK ADDRESS.

address mode

METHOD OF ADDRESSING INFORMATION AND INSTRUCTIONS; INSTRUCTIONS in a COMPUTER can refer to ADDRESSES in several different ways. See ABSOLUTE ADDRESS, INDIRECT ADDRESS and INDEXED ADDRESS.

address register

REGISTER IN A COMPUTER WHICH HOLDS AN ADDRESS; ADDRESS REGISTERS are HARDWARE REGISTERS which hold the ADDRESS of an INSTRUCTION or INFORMATION.

address space

THE AMOUNT OF MEMORY THAT CAN BE ACCESSED; The ADDRESS SPACE defines the amount of MEMORY with which a COMPUTER can work. The ADDRESS SPACE is the maximum size of a PROGRAM that can be held in MEMORY at one time, and therefore, implies the amount of MEMORY available to a USER. In a VIRTUAL STORAGE COMPUTER, the ADDRESS SPACE refers to the total amount of MEMORY available, both in MEMORY and on the DISK.

ADF

IBM APPLICATION GENERATOR; ADF is a PROGRAMMER-oriented SYSTEM which runs under the IMS DATA BASE MANAGEMENT SYSTEM. Stands for **A**pplication **D**evelopment **F**acility.

ADP

AUTOMATIC **D**ATA **P**ROCESSING; ADP is another term for DP or EDP. ADP, Inc., is a nationwide COMPUTER SERVICES ORGANIZATION which also offers international COMMUNICATIONS services.

ADRS

IBM REPORT WRITER; ADRS stands for **A** **D**epartmental **R**eporting **S**ystem.

AI

See **A**RTIFICIAL **I**NTELLIGENCE.

AIS/NET 1000

VALUE-ADDED COMMUNICATIONS SERVICE OF AMERICAN BELL; AIS/NET 1000 is a nationwide COMMUNICATIONS NETWORK which can perform PROTOCOL conversions between many different vendors' TERMINALS and COMPUTERS. Stands for **A**dvanced **I**nformation **S**ervice/NET 1000.

ALC

IBM ASSEMBLY LANGUAGE; Stands for **A**ssembly **L**anguage **C**oding.

ALGOL

PROGRAMMING LANGUAGE DESIGNED FOR SOLVING MATHEMATICAL PROBLEMS; ALGOL is a COMPILER language and stands for **ALGO**rithmic **L**anguage. ALGOL was developed as an international language for the expression of ALGORITHMS between individuals, as well as a PROGRAMMING LANGUAGE. ALGOL was introduced in the early 1960s and gained popularity in Europe more than in the United States.

algorithm

A FORMULA FOR SOLVING A PROBLEM; An ALGORITHM is a set of steps in a very specific order, such as a mathematical formula or PROGRAM LOGIC. Except for ARTIFICIAL INTELLIGENCE APPLICATIONS, most PROGRAMS are ALGORITHMIC PROGRAMS.

alphanumeric

ALPHABETIC AND NUMERIC; See CHARACTER.

ALU

ARITHMETIC **L**OGIC **U**NIT; The ALU is the CIRCUITRY in the COMPUTER that performs the arithmetic (add, subtract, multiply, divide) functions and the compare (equal, unequal, greater than, less than) functions. DATA is copied from MEMORY into the ALU for PROCESSING. Results of arithmetic calculations are stored back into MEMORY. Results of the compare are determined by a test INSTRUCTION which follows the compare INSTRUCTION in the PROGRAM. See MACHINE LANGUAGE.

AM

TRANSMISSION METHOD; AM stands for **A**mplitude **M**ODULATION, and is a method used to transmit AUDIO and DATA signals. The AM refers to the way the signal is blended into the CARRIER. The AM method MODULATES the CARRIER by raising and lowering the amplitude (strength) of the CARRIER WAVE. Contrast with FM (FREQUENCY MODULATION).

American National Standards Institute

See ANSI.

analog

AN ANALOGOUS REPRESENTATION OF REAL-WORLD EVENTS; ANALOG devices monitor real-world conditions, such as sound, temperature, and movement and convert them into an OUTPUT which resembles the real-world activity. The hands on an ANALOG watch rotate on the center of the watch face similar to our planet rotating on its axis. The telephone is an ANALOG device since it turns voice vibrations into analogous electrical vibrations. (Note: In time, ANALOG telephones may give way to DIGITAL telephones.)

ANALOG implies *continuous* operation, contrasted with DIGITAL, which is *broken up into numbers*. For example, a television signal is an ANALOG signal. It is an ANALOG of what the television camera originally perceived. The number of shades for the colors it perceives is infinite. On the other hand, when a DIGITAL CAMERA takes a picture, it splits up shades of color into numbers. In order to equal the speed and capabilities of ANALOG methods, DIGITAL techniques have to store and PROCESS enormous amounts of numbers.

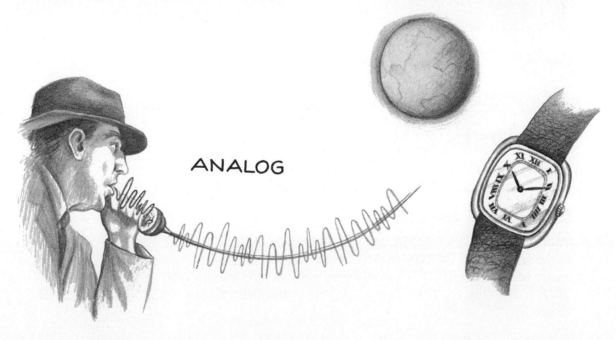

ANALOG

analog computer

COMPUTER WHICH ACCEPTS AND PROCESSES REAL-WORLD SIGNALS; INPUTS and OUTPUTS of ANALOG COMPUTERS are continuous signals, such as voltage fluctuations. Contrast with DIGITAL COMPUTER, which accepts only BINARY CODED INFORMATION. Most COMPUTERS are DIGITAL. As DIGITAL COMPUTERS get faster and less costly, they replace more functions performed by ANALOG COMPUTERS.

analog to digital converter

DEVICE THAT TURNS REAL-WORLD SIGNALS INTO DIGITAL PULSES; A-D CONVERTERS convert the continuous streams of ANALOG signals from instruments that monitor temperature, sound, air quality, etc., into DIGITAL CODES for INPUT into the COMPUTER. A DIGITAL TO ANALOG converter does the reverse conversion so that the COMPUTER OUTPUT can direct events in the real world. A-D and D-A CONVERTERS may be available on a single CHIP.

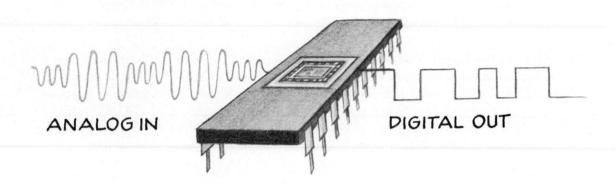

ANALOG IN   DIGITAL OUT

A-D CONVERTER

analyst

Same as SYSTEMS ANALYST.

and, or & not

PRIMARY BOOLEAN LOGICAL GATES IN DIGITAL CIRCUIT DESIGN; AND requires that both INPUTS (a AND b) be present in order to generate OUTPUT. OR requires that either INPUT (a OR b) be present to generate OUTPUT. NOT is an INVERTER— the OUTPUT is the opposite of the INPUT. See GATE and BOOLEAN SEARCH.

angstrom

UNIT OF MEASUREMENT; An ANGSTROM is approximately 1/250 millionth of an inch. ANGSTROMS are used to measure the elements in ELECTRONIC components on a CHIP.

ANSI

AMERICAN **N**ATIONAL **S**TANDARDS **I**NSTITUTE; An organization devoted to the development of American industry standards. Standards pertaining to the COMPUTER industry relate to INFORMATION and COMMUNICATIONS CODES and to PROGRAMMING and DATA MANAGEMENT languages. For example: ANSI COBOL or (ANS COBOL) is the ANSI-endorsed version of the COBOL PROGRAMMING LANGUAGE. Vendors developing ANS COBOL for their COMPUTERS must adhere to the language standards (verbs, nouns, grammar, etc.) as set forth by ANSI.

ANSI compatible

A STANDARD DEFINED BY THE AMERICAN NATIONAL STANDARDS INSTITUTE.

APL

PROGRAMMING LANGUAGE DESIGNED FOR SOLVING MATHEMATICAL PROBLEMS; APL stands for **A P**rogramming **L**anguage and was developed by Kenneth Iverson in the mid 1960s. APL is noted for its brevity and its MATRIX generation capabilities. APL is often used to develop mathematical MODELS. APL uses specific symbols for its language statements and requires a special APL KEYBOARD.

APLDI

IBM QUERY LANGUAGE; Stands for **APL D**ata Interface.

Apple II

PERSONAL COMPUTER SYSTEM; The APPLE II, introduced in 1977 by Apple Computer, Inc., was among the first MICROCOMPUTERS to be packaged as a consumer product. Its unique pop-off cover made it easy for USERS themselves to insert PRINTED CIRCUIT BOARDS. Many PLUG COMPATIBLE products were developed for the APPLE II, including CPU BOARDS. The APPLE II's PROCESSOR is a 6502; however, with the addition of a Z-80 BOARD, USERS can run both Apple and CP/M SOFTWARE (not simultaneously) in their APPLE II.

application

SPECIFIC USE FOR THE COMPUTER; Payroll, inventory, order entry and accounts receivable are examples of specific APPLICATIONS within business. The use of COMPUTERS is endless. Following are some broad APPLICATION areas:

Business— See DATA PROCESSING, WORD PROCESSING, OFFICE AUTOMATION and FINANCIAL PLANNING SYSTEM.

Engineering and design— See GRAPHICS, CAD, CADD and CAE.

Manufacturing— See CAM, NUMERICAL CONTROL, PROCESS CONTROL

Monitor and control— See HYBRID COMPUTERS and PROCESS CONTROL.

Simulation of real-world conditions— See SCIENTIFIC APPLICATIONS.

Analysis of objects— See IMAGE PROCESSING.

Education— See CAI and PLATO.

Entertainment— See VIDEOTEX and INTERACTIVE CABLE TV.

Information— See PERSONAL COMPUTER, INFORMATION UTILITY and VIDEOTEX.

application development language

PROGRAMMING LANGUAGE; An APPLICATION DEVELOPMENT LANGUAGE may refer to any CONVENTIONAL PROGRAMMING LANGUAGE. It also may refer to an extra-HIGH-LEVEL PROGRAMMING LANGUAGE, like a PROGRAM GENERATOR. APPLICATION DEVELOPMENT LANGUAGES developed around a specific DATA BASE MANAGEMENT SYSTEM provide the USER/PROGRAMMER with a language which is easier to implement than CONVENTIONAL PROGRAMMING.

application development system

INTEGRATED DEVELOPMENT SYSTEM; An APPLICATION DEVELOPMENT SYSTEM refers to series of PROGRAMS which comprise the entire PROGRAMMING and OPERATIONS environment of a COMPUTER SYSTEM. The APPLICATION DEVELOPMENT SYSTEM provides an OPERATING SYSTEM which is supported by one or more PROGRAMMING LANGUAGES. UTILITY PROGRAMS for PROGRAM development (like MEMORY DUMPS and DEBUGGING routines) are included, as well as routine DATA manipulation PROGRAMS (such as SORTS). PROGRAMS to create TEST DATA and/or standard FILES may also be part of an APPLICATION DEVELOPMENT SYSTEM. QUERY LANGUAGES and REPORT WRITERS may also be provided.

application generator

SOFTWARE THAT GENERATES A USER'S APPLICATION; An APPLICATION GENERATOR provides a HIGH-LEVEL NON-PROCEDURAL language which allows the USER/PROGRAMMER to *describe* the APPLICATION, rather than *program* the APPLICATION. APPLICATION GENERATORS may generate LINES OF CODE for an existing PROGRAMMING LANGUAGE or SYSTEM, or they may generate MACHINE LANGUAGE directly. APPLICATION GENERATOR, PROGRAM GENERATOR, DATA MANAGEMENT SYSTEM and FOURTH-GENERATION LANGUAGE are often used interchangeably.

application processor

A COMPUTER WHICH PROCESSES APPLICATION PROGRAMS; APPLICATION PROCESSOR refers to the COMPUTER that is PROCESSING DATA, in contrast with COMPUTERS which are handling control functions, such as FRONT END PROCESSORS or DATA BASE MACHINES.

application program

USER SPECIFIC PROGRAM; A DATA ENTRY PROGRAM for orders, a payroll UPDATE PROGRAM, an inventory QUERY PROGRAM and a sales REPORT PROGRAM are examples of business APPLICATION PROGRAMS. Contrast with SYSTEMS PROGRAM, such as the OPERATING SYSTEM or DATA BASE MANAGEMENT SYSTEM. APPLICATION PROGRAMS run under the control of an OPERATING SYSTEM (MASTER CONTROL PROGRAM).

application program library

COLLECTION OF APPLICATION PROGRAMS; The APPLICATION PROGRAM LIBRARY may be ON-LINE in the COMPUTER SYSTEM and available at all times, or OFF-LINE in the DATA LIBRARY.

application programmer

PROGRAMMER WHO DEVELOPS APPLICATION PROGRAMS; The majority of PROGRAMMERS are actually APPLICATION PROGRAMMERS. APPLICATION is mentioned when it is necessary to *specifically* reference this category of PROGRAMMER (as for example, for hiring purposes, or to contrast with SYSTEMS PROGRAMMER).

APT

NUMERICAL CONTROL PROGRAMMING LANGUAGE; APT is a HIGH-LEVEL PROGRAMMING LANGUAGE used to generate INSTRUCTIONS for NUMERICAL CONTROL machines. APT stands for **A**utomatic **P**rogrammed **T**ools.

architecture

See COMPUTER ARCHITECTURE and NETWORK ARCHITECTURE.

arithmetic logic unit

See ALU.

array

SERIES OF DATA IN ROW OR MATRIX FORM; An ARRAY refers to a TABLE of adjacent FIELDS in a PROGRAM, which may be viewed and PROCESSED as a single row of DATA ELEMENTS or as a series of rows and columns (MATRIX).

array processor

ARITHMETIC PROCESSOR; ARRAY PROCESSORS perform MATRIX arithmetic much faster than standard COMPUTERS. Certain mathematical problems, such as fluid dynamics or rotation of 3-D objects in COMPUTER GRAPHICS, are solved by calculations in MATRIX form. In an ARRAY PROCESSOR, DATA in MATRIX form (ARRAY form) are calculated faster since multiple operations are performed simultaneously on the DATA. TABLE LOOK-UP functions may also be performed faster in an ARRAY PROCESSOR.

The ARRAY PROCESSOR can be a stand-alone COMPUTER, or it can be connected to (or built into) an existing COMPUTER.

artificial intelligence

MACHINE INTELLIGENCE; ARTIFICIAL INTELLIGENCE (AI) refers to APPLICATIONS of the COMPUTER which, in operation, resemble human intelligence. There are different categories of uses which all fall into the AI domain. For instance, machines or ROBOTS with sensory capabilities which detect and recognize sound, pictures, textures, etc., are one category. Another category is KNOWLEDGE BASED SYSTEMS, which contain a base of knowledge about a subject and can assist us in solving a problem. KNOWLEDGE BASED SYSTEMS which have been developed from the experience of human experts are called EXPERT SYSTEMS and can perform such tasks as medical diagnoses. Eventually, KNOWLEDGE BASED SYSTEMS and EXPERT SYSTEMS will be developed to assist us in solving myriads of problems, and they will be incorporated into hand-held instruments like toys, games and appliances.

NATURAL LANGUAGE understanding and foreign language translation are also AI problems. AI will encompass many areas that have not been easily solved using traditional HARDWARE and SOFTWARE.

ARTIFICIAL INTELLIGENCE will be incorporated into 5th-generation COMPUTER SYSTEMS. By the 1990s, the average COMPUTER SYSTEM should not require USERS to remember a lot of complex CODES or COMMANDS. Rather, the USER should ask: "Can you help me with this type of problem?" The MASTER CONTROL PROGRAM (OPERATING SYSTEM) will be able to direct the USER to the appropriate EXPERT SYSTEM through a question and answer session.

AI PROGRAMMING is not magical; it does however, imply a change in rules and methods for the traditional APPLICATION PROGRAMMER. Normal APPLICATION PROGRAMS follow a fixed ALGORITHM: if this— do that. Given a set of INPUT conditions, the OUTPUT can be precisely determined. AI requires PROGRAM design with more imagination. New methods of PROGRAM organization and construction must be developed. AI PROGRAMS may require the use of HEURISTIC techniques, which are exploratory in nature and use trial and error methods. AI PROGRAMS are often PROGRAMMED in the LISP PROGRAMMING LANGUAGE, which allows the PROGRAM designer to concentrate on the problem-solving LOGIC more effectively than common languages like BASIC and COBOL.

In time, AI will probably become another abused buzzword to refer to any kind of PROGRAM that borders on USER-FRIENDLY operation. However, the "acid test" of an AI SYSTEM was defined years ago by Alan Turing (English COMPUTER pioneer): A machine has ARTIFICIAL INTELLIGENCE when there is no discernible difference between the conversation generated by the machine and that of an intelligent person.

Note: The term INTELLIGENCE by itself refers to PROCESSING capability. Therefore, every COMPUTER is "intelligent," since it can follow INSTRUCTIONS in a PROGRAM.

ASCII

STANDARD DIGITAL DATA CODE; ASCII is used extensively in MICROCOMPUTERS, MINICOMPUTERS and COMMUNICATIONS; ASCII, pronounced /as-kee/, is a 7-BIT CODE allowing 128 possible CHARACTER combinations. 32 of the 128 have been specified as control CHARACTERS for COMMUNICATIONS. ASCII is often stored in BYTES, where the 8th BIT may be used as the PARITY BIT. ASCII stands for **A**merican **S**tandard **C**ode for **I**nformation Interchange. ASCII and EBCDIC are the two major DATA CODES used in COMPUTERS.

ASM

ASSOCIATION FOR **S**YSTEMS **M**ANAGEMENT; Founded in 1947, the ASM is an international professional organization of over 9,000 SYSTEMS managers and ANALYSTS. ASM sponsors conferences in all phases of administrative SYSTEMS and management.

assembler

PROGRAM THAT TRANSLATES ASSEMBLY LANGUAGE INTO MACHINE
LANGUAGE; See ASSEMBLY LANGUAGE.

assembly language

PROGRAMMING LANGUAGE THAT LETS PROGRAMMERS WRITE THEIR
PROGRAMS AT THE MACHINE LANGUAGE LEVEL; ASSEMBLY PROGRAMMERS
must be thoroughly versed in their COMPUTER'S ARCHITECTURE and MACHINE
LANGUAGE. The ASSEMBLER PROGRAM translates each human-written
ASSEMBLY statement into the COMPUTER'S equivalent MACHINE LANGUAGE
INSTRUCTION (in BINARY). Unless well-documented, ASSEMBLY LANGUAGE
PROGRAMS can be extremely difficult to modify by another PROGRAMMER.
SYSTEM SOFTWARE (such as OPERATING SYSTEMS and DATA BASE
MANAGEMENT SYSTEMS) is usually written in ASSEMBLY LANGUAGE.

associative memory

PATTERN RECOGNITION STORAGE; ASSOCIATIVE MEMORY is similar to human
recognition. People see things by recognizing patterns. ASSOCIATIVE MEMORY
recognizes DATA by the actual patterns of the DATA itself. With this technique, there
is no need to keep track of ADDRESSES. Using specially designed CIRCUITS, the
DATA KEY is matched against all the stored KEYS at once. In essence, the
COMPUTER "sees" the DATA. ASSOCIATIVE MEMORY is a design objective for
ultra-fast ACCESS.

asynchronous communications

A CHARACTER AT A TIME; ASYNCHRONOUS COMMUNICATIONS is the
transmission and recognition of a single CHARACTER at a time. It is also called
START/STOP TRANSMISSION because each CHARACTER is treated as a unit, with a
BIT signalling the start of the CHARACTER BITS that follow, and one or more BITS
which signal the end of the CHARACTER transmitted. Contrast with SYNCHRONOUS
COMMUNICATIONS transmission whereby CHARACTERS are transmitted in groups.

ASYNCHRONOUS COMMUNICATIONS is a common method of transmission
between DUMB TERMINALS and COMPUTERS. For example, TERMINALS used with
most MINICOMPUTERS and MICROCOMPUTERS, as well as portable TIME-
SHARING TERMINALS, transmit and receive in ASYNCHRONOUS mode. Other than
PARITY checking, there is often little retransmission on error in ASYNCHRONOUS
mode. The terms ASCII PROTOCOL or TELETYPE PROTOCOL are often used to
refer to ASYNCHRONOUS COMMUNICATIONS.

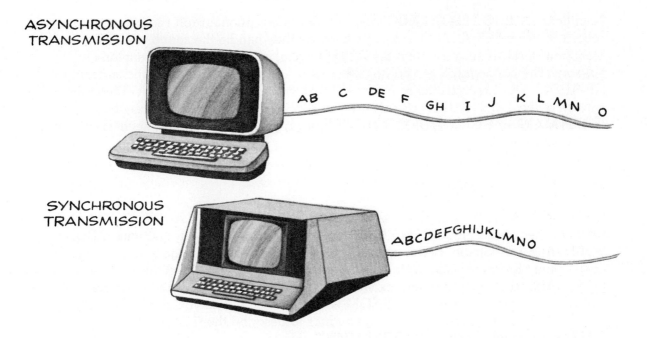

ASYNCHRONOUS
TRANSMISSION

AB C DE F GH I J K L M N O

SYNCHRONOUS
TRANSMISSION

ABCDEFGHIJKLMNO

ATM

AUTOMATIC **T**ELLER **M**ACHINE; ATMs are special-purpose banking TERMINALS which allow USERS to make deposits and withdrawals. ATMs can be stand-alone units or ON-LINE to a central COMPUTER SYSTEM. ATMs are activated by inserting a MAGNETIC CARD (cash card or credit card) in the machine which contains the USER'S identification number.

attached processor

TIGHTLY COUPLED ADDITIONAL PROCESSOR; An ATTACHED PROCESSOR is an additional CPU connected to the primary CPU in a MULTIPROCESSING environment. The ATTACHED PROCESSOR operates as an extension of the primary CPU and shares the SYSTEM SOFTWARE and PERIPHERAL devices.

attribute

Same as DATA ELEMENT.

audio

SOUND THAT CAN BE HEARD BY A HUMAN; AUDIO signal is a continuous vibration of air, generated by the human vocal cords or by a radio speaker. Although human voice is confined to a smaller range of vibrations, the maximum range the human ear can perceive is approximately from 15 to 20,000 vibrations per second (HERTZ). AUDIO vibrations, when displayed on a VIDEO SCREEN, look like rippling WAVES.

Traditional AUDIO ELECTRONIC devices, like radio, phonograph records, and tape recorders are called ANALOG devices because they handle the sound WAVES in an analogous form. Radios maintain the AUDIO signal as a vibration from antenna to speaker. The phonograph record holds the vibration carved into its plastic surface. An AUDIO TAPE records the sound WAVES as patterns of magnetic WAVES on the surface of the TAPE. AUDIO signals are PROCESSED in a COMPUTER by converting the ANALOG signal into a DIGITAL CODE using various techniques, such as PULSE CODE MODULATION.

audit software

SOFTWARE WHICH IS SPECIALIZED FOR AUDIT PURPOSES; AUDIT SOFTWARE refers to specialized PROGRAMS which perform a variety of audit functions. AUDIT SOFTWARE can sample a FILE or DATA BASE and automatically generate confirmation letters for mailing to outside customers or clients. Specialized AUDIT SOFTWARE REPORTS highlight exceptions to categories of DATA and alert the examiner to possible error. AUDIT SOFTWARE may provide a HIGH-LEVEL NON-PROCEDURAL language, allowing the auditor to describe the COMPUTER and DATA environment, without PROGRAMMING.

audit trail

RECORD OF TRANSACTIONS IN AN INFORMATION SYSTEM; AUDIT TRAILS provide a means of identification and verification of the activity of an INFORMATION SYSTEM. AUDIT TRAILS are the recording of TRANSACTIONS at various stages which can be used for tracing a SOURCE DOCUMENT through to final PROCESSING, and/or to verify the accuracy of the INFORMATION that is entered or altered. The TRANSACTION item count and the totals of numerical DATA can be used as controls.

auto dial/auto answer

AUTOMATIC TELEPHONE CONNECTION; The AUTO DIAL/AUTO ANSWER device is usually an integral part of the MODEM. Upon command of SOFTWARE, the AUTO/DIAL device opens the telephone line and dials up the telephone of the receiving COMPUTER to establish connection. The AUTO ANSWER device receives the telephone ring and accepts the call to establish connection.

automatic teller machine

See ATM.

automation

AUTOMATIC OPERATIONS; AUTOMATION usually implies the replacement of manual operations by COMPUTER SYSTEMS. OFFICE AUTOMATION refers to the integration of clerical tasks, such as typing and filing. Factory AUTOMATION refers to COMPUTER-driven assembly lines and warehouses. The term is used loosely to describe almost any task performed by machines rather than people.

auxiliary storage

EXTERNAL STORAGE IN THE COMPUTER SYSTEM; AUXILIARY STORAGE refers to storage devices, like DISK and TAPE, which are auxiliary to the COMPUTER'S MEMORY.

back end processor

Same as DATA BASE MACHINE.

background

LOWER PRIORITY PROGRAMS RUNNING IN THE COMPUTER; See
FOREGROUND/BACKGROUND.

backup

RESERVE FOR EMERGENCY; BACKUP DATA refers to an extra MACHINE
READABLE copy of a FILE or DATA BASE. BACKUP COMPUTER can refer to another
COMPUTER or COMPUTER SYSTEM that can be used if the main SYSTEM goes
DOWN. BACKUP power refers to an auxiliary SYSTEM that can be called upon if the
electrical power fails (See UPS).

Making BACKUP DISKS is a discipline that PERSONAL COMPUTER USERS *must*
learn.

backup & recovery

PROCEDURE FOR RECOVERING FROM AN OPERATIONAL FAILURE; BACKUP &
RECOVERY is a combination of manual and machine PROCEDURES which can
restore lost DATA in the event of a HARDWARE or SOFTWARE failure. BACKUP of
FILES, DATA BASES and PROGRAMS made routinely, and LOGS which keep track
of the COMPUTER'S operations are all part of a BACKUP & RECOVERY program.
See CHECKPOINT/RESTART.

BAL

IBM ASSEMBLY LANGUAGE; Stands for **BASIC ASSEMBLY LANGUAGE**.

band printer

LINE PRINTER THAT USES A BAND OF TYPE CHARACTERS AS ITS PRINTING MECHANISM; See PRINTER TECHNOLOGIES.

bandwidth

TRANSMISSION CAPACITY OF A CHANNEL; The BANDWIDTH is how much a transmission line will carry. BANDWIDTH refers to the maximum range of electrical vibrations per second that can be transmitted over an ANALOG CHANNEL. BANDWIDTH also refers to the maximum number of electrical pulses (BITS) per second that can be transmitted over a DIGITAL CHANNEL.

bar chart

GRAPHICAL REPRESENTATION OF INFORMATION; See BUSINESS GRAPHICS.

bar code

CHARACTERS CODED IN BAR FORM; The actual CODING of the BAR CODE is the width of the BAR, not the height. The extended height allows for easier recognition. See UPC (Universal Product Code).

base address

STARTING ADDRESS; The BASE ADDRESS is the location at which the beginning of a PROGRAM (or DATA) is stored. The BASE ADDRESS is added to the RELATIVE ADDRESS (from the PROGRAM) to determine the ABSOLUTE ADDRESS. See BASE/DISPLACEMENT METHOD.

baseband

CATEGORY OF COMMUNICATIONS NETWORK; BASEBAND NETWORKS are all DIGITAL NETWORKS which have a transmission BANDWIDTH of up to approximately 10 MEGABITS per second. Distances in a BASEBAND NETWORK are usually limited to within a couple of miles. BASEBAND NETWORKS use TWISTED PAIR wires or COAXIAL CABLE as the transmission medium. BASEBAND NETWORKS and BROADBAND NETWORKS are alternatives for LOCAL AREA NETWORK design. See BROADBAND.

base/displacement method

TECHNIQUE FOR RUNNING PROGRAMS IN DIFFERENT MEMORY LOCATIONS; The BASE/DISPLACEMENT method is a technique that allows a PROGRAM to be stored and EXECUTED anywhere in MEMORY. The ADDRESSES in the MACHINE LANGUAGE PROGRAM are augmented automatically by the SOFTWARE or HARDWARE at the time of EXECUTION. See BASE ADDRESS and RELOCATABLE CODE.

BASIC

PROGRAMMING LANGUAGE DESIGNED FOR SOLVING MATHEMATICAL AND BUSINESS PROBLEMS; BASIC was originally developed as an INTERACTIVE PROGRAMMING LANGUAGE for TIME-SHARING on large MAINFRAMES. BASIC is widely used on all sizes of COMPUTERS and has become extremely popular on MICROCOMPUTERS. There are many different versions of BASIC available with limited versions running on small hand-held COMPUTERS.

BASIC is available in both COMPILER and INTERPRETER form, the latter form being more popular and easier to use, especially for the first-time PROGRAMMER. In INTERPRETER form, the language is CONVERSATIONAL and can be used as a desktop calculator. In addition, it is easy to DEBUG a PROGRAM, since each LINE OF CODE can be tested one at a time.

BASIC is considered one of the easiest PROGRAMMING LANGUAGES to learn. For simple problems, BASIC PROGRAMS can be written "on the fly" at the TERMINAL. However, complex problems require PROGRAMMING technique, as in any CONVENTIONAL PROGRAMMING LANGUAGE. Since BASIC does not require a STRUCTURED PROGRAMMING approach, like PASCAL, and since there is no inherent DOCUMENTATION in the language, as in COBOL, BASIC PROGRAMS can be difficult to decipher later if the PROGRAM was not coherently designed.

BASIC was developed by John Kemeny and Thomas Kurtz in the mid 1960s at Dartmouth College, and stands for **B**eginners **A**ll-purpose **S**ymbolic **I**nstruction **C**ode.

batch

GROUP OF ITEMS; Any reference to BATCH PROGRAMS or BATCH JOBS refers to an activity involving a group of DOCUMENTS or RECORDS, rather than a single item. A BATCH PROGRAM searches or manipulates an entire group of DATA, such as a REPORT PROGRAM or SORT PROGRAM. A BATCH DATA ENTRY PROGRAM implies DATA ENTRY of a BATCH of DOCUMENTS. A REMOTE BATCH transmission refers to the sending of a bulk volume of DATA at one time.

BATCH opeations are often called OFF-LINE operations. Contrast with ON-LINE, REAL-TIME, INTERACTIVE and TRANSACTION PROCESSING.

batch processing

THE PROCESSING OF A GROUP OF TRANSACTIONS AT ONE TIME; In BATCH PROCESSING, TRANSACTIONS are collected in BATCHES and PROCESSED as a group. BATCH PROCESSING implies DATA collection and after-the-fact PROCESSING. Contrast with TRANSACTION PROCESSING, whereby a single TRANSACTION is entered and PROCESSED to completion as soon as it occurs. INFORMATION SYSTEMS are usually combinations of TRANSACTION and BATCH PROCESSING.

In an order processing INFORMATION SYSTEM, the TRANSACTION PROCESSING would be: Sales orders taken over the phone are immediately entered into a TERMINAL and checked against customer's credit and finished goods inventory. Picking lists are generated on the spot in the warehouse. After the merchandise is picked and shipped, the warehouse signals the completion of the order by entering a TRANSACTION in its TERMINAL.

The BATCH PROCESSING would be: At the end of the day, a PROGRAM scans the open orders in the SYSTEM and converts the completed orders to accounts receivable. Another PROGRAM prints the invoices. REPORTS are generated for the day's activities.

baudot code

COMMUNICATIONS CHARACTER CODE; Developed in the late 19th century by Emile Baudot, the BAUDOT CODE was one of the first standards for international telegraphy. The BAUDOT CODE uses five BITS to make up a CHARACTER.

baud (rate)

TRANSMISSION RATE OF A COMMUNICATIONS CHANNEL OR DEVICE; BAUD RATE often refers to a DIGITAL transmission speed equivalent to BITS per second. 1200 BAUD usually means 1200 BITS per second. However, BAUD RATE technically refers to the maximum physical switching speed of a COMMUNICATIONS CHANNEL. Using special transmission techniques, it is possible to transmit more BITS per second than the physical BAUD RATE of the CHANNEL. In these cases, BAUD RATE and BITS per second are not equivalent.

BCD

BINARY **C**ODED **D**ECIMAL; BCD is the storage of numbers in a COMPUTER whereby each decimal digit of the number (0 through 9) is converted into a single CHARACTER or BYTE. A 12-digit number would require 12 BYTES of storage (96 BITS). Contrast with plain BINARY whereby the entire decimal number is converted into a BINARY WORD which stores some fixed number of BITS (approx. 36 to 60). The size of the WORD determines the maximum value of the decimal number which can be manipulated. The COMPUTER can calculate the BINARY number faster than the BCD number.

BCD can also refer to PACKED DECIMAL, where two decimal digits are stored in one BYTE.

BCD may also refer to a variety of DATA CODES used on earlier COMPUTER models.

BDOS error

See READ ERROR AND WRITE ERROR.

benchmark

AN ACTUAL TEST OF HARDWARE OR SOFTWARE PERFORMANCE; A BENCHMARK serves as a comparison for evaluating the performance of different vendors' HARDWARE and/or SOFTWARE products.

beta test

FIRST INSTALLATION OF A NEW PRODUCT; A BETA TEST of HARDWARE or SOFTWARE usually implies first-time USER installations. The BETA TEST follows the TESTING that was performed by the vendor in-house. The BETA TEST is the first real live test of performance among normal USER conditions.

bidirectional printer

PRINTER THAT PRINTS FORWARD AND BACKWARD; A BIDIRECTIONAL PRINTER prints each alternate line backward instead of returning to the beginning of the line. A MEMORY BUFFER in the PRINTER holds two lines of DATA from the COMPUTER. When it finishes printing one line from left to right, it has the DATA for the next line so it can print it right to left.

binary

TWO; BINARY simply means *2*; however, it is the basis for the design of ELECTRONIC DIGITAL COMPUTERS. BINARY refers to INFORMATION or SOFTWARE in MACHINE READABLE form. See BINARY CODE and BINARY LANGUAGE.

binary chop

Same as BINARY SEARCH.

binary code

DIGITAL INFORMATION CODE; BINARY CODE is the fundamental principle behind
DIGITAL COMPUTER design. All INFORMATION (and INSTRUCTIONS) is
converted into BINARY numbers made up of the two BINARY digits *0* and *1* (BITS).
For example: When you depress the "A" key on your ASCII TERMINAL, the
TERMINAL automatically generates a one-BYTE BINARY number (01000001) which it
stores as a pattern of electric charges in its MEMORY cells (1 BIT = charge, 0 BIT =
no charge). It then transmits this BIT pattern as a pattern of electric impulses to the
COMPUTER. Each BIT is a duration of time (tiny fraction of a second). In that
duration, either a pulse of electricity or light (representing the 1 BIT) or no pulse
(representing the 0 BIT) is generated and transmitted. The COMPUTER (set at the
same pulse rate as the TERMINAL) accepts these patterns of pulses and stores them as
patterns of BITS in its MEMORY.

INFORMATION and INSTRUCTIONS on MAGNETIC TAPE & DISK are represented
as patterns of magnetic spots. We see the real CHARACTERS on our TERMINALS
and PRINTERS because these devices convert the BINARY patterns to real letters and
numbers.

The ELECTRONIC CIRCUITS that PROCESS these BINARY CODES are themselves
BINARY in concept: they are made up of on/off switches which are electrically
opened and closed. The switch itself is a TRANSISTOR. The current flowing through
one switch effects the operation of another switch, and so on. These switches open and
close in NANOSECONDS and PICOSECONDS (billionths and trillionths of a second).
The switch patterns are designed to detect and manipulate BINARY pulses according
to the rules of BOOLEAN LOGIC.

The BINARY concept is helpful for developing faster COMPUTERS. We concentrate
on improving the ELECTRONIC CIRCUITS that store and transmit the BIT. Greater
storage capacities are achieved by making the storage cell or magnetic spot smaller.
Faster transmission rates are achieved by shortening the time it takes to open or close
an ELECTRONIC switch and developing CIRCUIT paths that can handle the
increased speeds. We simply continue to refine the BINARY concept.

HOW BINARY NUMBERS WORK

BINARY numbers are not difficult. You can even have "math phobia" and still
understand how the BINARY method works in COMPUTERS.

BINARY means *2*. BINARY numbers work with only 2 digits, *0* and *1*, instead of the 10
digits, *0* thru *9*, in our decimal numbering system (decimal means *10*). One difference
between BINARY and decimal is that we have to "carry" more often in BINARY.

When you add *9* and *1* in decimal, you have a result of *0* and a carry of *1*. The *1* belongs in a new place to the left of the *0*:

$$\begin{array}{r} 9 \\ + 1 \\ \hline 10 \end{array}$$

Now follow counting to *10* by *1* in both BINARY and decimal. Note how the BINARY method has many more carries than the decimal method. In BINARY, *1* and *1* are *0* with a carry of *1*:

BINARY	decimal
0	0
+ 1	+ 1
1	1
+ 1	+ 1
10	2
+ 1	+ 1
11	3
+ 1	+ 1
100	4
+ 1	+ 1
101	5
+ 1	+ 1
110	6
+ 1	+ 1
111	7
+ 1	+ 1
1000	8
+ 1	+ 1
1001	9
+ 1	+ 1
1010	10

Study this carefully. If you have difficulty, put it down and try again (some other time). Eventually, you will get it. You'll be surprised!

BINARY is used in COMPUTERS because it is the simplest method there is for representing DATA ELECTRONICALLY. A pulse is either present or absent. It's much easier to build complicated ELECTRONIC CIRCUITS when their primary operation is just the detection of the presence or absence of current.

binary coded decimal

See BCD.

binary file

SOFTWARE IN MACHINE LANGUAGE FORM; A BINARY FILE or BINARY PROGRAM refers to a SOFTWARE PROGRAM in MACHINE LANGUAGE form which can be directly EXECUTED by the COMPUTER. A BINARY FILE is the same as OBJECT CODE.

binary search

A TECHNIQUE FOR LOCATING AN ITEM BY CONTINUOUSLY DIVIDING BY 2; The BINARY SEARCH only works on DATA that is in sequence. The KEY that is desired is compared to the DATA in the middle of the FILE or TABLE. The half that contains the DATA is then compared in the middle, and so on and so on, until the KEY is located or a small enough group is isolated that is then sequentially searched.

bionic

HUMAN-LIKE DEVICES; A BIONIC device is any device or machine which is patterned after principles found in humans or in nature. ROBOTS are BIONIC devices. BIONIC is also often used to refer to artificial devices implanted in humans and replacing or extending normal human functions.

bipolar

CATEGORY OF MICROELECTRONIC CIRCUIT DESIGN; The first TRANSISTOR and the first INTEGRATED CIRCUIT were designed using the BIPOLAR technique, which derives its name from the use of both positive and negative charges at the same time within the body of the TRANSISTOR. INTEGRATED CIRCUITS (CHIPS) employ the BIPOLAR design when fast speeds are required. The most common variety of BIPOLAR CHIP is called TTL (TRANSISTOR TRANSISTOR LOGIC). ECL (EMITTER COUPLED LOGIC) and I²L (INTEGRATED INJECTION LOGIC) are also part of the BIPOLAR family. BIPOLAR and MOS (METAL OXIDE SEMICONDUCTOR) are the two major categories of CHIP design. See CHIP.

bisync

CATEGORY OF SYNCHRONOUS COMMUNICATIONS PROTOCOLS; Stands for **binary sync**hronous.

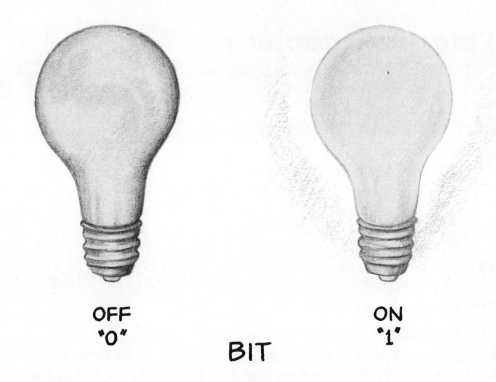

OFF
"0"

BIT

ON
"1"

bit

SMALLEST COMPONENT IN BINARY CODE; A BIT is a single BINARY digit in a
BINARY number (*0* or *1*). A BIT is physically a storage cell, a pulse, a magnetic spot, or
magnetic BUBBLE. Conceptually, a BIT can be thought of as a light bulb; either on or
off. BIT stands for **B**inary dig**IT**.

Groups of BITS make up storage units in the COMPUTER, called CHARACTERS,
BYTES, or WORDS, which are manipulated as a group. The most common storage unit
is the BYTE, which is made up of 8 BITS and is equivalent to one ALPHANUMERIC
CHARACTER. Capacities and speeds of all HARDWARE components, such as
MEMORY, DISKS, TAPES, etc., are measured and rated in BITS and BYTES. See
8-BIT/16-BIT/32-BIT COMPUTER and BINARY CODE.

bit map

AREA IN THE COMPUTER'S MEMORY RESERVED FOR GRAPHICS; The BIT MAP
holds the picture which is continuously transmitted to the VIDEO SCREEN. See
GRAPHICS (Raster Graphics).

bit mapped graphics

FULL GRAPHICS CAPABILITY; BIT MAPPED GRAPHICS refers to the RASTER GRAPHICS method for generating pictures. It implies a full GRAPHICS capability in contrast with CHARACTER GRAPHICS, which is a predefined set of GRAPHICS images. See GRAPHICS (Raster Graphics).

bit slice processor

LOGIC CHIP DESIGNED FOR CUSTOMER MODIFICATION AND INTEGRATION; BIT SLICE PROCESSORS are designed as elementary building blocks for the OEM builder. They contain very elementary CIRCUIT operations and are designed to be MICROPROGRAMMED for a specialized MACHINE LANGUAGE. BIT SLICE PROCESSORS are usually constructed to work on DATA 4 BITS at a time, but can be strung together in multiples to become larger PROCESSORS (8-BIT, 12-BIT, etc.).

black box

CONVERSION DEVICE; A BLACK BOX refers to a specialized HARDWARE device which converts one CODE into another. A BLACK BOX is a TRANSPARENT solution for interconnecting incompatible HARDWARE or SOFTWARE (it should not require changes to the HARDWARE or SOFTWARE in order to use it). BLACK BOXES are often used for PROTOCOL conversion, for example. The BLACK BOX was traditionally a customized device; however, today there are standard off-the-shelf BLACK BOXES designed to fix particular incompatibility situations.

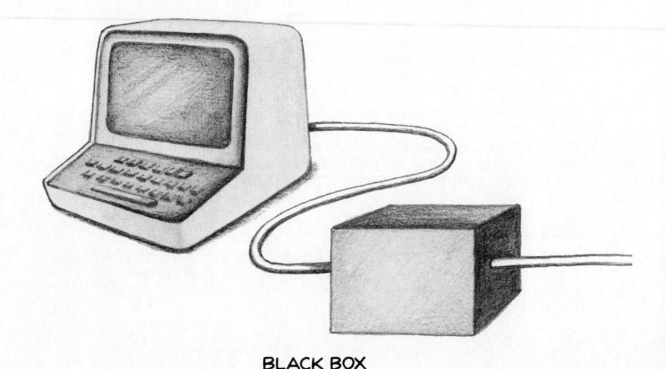

BLACK BOX

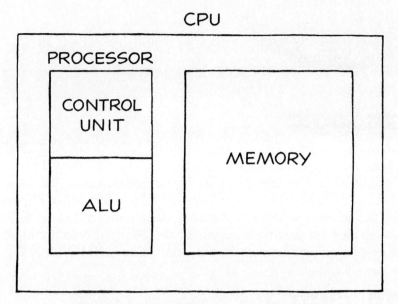

BLOCK DIAGRAM OF A CPU

block

A GROUP OF BITS, CHARACTERS OR RECORDS; On MAGNETIC TAPE & DISK, a BLOCK is a group of RECORDS stored and transferred as a single unit. In COMMUNICATIONS, a BLOCK is a contiguous group of BITS or CHARACTERS which are transmitted as a unit. BLOCK refers to a defined length of DATA.

block diagram

GENERALIZED DIAGRAM OF COMPONENTS AND INTERCONNECTIONS; Usually, BLOCK DIAGRAMS are simple squares or rectangles labeled to represent different HARDWARE or SOFTWARE components and their interconnections. PROGRAM FLOW CHARTS, INFORMATION SYSTEM FLOW CHARTS, CIRCUIT diagrams, and COMMUNICATIONS NETWORKS all have special symbols for their graphical representation.

blocking factor

THE NUMBER OF RECORDS IN A BLOCK.

board

See PRINTED CIRCUIT BOARD.

board level

IN PC BOARD FORM; A BOARD LEVEL device refers to components available on a PRINTED CIRCUIT BOARD instead of in a cabinet or finished housing. BOARD LEVEL COMPUTERS and CONTROLLERS are designed for the OEM or custom builder of COMPUTER SYSTEMS.

bomb

UNPLANNED PROGRAM TERMINATION; Same as ABEND.

Boolean logic

PRIMARY CONCEPTS IN DIGITAL COMPUTER DESIGN; DIGITAL COMPUTER CIRCUITS operate in a sequential fashion. Electrical pulses generated by the COMPUTER'S CLOCK are directed into CIRCUITS made up of LOGIC components, called GATES. The OUPUTS of the GATES are INPUTS to other GATES, and so on and so on. The rules governing the patterns of these pulses in and out of the GATES are BOOLEAN, named after the English mathematician, George Boole. In the mid 19th century, Boole developed his "mathematics of logic." See AND, OR & NOT.

Boolean search

A SEARCH FOR SELECTED INFORMATION; A request for INFORMATION that uses AND, OR and NOT conditions is called BOOLEAN. Example: Display all people in our company who have college degrees AND who speak Spanish OR French but have NOT been employed more than 5 years. A simple request may really be a BOOLEAN request: "Print every customer in district M7 who is 90 days overdue" really means: Print every customer who meets the conditions— in district M7 AND 90 days overdue! Be careful with the English words *and* and *or*, as they differ from the BOOLEAN AND and OR. If you wanted to express: "Show me everyone in departments 1 and 2" in a BOOLEAN QUERY LANGUAGE, you would have to express that statement as ORs, not ANDs. The person is not in both departments at the same time. Your expression would be something like: List Dept = 1 OR 2.

boot(strap)

INITIALIZE THE COMPUTER; The first button pressed when the COMPUTER is turned on is the BOOT or IPL (Initial Program Load) button. The BOOT causes the OPERATING SYSTEM to be LOADED into MEMORY. In some COMPUTERS, the BOOT occurs automatically after the power is turned on. Since the COMPUTER carries out its own INSTRUCTIONS, we need assistance in getting the first INSTRUCTIONS into the COMPUTER— BOOTSTRAPS help us get our boots on!

A COLD BOOT means the first BOOT after the power is turned on. A WARM BOOT means BOOTING again after the COMPUTER has been running. A WARM BOOT is often performed to reset the SYSTEM on PERSONAL COMPUTERS in order to start over because something went wrong, or as a matter of routine because of certain conditions, such as changing DISKS.

BPI

BITS **P**ER **I**NCH; BPI measures the PACKING DENSITY of BITS on a surface, such as a DISK or TAPE.

BPS

BITS **P**ER **S**ECOND OR **B**YTES **P**ER **S**ECOND; BPS measures the speed of INFORMATION transfer.

branch

GOTO INSTRUCTION; A BRANCH is another name for a GOTO INSTRUCTION.

broadband

CATEGORY OF COMMUNICATIONS NETWORK; BROADBAND NETWORKS are a BUS type of COMMUNICATIONS NETWORK (all devices connect to a common line) using COAXIAL CABLE as the COMMUNICATIONS CHANNEL. BROADBAND is noted for its large transmission capacities and long distances. BROADBAND COMMUNICATION has been used for many years by cable TV companies and is now gaining popularity as a LOCAL AREA NETWORK. BROADBAND NETWORKS can handle all varieties of transmission, including voice, VIDEO and DATA. MODEMS are required to connect all devices to the NETWORK, since BROADBAND only transmits in ANALOG form. Both ANALOG (voice and VIDEO) and DIGITAL (DATA) signals are MODULATED onto different CARRIERS via a technique called FREQUENCY DIVISION MULTIPLEXING (FDM). BROADBAND transmission exceeds the transmission capacity and distances associated with its often rivaled BASEBAND NETWORK counterpart.

BSC

BINARY **S**YNCHRONOUS **C**OMMUNICATIONS; See BISYNC.

BTAM

IBM COMMUNICATIONS ACCESS METHOD; Stands for **B**asic **T**elecommunications **A**ccess **M**ethod. BTAM is a LOW-LEVEL PROGRAM requiring detailed COMPUTER knowledge on the part of the PROGRAMMER.

bubble

A BIT IN BUBBLE MEMORY.

bubble chart

FLOW CHART USING BUBBLE-LIKE SYMBOLS; BUBBLE CHARTS are often used to depict DATA FLOW DIAGRAMS.

bubble memory

STORAGE FOR PROGRAMS AND INFORMATION; BUBBLE MEMORY is a storage technology which combines both SEMICONDUCTOR and magnetic recording techniques to create a SOLID STATE storage device. BUBBLE MEMORY is unique. Conceptually, it's a DISK that doesn't spin. Imagine a DISK that is held still, and the BITS on the surface spin around the DISK instead. BUBBLE MEMORY units are only a couple of square inches in size, and contain a THIN FILM magnetic recording layer. The BITS, called BUBBLES because of their globular shape, are electromagnetically generated in circular strings inside this layer. In order to READ or WRITE the BUBBLES, the strings of BUBBLES are made to rotate past the equivalent of a READ/WRITE HEAD in a DISK or TAPE DRIVE.

BUBBLE MEMORY holds its content without power, like DISK and TAPE. Although more expensive, it is considerably faster than FLOPPY DISKS and many HARD DISKS. It is often used in portable TERMINALS and COMPUTERS in place of DISKS for reduced weight and DOWNTIME due to the lack of motors and mechanical activity.

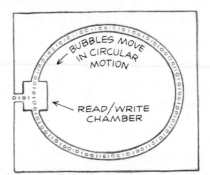

BUBBLES MOVE IN CIRCULAR MOTION

READ/WRITE CHAMBER

CONCEPTUAL PICTURE OF A
TRACK OF BUBBLE MEMORY

PORTABLE COMPUTER
WITH BUBBLE MEMORY

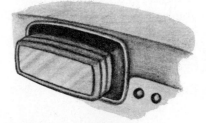

BUBBLE MEMORY
CASSETTE

bucket

A PLACE TO HOLD SOMETHING IN MEMORY; A BUCKET is a space reserved in the PROGRAM used to store something while in MEMORY. The BUCKET could accumulate numeric values or be used to store any kind of CHARACTERS. A bunch of BUCKETS could be a QUEUE to hold MESSAGES until they are PROCESSED. See COUNTER, BUFFER and PROGRAM.

buffer

STORAGE AREA WHICH TEMPORARILY HOLDS INFORMATION; BUFFERS in a PROGRAM are reserved areas which receive INFORMATION and hold it for PROCESSING. BUFFERS in COMMUNICATIONS PROGRAMS hold MESSAGES until the APPLICATION PROGRAMS can PROCESS them. BUFFERS in PERIPHERAL devices are units of MEMORY reserved for holding INFORMATION transmitted from the COMPUTER. For example: A PRINTER containing a BUFFER allows INFORMATION to be transmitted from the COMPUTER at high speed, while the PRINTER prints from the BUFFER at slow printing speeds. A BIDIRECTIONAL PRINTER has a BUFFER which holds two lines of CHARACTERS, so that it has the next line for printing backward. A KEYBOARD BUFFER allows the USER to type faster than the PROGRAM can accept the INPUT. See PROGRAM.

bug

AN ERROR IN SOFTWARE OR HARDWARE; PROGRAM BUGS can refer to errors or problems with PROGRAMS that don't work at all, or that are running but occasionally don't work right. The BUG could be the result of invalid PROGRAM LOGIC or the improper use of PROGRAMMING LANGUAGE statements. HARDWARE BUGS are improperly designed components; for example, a BUG in a CHIP is an invalid design of a CIRCUIT. A BUG usually refers to something that is incorrectly structured. A "GLITCH" usually refers to something that has temporarily gone wrong, like an intermittent HARDWARE failure.

bundled/unbundled

HARDWARE/SOFTWARE COMPONENTS PRICED TOGETHER/SEPARATELY; A BUNDLED SYSTEM implies one price for a combination of HARDWARE and/or SOFTWARE components. UNBUNDLED SYSTEMS have separate prices for each component.

bus

COMMON PATHWAY (CHANNEL) BETWEEN HARDWARE DEVICES; A BUS may refer to a common internal pathway between components in a COMPUTER, or it may refer to a COMMUNICATIONS NETWORK which uses a common CHANNEL (cable, wire, etc.) between all TERMINALS and COMPUTERS.

When BUS architecture is used in a COMPUTER, the PROCESSOR(S), MEMORY BANK(S), and PERIPHERAL CONTROL UNITS are all interconnected via one or more common BUSES.

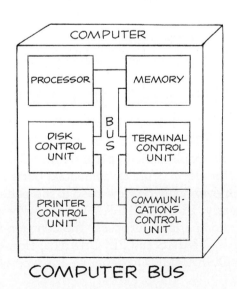

COMPUTER BUS

Typically, two BUSES are used, one called the ADDRESS BUS, the other called the DATA BUS. The ADDRESS BUS is used to select where DATA is located, and the DATA BUS is used to transfer the DATA. In a MICROCOMPUTER, the MOTHERBOARD contains the BUS which interconnects the PRINTED CIRCUIT BOARDS.

BUS COMMUNICATIONS NETWORKS imply a common pathway between all devices, rather than each TERMINAL or HARDWARE device connected to a central switch. BASEBAND and BROADBAND LOCAL AREA NETWORKS are BUS-type COMMUNICATIONS NETWORKS. See SHARED RESOURCE.

business analyst

BUSINESS SYSTEMS ANALYST; A BUSINESS ANALYST analyzes the operations of a department or functional unit with the purpose of developing a general SYSTEMS solution to the problem which may or may not require AUTOMATION. Solutions are primarily changes in operational PROCEDURES, including reallocation of human and machine resources. While a new or revised INFORMATION SYSTEM may be the solution to the problem, that is not the major thrust. The BUSINESS ANALYST can provide valuable insights into an operation for an INFORMATION SYSTEMS ANALYST.

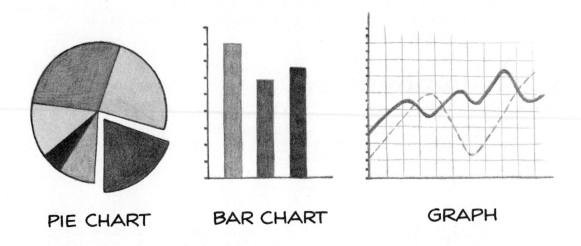

PIE CHART   BAR CHART   GRAPH

business graphics

TRANSLATION OF INFORMATON INTO GRAPHS AND CHARTS; When DATA/INFORMATION is charted in visual form, it can be assimilated faster by people, since people think in picture form. DATA relationships that can be easily spotted in picture form could go unnoticed buried between rows and columns of numbers. People can eventually become used to the patterns of their DATA and "see" it faster and more clearly. BUSINESS GRAPHICS can be printed on clear acetates which can be overlaid for comparison purposes. The common forms of BUSINESS GRAPHICS are GRAPHS, BAR CHARTS and PIE CHARTS. However, COMPUTER GRAPHICS can be PROGRAMMED to generate any type of image to represent DATA/INFORMATION.

byte

STORAGE UNIT EQUIVALENT TO A CHARACTER OF INFORMATION; A BYTE is a common unit of storage in a COMPUTER SYSTEM and is synonymous with a CHARACTER of DATA or TEXT. For example: 100,000 BYTES is the same as 100,000 CHARACTERS. BYTES can refer to the sizes of HARDWARE, SOFTWARE or INFORMATION. For example: A 1,000,000 BYTE DISK holds 1,000,000 BYTES of DATA. A 25,000 BYTE PROGRAM takes up 25,000 BYTES of storage. A 500,000 BYTE DATA BASE takes 500,000 BYTES of storage. BYTES are made up of 8 BITS. See BINARY CODE.

B5900

MAINFRAME SERIES MANUFACTURED BY BURROUGHS CORPORATION; Burroughs COMPUTER SYSTEMS are prefixed with a B, such as the B7900, etc.

C

HIGH-LEVEL STRUCTURED PROGRAMMING LANGUAGE DEVELOPED BY BELL LABORATORIES; C is a COMPILER language which is noted for its ability to handle conditions that normally would have to be written in an ASSEMBLY LANGUAGE. The UNIX OPERATING SYSTEM is written in C.

cabletext

VIDEOTEX SERVICE USING COAXIAL CABLE; See VIDEOTEX.

cache memory

EXTREMELY FAST MEMORY USED FOR TRANSFERS OF INFORMATION; CACHE MEMORY is used in CPUs for certain extra-high-speed functions.

CAD

COMPUTER AIDED DESIGN; CAD SYSTEMS are used to design myriads of consumer and industrial products, from a machine part to an interior design to an airplane. CAD SOFTWARE is specialized for the particular class of product designed, such as architectural, electrical or mechanical. CAD SOFTWARE PACKAGES are also specialized for specific products such as PRINTED CIRCUIT BOARD design and INTEGRATED CIRCUIT (CHIP) design. CAD SYSTEMS are often TURNKEY SYSTEMS developed by vendors who may develop or integrate SOFTWARE into standard or optimized HARDWARE. Except in certain cases, CAD SYSTEMS rely extensively on GRAPHICS. See CADD and CAE.

CAD/CAM

INTEGRATION OF DESIGN AND MANUFACTURING; CAD/CAM SYSTEMS imply that the products designed in the CAD SYSTEM are direct INPUT to the CAM SYSTEM. An example of CAD/CAM is a machine part designed in a CAD SYSTEM, which, after design, becomes direct INPUT to a NUMERICAL CONTROL PROGRAMMING LANGUAGE (which then generates the MACHINE INSTRUCTIONS to control the fabrication of the part).

CADD

COMPUTER AIDED DESIGN AND DRAFTING; CADD SYSTEMS are CAD SYSTEMS with additional features for the drafting function, such as dimensioning (size annotations on standard engineering drawings) as well as TEXT (description and notes) entry.

CAE

COMPUTER AIDED ENGINEERING; CAE SYSTEMS analyze designs (which may have been created in CAD SYSTEMS) which have been entered into the COMPUTER SYSTEM. Different kinds of engineering analyses can be performed, such as structural analysis and ELECTRONIC CIRCUIT analysis.

CAI

COMPUTER ASSISTED INSTRUCTION; CAI APPLICATIONS are designed for teaching all varieties of subjects to young and old alike. Any combination of GRAPHICS, VOICE RESPONSE, and TOUCH-SENSITIVE SCREENS may be used to enhance the INTERACTIVE dialogue between student and machine. CAI takes many forms, from hand-held devices that are used for exercises in spelling, reading, and mathematics to sophisticated COURSEWARE developed for PERSONAL COMPUTERS.

COMPUTERS have infinite patience with a student, and as a result, make excellent teachers. In addition, the COMPUTER can tailor the curriculum to the student's ability to absorb the material. In the future, CAI, combined with ARTIFICIAL INTELLIGENCE techniques, will prove to be an effective educational assistant for our teachers.

CAM

COMPUTER AIDED MANUFACTURING; CAM is an extensive category of automated manufacturing SYSTEMS and techniques, including NUMERICAL CONTROL, PROCESS CONTROL, ROBOTICS and materials requirements planning (MRP).

canned program

OFF-THE-SHELF PROGRAM; CANNED PROGRAMS imply a fixed solution to a problem and may also imply that little or no modifications can be made. Synonymous with SOFTWARE PACKAGE.

capacitor

ELECTRONIC COMPONENT THAT STORES A CHARGE; CAPACITORS are available as DISCRETE COMPONENTS and are also built into CHIPS. CAPACITORS are used for a wide variety of electrical storage functions, such as power supplies and cells in DYNAMIC MEMORIES.

CAR

COMPUTER ASSISTED RETRIEVAL SYSTEM; CAR SYSTEMS refer to TEXT DOCUMENTS or DATA RECORDS stored on paper or on MICROFORM which use the COMPUTER to keep track of them. The COMPUTER maintains an INDEX of the stored items and is used to derive the location of a requested item. The USER must manually retrieve the item from the location indicated by the COMPUTER, which may be on a shelf, in a bin, or on a particular MICROFORM.

card

See PRINTED CIRCUIT BOARD, MAGNETIC CARD and PUNCHED CARD.

card punch

PERIPHERAL OUTPUT DEVICE; The CARD PUNCH punches holes into a deck of PUNCHED CARDS by receiving OUTPUT from the COMPUTER. CARDS are punched at a rate of approximately 100 to 300 CARDS per minute. A CARD PUNCH may also refer to a KEYPUNCH MACHINE.

card reader

PERIPHERAL INPUT DEVICE; The CARD READER READS a deck of PUNCHED CARDS into the COMPUTER. The PUNCHED CARD CODE is detected by patterns of light streaming through the holes in the PUNCHED CARD. PUNCHED CARDS are READ at a rate of approximately 500 to 2,000 CARDS per minute. A CARD READER may also refer to a MAGNETIC CARD READER.

carriage return

TYPEWRITER RETURN KEY; The CARRIAGE RETURN causes the carriage, type ball, or DAISY WHEEL to return to the left margin of the next line. The CARRIAGE RETURN is called the RETURN KEY on a TERMINAL KEYBOARD.

carrier

UNIQUE TRANSMISSION SIGNAL; The CARRIER method is the technique which allows TV, radio, telephone, and DIGITAL DATA to be transmitted over the air. It also allows for the transmission of several of these kinds of signals simultaneously over a single COMMUNICATIONS CHANNEL, such as a COAXIAL CABLE. Essentially, a CARRIER is a uniform vibration which is used to establish recognition between sender and receiver. Each CARRIER is a uniquely assigned FREQUENCY range. For example, each radio and TV station has an assigned CARRIER which will not interfere with any others in the proximity. COMMUNICATION SATELLITES use CARRIERS which are different from radio, TV, etc.

The DATA or voice (or TV or radio program) signal is MODULATED onto the CARRIER for transmission. (DIGITAL DATA is MODULATED into ANALOG form for transmission via this method.) The receiving device locks-in to a particular FREQUENCY and proceeds to filter out the CARRIER to obtain the original signal. This process is called DEMODULATION, and is accomplished by the TV, AM or FM tuner, or COMMUNICATIONS MODEM.

When multiple CARRIERS are transmitted over a physical COMMUNICATIONS CHANNEL (cable, wire, etc.), the process is called FREQUENCY DIVISION MULTIPLEXING (FDM). This is used extensively in the telephone SYSTEM, as well as in BROADBAND NETWORKS.

cartridge

REMOVABLE TAPE, HARD DISK OR CHIP MODULE; See DISK CARTRIDGE.

TAPE CARTRIDGE

TAPE CASSETTE

cassette (tape)

SELF-CONTAINED UNIT OF REEL-TO-REEL TAPE; CASSETTE TAPE is used for the storage of PROGRAMS and INFORMATION for COMPUTERS. Standard AUDIO CASSETTE TAPE recorders may be used by PERSONAL COMPUTERS in which the BINARY CODE is stored as a series of AUDIO tones. The TAPE CONTROL UNIT in the PERSONAL COMPUTER handles the DIGITAL TO ANALOG and ANALOG TO DIGITAL conversions. DIGITAL CASSETTE TAPE units are more reliable and faster than the AUDIO unit.

CATV

COMMUNITY ANTENNA TV; CATV was the original name for cable TV. A single antenna, usually placed at the highest location within the community, picks up TV signals for the residents of the community. CATV often refers to cable TV or to the types of cable used for cable TV. See INTERACTIVE CABLE TV and COAXIAL CABLE.

CBEMA

COMPUTER AND **B**USINESS **E**QUIPMENT **M**ANUFACTURERS **A**SSOCIATION;
CBEMA is a professional membership organization composed of COMPUTER vendors
and business equipment manufacturers and suppliers. Founded in 1916, CBEMA is
concerned with the development of standards for DATA PROCESSING and business
equipment, both in the United States and abroad.

CBX

COMPUTERIZED **B**RANCH **EX**CHANGE; CBX may refer to a PABX controlled by a
COMPUTER or to a DIGITAL PABX.

CCD

ELECTRONIC MEMORY; **C**HARGE **C**OUPLED **D**EVICES are a special type of MOS
(METAL OXIDE SEMICONDUCTOR) TRANSISTOR which can store patterns of charges
(BINARY CODE) in a sequential fashion. CCDs are also used in television and OPTICAL
SCANNING devices since they can be charged by light as well as by electricity.

CCIA

COMPUTER AND **C**OMMUNICATIONS **I**NDUSTRY **A**SSOCIATION; Members are
vendors of MAINFRAMES, PERIPHERALS and COMMUNICATIONS equipment and
services, as well as SOFTWARE HOUSES, SERVICE BUREAUS, leasing and FIELD
SERVICE organizations. CCIA keeps members advised of governmental legislation,
rules and regulations, international trade, capital formation and tax policy, federal
procurement and industry standards, as it relates to the COMPUTER and
COMMUNICATIONS industry.

CCITT

CONSULTATIVE **C**OMMITTEE FOR **I**NTERNATIONAL **T**ELEPHONY AND
TELEGRAPHY; The CCITT is one of four permanent organs of the International
Telecommunications Union (ITU), headquartered in Geneva Switzerland. The ITU,
founded in 1865, is an international organization with over 150 member countries.
CCITT sets international COMMUNICATIONS standards.

CCP

CERTIFICATE IN **C**OMPUTER **P**ROGRAMMING; Certificate awarded for successful
completion of an examination in COMPUTER PROGRAMMING, offered by the Institute
of Certification of Computer Professionals (ICCP).

CDC

CONTROL **D**ATA **C**ORPORATION.

CDP

CERTIFICATE IN **D**ATA **P**ROCESSING; Certificate awarded for successful completion of an examination in HARDWARE, SOFTWARE, SYSTEMS ANALYSIS and PROGRAMMING, management and accounting, offered by the Institute of Certification of Computer Professionals (ICCP).

central processing unit

See CPU.

central processor

PRIMARY PROCESSOR IN THE COMPUTER; CENTRAL PROCESSOR refers to the PROCESSOR by itself, excluding MEMORY.

centralized processing

COMPUTERS IN A CENTRALIZED LOCATION; CENTRALIZED PROCESSING implies a single DATACENTER wherein all INFORMATION PROCESSING is performed. TERMINALS may be located throughout the organization and in remote locations; however, they all connect (are ON-LINE) to the centralized COMPUTER(S).

chain printer

LINE PRINTER THAT USES TYPE CHARACTERS LINKED TOGETHER IN A CHAIN AS ITS PRINTER MECHANISM; See PRINTER TECHNOLOGIES.

channel

A PATH BETWEEN TWO DEVICES; COMPUTER CHANNELS are high-speed pathways between the COMPUTER and the CONTROL UNITS of PERIPHERAL devices, or between two COMPUTERS directly connected (MULTIPROCESSING). COMPUTER CHANNELS are either metal wire or OPTICAL FIBER. COMMUNICATIONS CHANNELS are pathways between remote TERMINALS and COMPUTERS. A CHANNEL may also refer to a CARRIER, such as a SATELLITE CHANNEL or a TV CHANNEL. See COMMUNICATIONS CHANNEL, SELECTOR CHANNEL, MULTIPLEXOR CHANNEL and BUS.

character

AN ALPHANUMERIC; A CHARACTER is an alphabetic letter, numeric digit, or special symbol such as a decimal point or comma. A CHARACTER may also refer to a storage space which holds a CHARACTER (usually a BYTE). For example: 50,000 CHARACTERS of MEMORY is the same as 50,000 BYTES of MEMORY.

character graphics

PREDEFINED SET OF GRAPHICS SHAPES; CHARACTER GRAPHICS are a set of predefined shapes, which are strung together to create GRAPHICS images. The GRAPHICS CHARACTERS are an extension of the standard set of alphabetic and numeric CHARACTERS that can be generated by the TERMINAL. Each GRAPHICS CHARACTER takes up one space on the SCREEN, just like a letter or digit. CHARACTER GRAPHICS are a simple way of generating GRAPHICS on a standard TERMINAL. Contrast with RASTER GRAPHICS or VECTOR GRAPHICS.

character printer

SERIAL PRINTER OR LETTER QUALITY PRINTER; See PRINTER.

charge coupled device

See CCD.

check digit

A DIGIT GENERATED FROM AN ORIGINAL NUMBER TO ENSURE ACCURACY; A CHECK DIGIT is calculated from the original digits in the number and is added to and maintained as part of the number all the time. When the number is keyed into the COMPUTER, a validation routine in the PROGRAM recalculates the CHECK DIGIT. If the CHECK DIGIT entered is not the same as the calculated digit, it is considered an erroneous INPUT. The digits in the number might have been transposed in keying, or the number may just be incorrect. CHECK DIGITS are applied to numbers that identify RECORDS such as customer number, vendor number, employee number, etc., to ensure that the proper account is selected and UPDATED.

checkpoint/restart

COMPUTER SYSTEM RECOVERY METHOD; A CHECKPOINT is a point where the status of a PROGRAM (or all the PROGRAMS) running in the COMPUTER is saved in the event of COMPUTER failure. Periodically, the COMPUTER MEMORY containing the PROGRAMS is copied onto a DISK or TAPE along with a notation of the last INSTRUCTION that was PROCESSED by the COMPUTER. In the event of a power failure, or HARDWARE or SOFTWARE failure, the PROGRAM(S) can be RESTARTED from the last CHECKPOINT after the problem is corrected. A RESTART PROGRAM copies the last CHECKPOINT into MEMORY and directs the COMPUTER to the appropriate next INSTRUCTION. It's like going back in time and starting over.

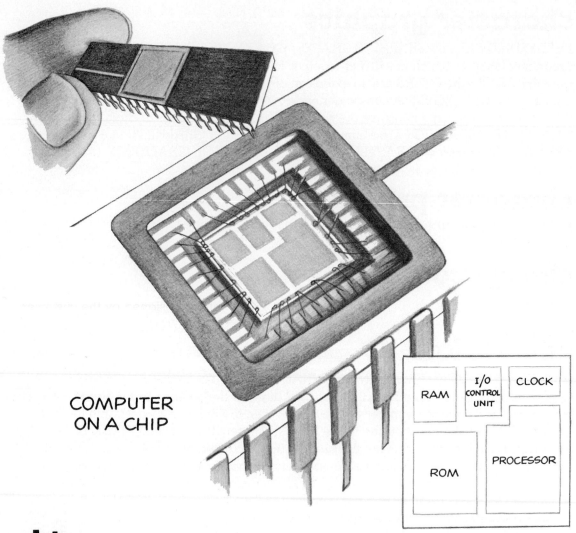

COMPUTER
ON A CHIP

RAM	I/O CONTROL UNIT	CLOCK
ROM		PROCESSOR

chip

MINIATURIZED ELECTRONIC CIRCUITS; A CHIP, from approximately 1/16" square to 3/8" square, and approximately 1/30" thick, contains from a handful to several hundred thousand ELECTRONIC components (TRANSISTORS, RESISTORS, etc.). The terms CHIP, INTEGRATED CIRCUIT and MICROELECTRONIC are synonymous.

TYPES OF CHIPS BY FUNCTION

LOGIC CHIP— A single CHIP can perform some or all of the functions of a PROCESSOR. A MICROPROCESSOR is an entire PROCESSOR on a single CHIP. One or more MICROPROCESSORS are used in a portable or desktop COMPUTER. Larger COMPUTERS may employ several types of MICROPROCESSORS, as well as hundreds and even thousands of specialized LOGIC CHIPS.

MEMORY CHIP— MEMORY CHIPS contain from several hundred to hundreds of thousands of BITS (storage cells). RAM CHIPS are the COMPUTER'S primary internal working storage and require constant power to keep their BITS charged. FIRMWARE

CHIPS, such as ROMs, PROMs, EPROMs, and EEPROMs are permanent MEMORY CHIPS and hold their content without power.

COMPUTER ON A CHIP— A single CHIP can contain the PROCESSOR, RAM, ROM, an INPUT/OUTPUT CONTROL UNIT, and a timing CLOCK. A COMPUTER ON A CHIP is used in myriads of consumer and industrial products.

ANALOG/DIGITAL CONVERTER— A single CHIP can perform ANALOG/DIGITAL and/or DIGITAL/ANALOG conversion of signals, such as a CODEC in a telephone.

Special Purpose CHIPS— CHIPS used for low-cost, mass-merchandised items, like DIGITAL watches and calculators; are often designed from the ground up to obtain the most economical product. CHIPS for higher cost products, like VIDEO game COMPUTERS, may be designed from scratch as well.

LOGIC ARRAY and GATE ARRAY— These types of CHIPS contain LOGIC GATES that have not been tied together yet. A final set of steps applies the top metal layer onto the CHIP and strings the LOGIC GATES together in the pattern designed by the customer. This method eliminates much of the fabrication design time, as well as the actual fabrication time for producing the CHIP.

BIT SLICE PROCESSORS— BIT SLICE CHIPS contain elementary ELECTRONIC CIRCUITS which serve as building blocks for the COMPUTER architect. They are used to custom-build a PROCESSOR for specialized purposes.

EVOLUTION OF THE CHIP

The SEMICONDUCTOR Industry was formally born after the invention of the TRANSISTOR by John Bardeen, Walter Braittain and William Schockley of Bell Laboratories in 1947. The TRANSISTOR was the first device to incorporate SEMICONDUCTOR materials in its design and fabrication. In the 1950s, the TRANSISTOR slowly began to replace the bulky VACUUM TUBES used in radio and television as ELECTRONIC amplifiers. The SEMICONDUCTOR TRANSISTOR also rapidly obsoleted the 1st-generation COMPUTERS that used thousands of VACUUM TUBES in their DIGITAL CIRCUITS (the VACUUM TUBE acted as an on/off switch). By the early 1960s, COMPUTER size was reduced dramatically because of the TRANSISTOR.

TRANSISTORS were DISCRETE COMPONENTS, each one packaged as a single unit and then soldered onto a PRINTED CIRCUIT BOARD to interconnect with other TRANSISTORS and DISCRETE COMPONENTS. Since hundreds of TRANSISTORS were fabricated on a single base, cut apart and packaged separately, only to be reconnected again, the next step was more evolutionary than the revolutionary concept of the TRANSISTOR. The INTEGRATED CIRCUIT is simply an entire ELECTRONIC CIRCUIT fabricated at one time, incorporating all the required TRANSISTORS and components plus the interconnections between them in their prescribed sequence. Jack Kilby (of Texas Instruments) and Robert Noyce (of Fairchild Semiconductor) conceived the INTEGRATED CIRCUIT in the late 1950s.

Since the first CHIPS of the 1960s, the number of ELECTRONIC components that have been microminiaturized onto a single CHIP has been increasing every year, from SSI (Small Scale Integration) to MSI (Medium Scale Integration) to LSI (Large Scale Integration) to VLSI (Very Large Scale Integration) to SLSI (Super Large Scale Integration). In the 1980s, the physical space occupied by one hundred thousand TRANSISTORS on a CHIP takes up the same space as one TRANSISTOR used in the 1960s.

A byproduct of miniaturization is speed: the shorter the distance a pulse has to travel, the faster it gets there; the smaller the components making up the TRANSISTOR switch, the faster the switch switches. Internal movements inside the tiny CHIP are measured in NANOSECONDS and PICOSECONDS (billionths and trillionths of a second).

The real significance of the CHIP was its ability to be used, not just for PROCESSING CIRCUITRY (LOGIC CHIPS), but for MEMORIES as well. Before CHIP MEMORY, MEMORIES were made of magnetic CORES; before CORES, such arcane methods as tubes filled with liquid mercury were used. Using various ELECTRONIC component design techniques, storage cells were created of the same SEMICONDUCTOR material as the TRANSISTORS used for LOGIC CIRCUITS. As a result, everything that made up a COMPUTER could be made out of the same material. Being able to fabricate an entire COMPUTER on a single CHIP opened up new worlds of uses for COMPUTERS in appliances, toys, games, and hand-held devices of all varieties. Along with a certain amount of RAM MEMORY (working storage) to accept INPUT from the USER, these tiny COMPUTERS use permanent MEMORIES (ROMS) to hold the PROGRAM that the PROCESSOR will EXECUTE. Who would have believed in 1951, when the awesome-looking UNIVAC I was unveiled to the public, that COMPUTERS would be built into credit cards thirty years later? (See SMART CARD.)

THE MAKING OF A CHIP

ELECTRONIC CIRCUITS in DIGITAL COMPUTERS are pathways that carry pulses of electricity from one point to another. The pulses flow through on/off switches like a light switch on the wall, except that the switch itself is electrically activated. The current flowing out of one switch effects the opening or closing of another switch, and so on and so on. The fact that anything meaningful happens is because the CIRCUIT is designed using BOOLEAN LOGIC. BOOLEAN LOGIC is a set of rules for detecting the presence or absence of combinations of pulses.

CIRCUIT designers use building blocks of BOOLEAN LOGIC to create new types of DIGITAL CIRCUITS. This LOGICAL design is then converted into an ELECTRONIC design using components like TRANSISTORS, DIODES, RESISTORS, etc., which duplicate the BOOLEAN LOGIC conditions with the flow of electricity. COMPUTER SOFTWARE can aid this conversion. However, there is yet one more step: the ELECTRONIC design must still be converted into the actual physical CIRCUIT design that will be fabricated onto a CHIP. Specialized INTEGRATED CIRCUIT design SOFTWARE generate the form and placement of the physical ELECTRONIC components, as well as the immense interconnected maze of pathways between them, which looks like a "plumber's nightmare." This mass of "plumbing" is printed on oversized drawings for people to inspect. After corrections are made, a picture of the "plumbing" is burned into a photographic plate in microminiaturized form, and replicated several hundred times so that many CHIPS can be made together. The CHIP is built up in layers and a separate PHOTOMASK is used to isolate each layer to be worked on. Literally, millions of TRANSISTORS are constructed, layer by layer, at the same time.

The base material from which CHIPS are made is primarily SILICON, although materials like sapphire and gallium arsenide are also used. SILICON is purified in a molten state and is then DOPED (chemically combined with other materials) to alter its electrical properties. The result is a SILICON crystal of either P-type (positive) or N-type (negative) which looks like a long salami about 4 or 5 inches in diameter. Thin slices are cut from the "salami," called WAFERS, and are the basic raw material for the CHIP-making process.

The actual CHIP fabrication starts by chemically creating a layer of SILICON dioxide on the surface of the WAFER to act as an insulator. The WAFER is then coated with a film that is exposed to the first PHOTOMASK. The design transferred to the WAFER is etched into the SILICON dioxide layer, exposing the SILICON base in specific areas. Through a process called diffusion, chemicals (under heat and pressure) are shot into the exposed areas of the SILICON, DOPING the layers beneath the surface.

Through multiple stages of PHOTOMASKING, etching, and diffusion, the various layers of each of the components on the CHIP are built. The final stage lays the top metal layer (usually aluminum), which interconnects the TRANSISTORS and other components on the CHIP to each other and to the outside world.

The finished CHIPS are tested on the WAFER and those failing the test are marked for elimination. The CHIPS are then sliced out of the WAFER and the good ones are placed into their final package, such as a DIP (Dual Inline Package). Tiny wires bond the pads on the CHIP to the connectors on the mounting package. The package is then sealed and tested again. The number of CHIPS that make it through all the testing steps is often less than the number that fail.

The CHIP-making business is an extremely precise one. Many operations are performed in a "clean room," since particles in the air could mix with the microscopic mixtures being created and easily render a CHIP or WAFER worthless.

In order to miniaturize the elements of an ELECTRONIC component still further, the PHOTOMASK will have to be made with x-rays or other beams which are more narrow than light. Eventually, we may etch the patterns of the CIRCUIT directly onto the CHIP itself, thereby eliminating the entire photographic MASKING process.

During the 1980s, we will build several million TRANSISTORS on a single CHIP (each TRANSISTOR made up of several discrete elements). Instead of adding more TRANSISTORS horizontally on a CHIP, we will build the CHIP in overlapping layers vertically. It is entirely conceivable that by the turn of the century, the LOGIC and MEMORY of an entire MAINFRAME will be built within a cube 1 inch square!

chip card

See SMART CARD.

CICS

IBM SYSTEM SOFTWARE FOR ON-LINE OPERATIONS; CICS is a widely used SYSTEM for the management of ON-LINE APPLICATIONS in IBM COMPUTERS. CICS provides for the creation of a MULTI-USER, ON-LINE environment within the traditional BATCH PROCESSING IBM OPERATING SYSTEMS. CICS, like JCL, has its own variety of COMMANDS and features, and people involved with CICS are often called CICS PROGRAMMERS. CICS falls into the TP MONITOR category and stands for **C**ustomer Information **C**ontrol **S**ystem.

circuit

AN ELECTRONIC PATHWAY; A CIRCUIT may refer to a LOGIC CIRCUIT, which controls and performs functions in a DIGITAL COMPUTER SYSTEM. A CIRCUIT may also refer to a COMMUNICATIONS CHANNEL. See ELECTRONIC CIRCUIT and COMMUNICATIONS CHANNEL.

circuit switching

CONNECTING COMMUNICATIONS CHANNELS TOGETHER; CIRCUIT SWITCHING causes a physical connection to take place between the sending and receiving CHANNELS. CIRCUIT SWITCHING is used to switch ANALOG COMMUNICATIONS CHANNELS.

clock

INTERNAL TIMING DEVICE WITHIN THE CPU; There are several varieties of CLOCKS:

The CPU CLOCK is a timing device which generates a uniform number of electrical vibrations per second (often a quartz crystal is used). These electrical vibrations are used to create MACHINE CYCLES (to control the CPU) and DIGITAL pulses which traverse through the ELECTRONIC CIRCUITS.

The REAL-TIME CLOCK is a time-of-day CLOCK which keeps track of regular hours, minutes and seconds and makes this DATA available to the PROGRAMS running in the COMPUTER.

The TIME-SHARING CLOCK is a timer set to INTERRUPT the CPU at regular intervals in order to provide equal time to multiple USERS on the COMPUTER.

The CLOCK in a SYNCHRONOUS COMMUNICATIONS device maintains the uniform transmission of DATA between the sending and receiving TERMINALS and COMPUTERS.

CMOS

TYPE OF MICROELECTRONIC CIRCUIT DESIGN; CMOS INTEGRATED CIRCUITS
are widely used for PROCESSORS (LOGIC CHIPS) and MEMORIES. The CMOS
technique uses a PMOS and NMOS TRANSISTOR connected in a complimentary
fashion, which results in using less power to operate. CMOS CHIPS are valuable for
portable, battery-operated devices. Stands for **C**omplimentary **MOS** and is pronounced
/see-moss/.

CMS

INTERACTIVE PROGRAM MODULE FOR THE IBM VM OPERATING SYSTEM; CMS
runs under IBM's VM OPERATING SYSTEM and is used for both TIME-SHARING and
INTERACTIVE PROGRAM DEVELOPMENT. CMS stands for **C**onversational **M**onitor
System.

coax

ABBREVIATION FOR COAXIAL CABLE.

coaxial cable

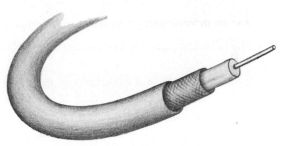

COMMUNICATIONS MEDIUM; COAXIAL
CABLE is a two-wire cable constructed as
follows: An insulated wire runs through the
middle of the cable. A second wire

COAXIAL CABLE

surrounds the insulation of the inner wire like a sheath, which is constructed of either a
solid or mesh metal. The outer insulation wraps the second wire. There are many
varieties of COAXIAL CABLE. COAXIAL CABLE has a greater BANDWIDTH
(transmission capacity) than standard telephone wires (TWISTED PAIRS).

COBOL

PROGRAMMING LANGUAGE USED PRIMARILY IN BUSINESS APPLICATIONS;
COBOL is a COMPILER language and stands for **CO**mmon **B**usiness **O**riented
Language. COBOL was one of the first HIGH-LEVEL LANGUAGES developed.
Formally adopted in 1960, it stemmed from a language called Flowmatic in the mid
1950s. COBOL has been the most widely used PROGRAMMING LANGUAGE on
MAINFRAMES (for business APPLICATIONS) and has been used extensively on
MINICOMPUTERS as well. The COBOL language provides a certain amount of
DOCUMENTATION standardization. COBOL is excessively wordy, usually requiring
more writing than other PROGRAMMING LANGUAGES. As a result, it may be easier
to understand another person's COBOL PROGRAM.

COBOL is structured into four divisions:

IDENTIFICATION DIVISION: The PROGRAM is identified.

ENVIRONMENT DIVISION: The SOURCE and OBJECT COMPUTERS are identified.

DATA DIVISION: BUFFERS, CONSTANTS and work areas are identified.

PROCEDURE DIVISION: The PROCESSING is described (PROGRAM LOGIC).

CODASYL

CONFERENCE ON **DA**TA **SY**STEMS **L**ANGUAGES; Organization devoted to the development of DATA languages. COBOL is a product of CODASYL.

code

INFORMATION IN VARIOUS FORMS; CODE may refer to any of the following:

SOURCE LANGUAGE and MACHINE LANGUAGE are often referred to as SOURCE CODE and MACHINE CODE. The size of a PROGRAM is often given in LINES OF CODE.

INFORMATION converted into DIGITAL form is called CODE. For example, EBCDIC or ASCII is a DIGITAL CODE or DATA CODE. DIGITIZED voice is CODED voice. The first DIGITAL CODE was Morse CODE.

INFORMATION which has been synthesized is called CODE; for example, a part CODE or customer CODE is a condensed representation of INFORMATION values. SPEECH SYNTHESIS is CODED speech.

CODE refers to a signal which has been ENCRYPTED or SCRAMBLED for SECURITY purposes.

codec

VOICE CONVERSION CHIP; A CODEC is a CHIP used in a telephone to convert human voice to DIGITAL voice using the PULSE CODE MODULATION technique. The CODEC converts DIGITAL voice back into sound waves for listening. CODEC stands for **cod**er-**dec**oder. A CODEC is a voice A-D/D-A CONVERTER.

coder

PERSON OR MACHINE THAT CREATES CODE; A CODER usually refers to a PROGRAMMER who is writing LINES OF CODE in a PROGRAM. In this case, CODER often connotes a junior PROGRAMMER, or an individual who has not designed the PROGRAM LOGIC.

cold boot

INITIALIZATION OF THE COMPUTER; A COLD BOOT is the first BOOT performed after the power is turned on.

color graphics

PICTURE IMAGES IN COLORS; See PIXEL and RASTER GRAPHICS.

collator

HARDWARE OR SOFTWARE THAT MERGES DATA TOGETHER; PUNCHED CARD COLLATORS merge two decks of PUNCHED CARDS into one or more stacks. A UTILITY PROGRAM can merge RECORDS and FILES together in a COMPUTER SYSTEM.

COM

COMPUTER **O**UTPUT **M**ICROFILMING; COM units create MICROFILM or MICROFICHE directly from COMPUTER-generated OUTPUT. The COMPUTER OUTPUT for the COM unit is the same as COMPUTER OUTPUT for the PRINTER. The REPORT has already been FORMATTED with rows and columns of DATA. Using either traditional camera methods, which take a picture of a image generated on a CRT, or by using LASERS which write images directly, COM units create a film image of each page of the REPORT. It may also be able to add additional graphics on the page, such as lines and company logos, etc. COM units can be stand-alone devices or ON LINE to a COMPUTER.

command

USER DIRECTIVE; COMMANDS are language statements designed into a SOFTWARE PROGRAM, which when entered by the USER cause a function to occur in the COMPUTER. For example: "dir" in the CP/M OPERATING SYSTEM is the USER COMMAND to display the **dir**ectory of FILES on the DISK. The OPERATING SYSTEM follows the COMMAND by EXECUTING a SUBROUTINE (which contains several hundred MACHINE LANGUAGE INSTRUCTIONS) to display the directory. A COMMAND is a LOGICAL statement; the resulting EXECUTION is the PHYSICAL response. COMMANDS may also refer to statements in a PROGRAMMING LANGUAGE.

command driven

INTERACTIVE PROGRAM TECHNIQUE; COMMAND DRIVEN PROGRAMS require that the USER learn a set of COMMANDS to be used when INTERACTING with the PROGRAM. Contrast with MENU DRIVEN PROGRAMS wherein all the options are displayed and the USER simply selects an option. The COMMAND DRIVEN technique is usually harder to learn, but may be more flexible later on. The MENU DRIVEN PROGRAM is easy to use, but any options desired outside of the MENU cannot be taken. PROGRAMS can also be designed to incorporate both methods. A MENU can be displayed showing all the COMMANDS that can be entered. That would still be primarily a COMMAND DRIVEN PROGRAM.

common carrier

GOVERNMENT REGULATED ORGANIZATION THAT PROVIDES TELECOMMUNICATIONS SERVICES FOR PUBLIC USE, SUCH AS AT&T, THE TELEPHONE COMPANIES, ITT, MCI, SBS AND WESTERN UNION.

communications

TRANSFER OF INFORMATION BETWEEN DEVICES OVER A COMMUNICATIONS SYSTEM; COMMUNICATIONS includes the COMMUNICATIONS NETWORK and all related HARDWARE and SOFTWARE. COMMUNICATIONS are required between remote TERMINALS and COMPUTERS, and between COMPUTER SYSTEMS in a DISTRIBUTED PROCESSING/OFFICE AUTOMATION environment. TERMINALS and PRINTERS that are directly cabled to the COMPUTER often do not utilize COMMUNICATIONS.

DATA COMMUNICATIONS refers to DATA and TEXT COMMUNICATIONS. TELECOMMUNICATIONS refers to all forms of COMMUNICATIONS, including voice conversations, FACSIMILE and TELECONFERENCING. TELEPROCESSING is the IBM term for DATA COMMUNICATIONS/DATA PROCESSING.

DIGITAL vs ANALOG COMMUNICATIONS

DIGITAL COMMUNICATIONS is the transmission of BINARY CODE. BINARY CODE is a CODE made up of the two digits, *0* and *1*, which transmit as the presence or absence of an electric or light pulse. When a long-distance COMMUNICATIONS CHANNEL is constructed for pure DIGITAL transmission, it is set up with regeneration points every so many miles. As the pulses get weak, they are analyzed at each regeneration point and created anew at that point. Any NOISE (unwanted signal) that inadvertently got mixed into the transmission is filtered out at these regeneration stations. Contrast with the traditional ANALOG CHANNELS of the telephone SYSTEM which do not have built-in regeneration stations. Instead, they have amplifiers built into the CHANNEL, which amplify the NOISE along with the voice or DATA signal. Traditional ANALOG transmission limits the maximum transfer rate because the MODEM at the receiving end has to distinguish between the BITS and the NOISE (which get thoroughly garbled together). ANALOG transmission of DIGITAL DATA is limited to several thousand BITS per second (in a VOICE GRADE line). Pure DIGITAL transmission over metal wire can reach several million BITS per second, and over OPTICAL FIBER, hundreds of millions of BITS per second.

Traditional ANALOG lines can be altered to transmit DIGITAL DATA by various techniques, including the replacement of the ANALOG amplifiers with DIGITAL repeaters. Note: An ANALOG NETWORK, designed from the beginning for the transmission of DIGITAL DATA, can transmit at very high speeds. For example: BROADBAND NETWORKS carry DIGITAL DATA in ANALOG form at very high speeds for distances of several miles.

COMMUNICATIONS AND COMPUTERS

Traditionally, COMMUNICATIONS (or TELECOMMUNICATIONS) has been a separate department, concentrating on telephone operations within an organization, separate and distinct from the DATA PROCESSING department. As DATA PROCESSING extends itself into DISTRIBUTED PROCESSING/OFFICE AUTOMATION, the backbone behind its operations is effective COMMUNICATIONS NETWORKS. Since the telephone PABX may now handle DATA (which until recently only handled voice), and in fact, may even cause the telephones to generate DIGITAL voice signals, the difference between COMMUNICATIONS and COMPUTERS has begun to blur. As a result, the traditional lines of authority and control over COMPUTERS and COMMUNICATIONS has become an organizational issue in many a company.

communications channel

PHYSICAL PATHWAY OVER WHICH INFORMATION IS TRANSFERRED; Public and private telephone lines, MICROWAVE and SATELLITE CHANNELS, OPTICAL FIBERS, COAXIAL CABLE and TWISTED PAIRS are all forms of COMMUNICATIONS CHANNELS. A COMMUNICATIONS CHANNEL is also called a CIRCUIT or a "line." A COMMUNICATIONS CHANNEL differs from a COMPUTER CHANNEL. It is usually a serial transmission device; the COMPUTER CHANNEL is usually parallel. It is traditionally slower than the COMPUTER CHANNEL; however, as higher-speed LOCAL AREA NETWORKS are developed, the speed of a COMMUNICATIONS CHANNEL will approach the speed of a COMPUTER CHANNEL.

communications network

COMMUNICATIONS CHANNEL(S) OF ONE OR MORE TYPES DESIGNED TO CONNECT TWO OR MORE DEVICES TOGETHER; All HARDWARE and SOFTWARE used to link the CHANNELS together and support the COMMUNICATIONS within the NETWORK itself is considered part of the COMMUNICATIONS NETWORK. See NETWORK ARCHITECTURE.

communications protocol

COMMUNICATIONS STANDARD; A PROTOCOL is a set of HARDWARE and SOFTWARE features and PROCEDURES which allow a TERMINAL or COMPUTER to exchange MESSAGES between another TERMINAL or COMPUTER via a COMMUNICATIONS NETWORK.

PROTOCOLS are designed in layers, the first two of which are *mandatory* in order to communicate from one device to another:

> Layer 1 (called the electrical INTERFACE) defines the actual set of wires, plugs and electrical signals which connect the sending and receiving devices to the COMMUNICATIONS NETWORK. The RS-232 INTERFACE is the typical standard for this bottom layer.

> Layer 2 (called the DATA link control) is responsible for the physical movement of a BLOCK of DATA from one device to another, and includes all the ERROR CHECKING necessary to ensure an accurate transmission. This layer is the most commonly referenced in COMMUNICATIONS. Typical low-speed PROTOCOLS are called ASCII PROTOCOLS; typical high-speed PROTOCOLS are called BISYNC, HDLC and SDLC.

> Layer 3 (called the NETWORK layer) establishes the connection between two parties that are not directly connected together. This layer is the common function of the telephone SYSTEM, for example. When an X.25 PACKET SWITCHING NETWORK performs this function, the actual route that has been established from one device to another is called a VIRTUAL CIRCUIT.

> Layer 4 (called the session layer) is a collection of rules for how the interaction between two COMPUTERS, or between the USER and the COMPUTER, is conducted after the connection is made. The LOG-ON begins the session layer and the LOG-OFF ends it. Rules in this layer depend on the vendor and the USER.

CATEGORIES OF DATA LINK PROTOCOLS

ASYNCHRONOUS PROTOCOLS:
Originating from the mechanical TELETYPEWRITERS (the first DATA COMMUNICATIONS TERMINALS), ASYNCHRONOUS PROTOCOLS are widely used in DUMB TERMINALS connected to TIME-SHARING COMPUTERS, as well as in in-house MINICOMPUTERS and MICROCOMPUTERS. The garden variety ASYNCHRONOUS PROTOCOL (called a TELETYPE PROTOCOL or ASCII PROTOCOL) usually has limited ERROR CHECKING; however, proprietary ASYNCHRONOUS PROTOCOLS may have extensive ERROR CHECKING.

SYNCHRONOUS PROTOCOLS:
Developed for higher speeds and higher volumes of transmission than ASYNCHRONOUS PROTOCOLS, SYNCHRONOUS PROTOCOLS have extensive

ERROR CHECKING and require specialized TERMINALS for use. Examples are the BISYNCHRONOUS PROTOCOLS (a large family of PROTOCOLS, including IBM's 3270 and 2780/3780), HDLC (an international standard), IBM's SDLC and Digital Equipment Corporation's DDCMP.

Consider two COMPUTERS "talking" to each other in this representative DATA link PROTOCOL:

> Are you there? **Yes I am.** Are you ready to receive? **Yes I am.** Here comes the MESSAGE— did you get it? **Yes I did.** Here comes the next part— did you get it? **No I didn't.** Here it comes again— did you get it? **Yes I did.** There is no more— Goodbye. **Goodbye.**

(Get the idea?)

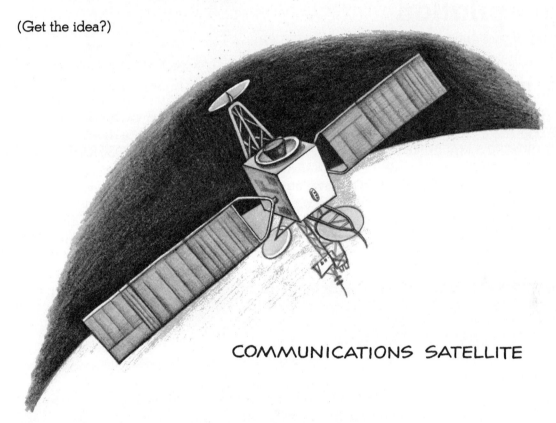

COMMUNICATIONS SATELLITE

communications satellite

RADIO RELAY STATION IN ORBIT; COMMUNICATIONS SATELLITES (approximately 22,300 miles above the earth) are designed to travel at the same rate of speed as the earth, so they appear stationary to us. SATELLITES contain many COMMUNICATIONS CHANNELS which receive ANALOG and DIGITAL signals from EARTH STATIONS. (Note: DIGITAL CODE is transmitted within a CARRIER.) The signals are amplified and transmitted back to earth, covering either a small geographical area (called a spot beam) or almost a third of the earth's surface. In the latter case, private INFORMATION is often ENCRYPTED so that other parties cannot understand it even if they receive it. See TRANSPONDER.

COMPACT II

NUMERICAL CONTROL PROGRAMMING LANGUAGE; COMPACT II is a HIGH-LEVEL PROGRAMMING LANGUAGE used to generate INSTRUCTIONS for NUMERICAL CONTROL devices.

compatibility

See STANDARDS & COMPATIBILITY, DOWNWARD COMPATIBLE and UPWARD COMPATIBLE.

compilation

COMPILING OF A PROGRAM; See COMPILER.

compiler

A HIGH-LEVEL PROGRAMMING LANGUAGE TRANSLATOR; A COMPILER is a PROGRAM that translates the PROGRAMMING LANGUAGE into a particular COMPUTER'S MACHINE LANGUAGE. ALGOL, BASIC, COBOL, FORTRAN, PASCAL and PL/I are COMPILER PROGRAMMING LANGUAGES. Some PROGRAMMING LANGUAGES are available in both COMPILER and INTERPRETER form. A COMPILED version implies one which has been translated and is ready to EXECUTE in the COMPUTER. The COMPILED version is faster than the INTERPRETED version, since the INTERPRETER must translate while it is EXECUTING. A COMPILER must generate a MACHINE LANGUAGE PROGRAM that will EXECUTE in a particular COMPUTER, and it must also generate that PROGRAM in a form compatible with a particular OPERATING SYSTEM, as well.

composite video

STANDARD VIDEO SIGNAL; COMPOSITE VIDEO signals are commonly used between COMPUTERS and VIDEO MONITORS. Technically, it means that certain synchronization signals are mixed with the display signals. It also means that in most cases only a single wire is required. See MONITOR.

computer

A PROGRAMMABLE MACHINE THAT PROCESSES INFORMATION; The machine is the HARDWARE and the PROGRAM is the SOFTWARE. A COMPUTER is designed as a general-purpose machine which performs specific functions when a set of INSTRUCTIONS (called a PROGRAM) are stored in its MEMORY. These INSTRUCTIONS, which are developed by PROGRAMMING, tell the machine exactly what to do in precise detail. Every action taken by the COMPUTER is due to INSTRUCTIONS telling it what to do. The COMPUTER repeats the same INSTRUCTIONS over and over again each time a particular task is required by the USER.

The COMPUTER does work for us by performing INPUT/OUTPUT and PROCESSING functions:

INPUT/OUTPUT

The COMPUTER can selectively receive INFORMATION into its MEMORY from any PERIPHERAL device or COMMUNICATIONS CHANNEL attached to it. It can also send a copy of INFORMATION from MEMORY out to any PERIPHERAL or COMMUNICATIONS CHANNEL attached to it.

THE 3 C's

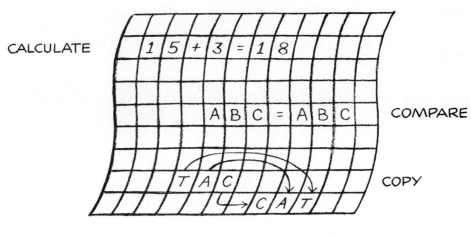

"ELECTRONIC PAPER"

PROCESSING (THE 3 C's*)

Once the INFORMATION is stored in MEMORY, the COMPUTER can (1) **calculate**, (2) **compare** and (3) **copy** the INFORMATION:

The COMPUTER can **calculate** by adding, subtracting, multiplying and dividing the INFORMATION. The COMPUTER can analyze and evaluate INFORMATION by **comparing** it with known values or with other INFORMATION. And the COMPUTER can **copy** the INFORMATION any number of times throughout MEMORY in any sequence desired. For example:

The COMPUTER SORTS by **comparing** the KEY FIELDS in two RECORDS at a time and then **copying** the lower KEY in front of the higher KEY.

The COMPUTER locates the proper RECORD on a DISK by **comparing** the KEY entered by the USER with an INDEX of stored KEYS.

In WORD PROCESSING, inserting new TEXT CHARACTERS into existing TEXT is accomplished by **copying** the CHARACTERS over one BYTE to the right to make room for each inserted CHARACTER. Deletion is accomplished by **copying** the remaining CHARACTERS on top of the CHARACTERS to be deleted.

A QUERY LANGUAGE statement that says: "Sum salary for title = nurse" causes the COMPUTER to **compare** the title FIELD in each RECORD for "nurse" and then add (**calculate**) the salary FIELD into a COUNTER for each match.

REMEMBER THE 3 C's* NEXT TIME YOU WONDER IF A COMPUTER CAN SOLVE A PROBLEM. On a piece of paper, identify your INFORMATION. The COMPUTER'S MEMORY *is* ELECTRONIC PAPER. If you can solve your problem by **calculating**, **comparing** and **copying**, the COMPUTER can help you do it faster.

(***The 3 C's** is a trademark and service mark of FREEDMAN ASSOCIATES and THE COMPUTER LANGUAGE COMPANY INC.)

HOW THE COMPUTER WORKS (THE STORED PROGRAM CONCEPT)

COMPUTER HARDWARE is primarily a PROCESSOR and MEMORY. The PROCESSOR is really the COMPUTER and the MEMORY is the working storage for the COMPUTER. The PROGRAM (in MACHINE LANGUAGE) is copied into MEMORY from a DISK, TAPE, or other source before anything can happen. Once the PROGRAM is stored in MEMORY, the PROCESSOR is directed to go to the first INSTRUCTION in the PROGRAM and begin. The PROCESSOR copies the INSTRUCTION from MEMORY into its ELECTRONIC CIRCUIT, called the CONTROL UNIT, and matches it against its built-in INSTRUCTION SET. If the INSTRUCTION is CODED properly, the PROCESSOR performs the INSTRUCTION (EXECUTES it). If the INSTRUCTION is not CODED properly, the PROCESSOR ABENDS (**ab**normally **ends**).

The INSTRUCTIONS in the PROGRAM direct the PROCESSOR to INPUT, OUTPUT and PROCESS INFORMATION. INPUT/OUTPUT is the actual physical transfer of INFORMATION between MEMORY and the PERIPHERAL devices or COMMUNICATIONS CHANNELS. PROCESSING is performed by **calculating**, **comparing** and **copying** selected INFORMATION brought into the PROGRAM.

The PROCESSOR EXECUTES the PROGRAM by keeping track of where in MEMORY it got the last INSTRUCTION. The PROCESSOR goes back into the PROGRAM in MEMORY and copies in the next INSTRUCTION, and so on, one INSTRUCTION at a time, again and again. The COMPUTER can EXECUTE INSTRUCTIONS extremely fast, from many thousands to many millions of INSTRUCTIONS per second. It accomplishes this because of the speed at which ELECTRONIC components can change their state (on to off, off to on). We can take advantage of this speed by running more than one PROGRAM in the COMPUTER at the same time. While one PROGRAM is waiting for INPUT (a USER may be thinking about what to enter at the TERMINAL) the OPERATING SYSTEM directs the COMPUTER to PROCESS in another PROGRAM. COMPUTERS

THE COMPUTER GLOSSARY

can be designed so that the INFORMATION transfers (INPUTS and OUTPUTS) are overlapped with PROCESSING (INSTRUCTIONS being EXECUTED).

It can take thousands of MACHINE INSTRUCTIONS to perform very routine tasks, such as storing and retrieving INFORMATION on a DISK or TAPE. A large COMPUTER could easily EXECUTE a million INSTRUCTIONS to search for and display a RECORD at your TERMINAL.

COMPUTERS COME IN MANY SIZES

COMPUTERS may be as small as a single CHIP, or may be six feet high and weigh thousands of pounds. The difference between them is in the amount of work they can perform in the same time frame. A single CHIP COMPUTER is called a COMPUTER ON A CHIP. A hand-held educational or entertainment game may use a MICROPROCESSOR which requires additional CHIPS (MEMORY) for its operation. A desktop MICROCOMPUTER may contain one or more MICROPROCESSORS, as well as MEMORY and other CHIPS. A MINICOMPUTER may contain specialized LOGIC CHIPS and/or use a number of MICROPROCESSORS. MAINFRAMES use specialized LOGIC CHIPS and/or many varieties of MICROPROCESSORS.

COMPUTER categories, from smallest to largest are:

COMPUTER ON A CHIP (4-BIT, 8-BIT, 16-BIT)
MICROPROCESSOR (8-BIT, 16-BIT)
MICROCOMPUTER (8-BIT, 16-BIT)
SUPERMICRO or MICROMINI (16-BIT)
MINICOMPUTER (16-BIT)
SUPERMINI or MICROMAINFRAME (32-BIT)
MAINFRAME (32-BIT, 32-BIT +)
SUPERCOMPUTER (32-BIT +)

GENERATIONS OF COMPUTER SYSTEMS

1st-generation COMPUTER SYSTEMS (beginning approximately 1950) employed VACUUM TUBES as the primary switching component in the PROCESSOR. MEMORIES were constructed of liquid mercury delay lines or MAGNETIC DRUMS (UNIVAC I and IBM 650 are examples).

2nd-generation SYSTEMS began around the late 1950s and used TRANSISTORS in place of VACUUM TUBES and MEMORIES were made of magnetizable CORES (IBM 1401 and Honeywell 800 are examples). Size was reduced and reliability was improved significantly in 2nd-generation SYSTEMS. 2nd-generation was primarily a BATCH PROCESSING environment with a single PROGRAM running at one time.

3rd-generation COMPUTERS, beginning in the mid 1960s, introduced PROCESSORS made of INTEGRATED CIRCUITS (IBM 360 and CDC 6400 are examples). 3rd-generation also introduced SYSTEM SOFTWARE technologies like OPERATING SYSTEMS and DATA BASE MANAGMENT SYSTEMS. ON-LINE SYSTEMS were widely developed throughout the 3rd-generation, although most PROCESSING was still BATCH oriented.

The 4th-generation is more evolutionary than revolutionary. Starting in the mid to late 1970s, 4th-generation COMPUTER LOGIC and MEMORY were built almost entirely of CHIPS which contain extremely large numbers of ELECTRONIC components. 4th-generation embraces extensive integration of small and large COMPUTERS together in a DISTRIBUTED PROCESSING/OFFICE AUTOMATION environment. 4th-generation integrates the USER into the COMPUTER environment with NON-PROCEDURAL languages like QUERY LANGUAGES and REPORT WRITERS, and the so-called USER-FRIENDLY PROGRAM.

The 5th-generation ought to become formalized by the 1990s. VLSI and SLSI technologies will put current-day MAINFRAMES on everyone's desk. OPTICAL FIBERS, VIDEODISCS and technologies now in the research labs, will be used to construct 5th-generation COMPUTER SYSTEMS. ARTIFICIAL INTELLIGENCE techniques will be incorporated into every type of APPLICATION. By the turn of the century, a COMPUTER should be able to converse rather intelligently with a person.

computer aided design

See CAD.

computer aided engineering

See CAE.

computer aided manufacturing

See CAM.

computer architecture

DESIGN OF A COMPUTER; COMPUTER ARCHITECTURE is based on the type of PROGRAMS that will run in it and the number of different PROGRAMS that are expected to be run at the same time. The design will determine how the COMPUTER will service the concurrent activities (INTERRUPTS, PARALLEL PROCESSING, etc.), the amount of MEMORY required, and the size of the internal CHANNELS that transfer DATA and INSTRUCTIONS back and forth (DATA BUS and ADDRESS BUS).

Non-stop operation may be a design objective which will influence the construction of every component in the COMPUTER. Specialized machines, like ARRAY PROCESSORS and DATA BASE MACHINES, require different architectures than standard COMPUTERS in order to facilitate faster PROCESSING.

Providing a foundation for the EXECUTION of all the functions in the COMPUTER will be the design of its INSTRUCTION SET (called its NATIVE LANGUAGE). Sometimes COMPUTERS are built with a fixed INSTRUCTION SET; others are built with ability to later enhance or modify the INSTRUCTION SET.

A major design criterion is the tradeoff between HARDWARE and SOFTWARE functions. Functions left to be implemented in SOFTWARE will slow down the machine. However, functions implemented in SOFTWARE can be modified more easily than in HARDWARE. For example, if a multiply INSTRUCTION is not implemented in HARDWARE, a PROGRAM SUBROUTINE must perform the multiplication. The HARDWARE will have to EXECUTE many PROGRAM INSTRUCTIONS to perform the multiplication, instead of multiplying in its ELECTRONIC CIRCUITS. More and more SYSTEM SOFTWARE functions in OPERATING SYSTEMS and DATA BASE MANAGEMENT SYSTEMS are being removed from the SOFTWARE and implemented in HARDWARE.

computer designer

COMPUTER ARCHITECT; A COMPUTER DESIGNER is a person who designs the ELECTRONIC structure of a COMPUTER.

computer graphics

See GRAPHICS.

computer literacy

COMPUTER AND INFORMATION SYSTEM COMPREHENSION; COMPUTER LITERACY implies a reasonable comprehension level about COMPUTERS and how to use them. It includes a working vocabulary about COMPUTER and INFORMATION SYSTEM components, the fundamental principles of COMPUTER PROCESSING, and a perspective for how non-technical people can manage in the world of technology. COMPUTER LITERACY does not imply an understanding of how DIGITAL CIRCUITS work, but it does imply an understanding of the basic reasons for SYSTEMS ANALYSIS & DESIGN, APPLICATION PROGRAMMING, SYSTEMS PROGRAMMING and DATACENTER OPERATIONS. COMPUTER LITERACY requires that USERS define their INFORMATION requirements effectively and that they have an understanding of DECISION SUPPORT SYSTEM tools, like QUERY LANGUAGES, REPORT WRITERS, DATA MANAGEMENT SYSTEMS and FINANCIAL PLANNING SYSTEMS.

computer on a chip

CPU ON A CHIP; A COMPUTER ON A CHIP contains a CPU, RAM, ROM, CLOCK, and I/O CONTROL UNIT on a single CHIP.

computer output microfilm

See COM.

computer power

PERFORMANCE OF A CPU; COMPUTER POWER is expressed in different ways, but essentially refers to the COMPUTER'S THROUGHPUT, which is its effective capacity to do work. COMPUTER POWER may be expressed in MIPS ratings, which refers to how many millions of INSTRUCTIONS the COMPUTER can EXECUTE in one second. It can also be expressed as internal CPU size, such as 8-BIT, 16-BIT, etc. A COMPUTER'S effective capability is also a combination of its HARDWARE and the SOFTWARE running in it. The net effect of a particular PROGRAM running in the COMPUTER can be expressed as "powerful," as well.

computer science

THE FIELD OF COMPUTER HARDWARE AND SOFTWARE; The COMPUTER SCIENCES include SYSTEMS ANALYSIS & DESIGN, APPLICATION and SYSTEM SOFTWARE design and PROGRAMMING. The COMPUTER SCIENCES touch on (but do not delve into) the INFORMATION SCIENCES— the study of INFORMATION and its uses.

computer services organization

PROCESSING, SOFTWARE AND/OR PROFESSIONAL SERVICES ORGANIZATION; A COMPUTER SERVICES ORGANIZATION can be a SERVICE BUREAU that provides TIME-SHARING and BATCH PROCESSING services, a SOFTWARE HOUSE, SYSTEMS HOUSE or OEM that provide SOFTWARE development services, or a consulting firm that provides individual management or technical personnel for COMPUTER-related activities. See SERVICE BUREAU and ADAPSO.

computer system

THE COMPUTER (CPU), ALL THE PERIPHERAL DEVICES ATTACHED TO IT (TERMINALS, PRINTERS, DISKS AND TAPES) AND THE OPERATING SYSTEM (MASTER CONTROL PROGRAM); COMPUTER SYSTEMS fall into ranges called MICROCOMPUTERS, MINICOMPUTERS and MAINFRAMES (roughly small, medium and large).

COMPUTER SYSTEMS are sized for the total USER workload, which is primarily based on: (1) the number of USER TERMINALS required, (2) the amount and nature of work that must be performed simultaneously by USERS at each TERMINAL (light work = INTERACTIVE, heavy work = BATCH), and (3) the amount of ON-LINE DISK STORAGE necessary to hold the INFORMATION. A single COMPUTER SYSTEM usually has a maximum amount of MEMORY and a maximum amount of PERIPHERALS (TERMINALS and DISKS, etc.) that can be physically attached to it.

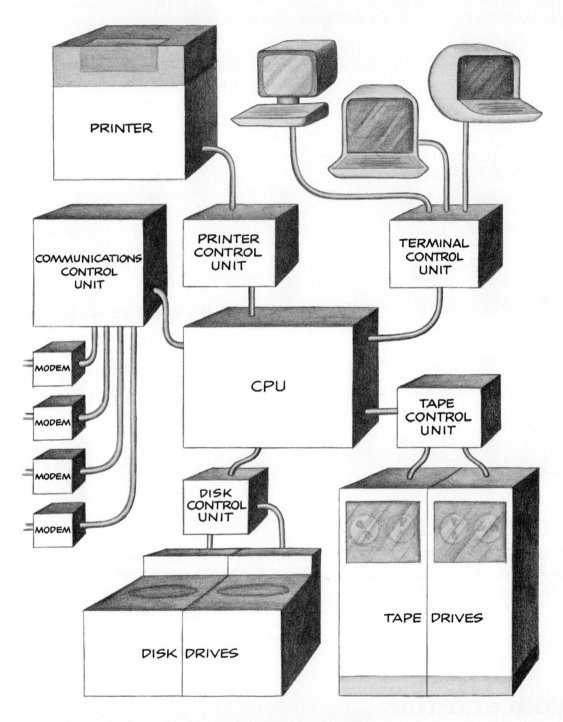

COMPUTER SYSTEM

COMPUTER SYSTEM FEATURES

Following are the major features of a COMPUTER SYSTEM which can be used as a guide to COMPUTER SYSTEM selection and evaluation:

Feature:	Significance:
ARCHITECTURE and MACHINE LANGUAGE of CPU	(compatibility with available and future HARDWARE and SOFTWARE)
Maxium number of TERMINALS	(number of individual USER TERMINALS)
Maximum amount of MEMORY	(capacity to do work)
Maximum amount of ON-LINE DISK	(available INFORMATION capacity at all times)
OPERATING SYSTEM	(how COMPUTER environment is managed)
COMMUNICATIONS PROTOCOLS	(available ACCESS to NETWORKS and other COMPUTERS)
PROGRAMMING LANGUAGES	(choice of development tools and future transportability to other COMPUTERS)
FAIL-SAFE design	(non-stop operation)

concatenation

CHAINING TOGETHER; CONCATENATION links together DATA STRUCTURES, such as FIELDS, RECORDS, and FILES. In order to SORT a group of separate FILES into one sequence, they must be CONCATENATED first (if the SORT PROGRAM will not accept multiple FILES). If city and state are FIXED LENGTH FIELDS in a RECORD, the FIELDS must be CONCATENATED with a comma and a "blank squash" to get "New York, NY" instead of "New York   NY." SPEECH SYNTHESIS units CONCATENATE PHONEMES into speech.

concentrator

COMMUNICATIONS HARDWARE; A CONCENTRATOR joins several COMMUNICATION CHANNELS into a single COMMUNICATIONS CHANNEL. A CONCENTRATOR is similar to a MULTIPLEXOR, except that it does not spread the signals out again on the other end. The receiving device (COMPUTER) performs that function.

conditioning

ELECTRONIC FINE-TUNING OF A TELEPHONE LINE; CONDITIONING is a telephone term for balancing a PRIVATE LINE for maximum transmission of DIGITAL DATA.

connect time

THE TIME A USER AT A TERMINAL IS LOGGED-ON TO A COMPUTER; See SERVICE BUREAU.

console

COMPUTER OPERATOR'S TERMINAL; The CONSOLE usually refers to the VIDEO TERMINAL used by the COMPUTER OPERATOR or the SYSTEMS PROGRAMMER to control the COMPUTER SYSTEM. This type of CONSOLE could contain special keys not available on the USER TERMINAL. The term is also used to refer to the USER'S TERMINAL or SCREEN on a PERSONAL COMPUTER (since the USER is the OPERATOR). CONSOLE is also used to refer to any VIDEO TERMINAL.

constant

INFORMATION IN A PROGRAM WITH FIXED VALUES; REPORT titles, CONVERSATIONAL messages for USERS at a TERMINAL, or values used for PROCESSING the INPUT are all examples of CONSTANTS in a PROGRAM. See PROGRAM.

consultant

TECHNICAL SPECIALIST; CONSULTANTS come from internal consulting groups or from an outside consulting firm. They can act as advisors or they can perform detailed SYSTEMS ANALYSIS & DESIGN. CONSULTANTS can help USERS formulate their INFORMATION requirements and produce a generalized or detailed set of specifications from which HARDWARE or SOFTWARE vendors can respond. CONSULTANTS are often used as project advisors throughout the SYSTEM DEVELOPMENT CYCLE.

control key

FUNCTION KEY; The CONTROL KEY on the KEYBOARD is used like a typewriter shift key. The CONTROL KEY is depressed along with another key, and the combination is sensed as a unique INPUT (and a special CODE is generated). CONTROL KEY functions are used extensively in PERSONAL COMPUTERS for APPLICATIONS like WORD PROCESSING. See KEYBOARD.

control unit

HARDWARE COMPONENTS WHICH DIRECT COMPUTER AND PERIPHERAL
ACTIVITIES; The CONTROL UNIT in the PROCESSOR performs the primary
COMPUTER functions. It locates, analyzes and directs the EXECUTION of each
INSTRUCTION in the PROGRAM. PERIPHERAL CONTROL UNITS, upon signals from
the CPU, carry out the physical INFORMATION transfers between the PERIPHERALS
and the CPU. In small COMPUTERS, PERIPHERAL CONTROL UNITS may be
contained on the same PC BOARD as the CPU, or they may be housed on separate PC
BOARDS. In large MAINFRAMES, PERIPHERAL CONTROL UNITS are often stand-
alone units.

controller

Same as CONTROL UNIT.

conventional programming

PROCEDURAL PROGRAMMING LANGUAGES; COMPILERS and INTERPRETERS
like COBOL, FORTRAN, and BASIC are CONVENTIONAL PROGRAMMING
LANGUAGES. They require knowledge of COMPUTER and INFORMATION
PROCESSING concepts and techniques. Languages which are not considered
CONVENTIONAL PROGRAMMING are found in PROGRAM and APPLICATION
GENERATORS, DATA MANAGEMENT SYSTEMS, FINANCIAL PLANNING SYSTEMS,
QUERY LANGUAGES and REPORT WRITERS.

conversational

INTERACTIVE DIALOGUE BETWEEN THE USER AT A TERMINAL AND THE
COMPUTER; See PEOPLE/MACHINE INTERFACE.

conversion

CHANGING FROM ONE SYSTEM TO ANOTHER; DATA CONVERSION may refer to a
change in FILE or DATA BASE FORMAT, or a change in storage media FORMAT (DISK
to TAPE, 7-TRACK TAPE to 9-TRACK TAPE, etc.). CODE CONVERSION is a change of
DATA CODE (ASCII to EBCDIC, etc.). PROGRAM CONVERSION refers to changing
the PROGRAMMING LANGUAGE or changing SOFTWARE INTERFACES between
APPLICATION PROGRAMS and SYSTEM SOFTWARE. COMPUTER SYSTEM
CONVERSION refers to a change in CPU and PERIPHERALS. INFORMATION SYSTEM
CONVERSION refers to DATA CONVERSION and the installation of new APPLICATION
PROGRAMS.

core (storage)

MEMORY (RAM); MEMORY (working storage) in a COMPUTER during the 1960s was usually constructed of tiny magnetic CORES. The direction of the current in the CORE represented the *0* or *1* BIT. As a result, MEMORY is often still referred to as CORE or CORE STORAGE. (Note: CORES are still used for various specialized APPLICATIONS.)

cost/benefits analysis

PROJECTION OF COSTS AND BENEFITS; Costs for the development and use of an INFORMATION SYSTEM include all the human and machine resources in the SYSTEM DEVELOPMENT CYCLE as well as: costs for people and utilities to run the SYSTEM, on-going HARDWARE and SYSTEM SOFTWARE MAINTENANCE, APPLICATION PROGRAM MAINTENANCE, storage media, and paper supplies. Tangible benefits can be viewed by estimating the cost savings of both human and machine resources to run the new SYSTEM versus the old SYSTEM. Intangible benefits, such as improved customer service, improved employee relations, or more effective competition in the marketplace may ultimately provide larger payback than the tangible benefits, yet are the hardest to justify. Justification for intangible benefits relies heavily on expert management judgement.

counter

A FIELD RESERVED IN A PROGRAM FOR CALCULATING; A COUNTER can be used for calculations or for keeping track of things. Except for exceeding the MEMORY size of the COMPUTER in which it will be run, there is usually very little limitation to the number of COUNTERS that can be reserved in a PROGRAM.

courseware

EDUCATIONAL SOFTWARE PROGRAMS; COMPUTER PROGRAMS that teach may be referred to as COURSEWARE instead of SOFTWARE.

CP

CENTRAL **P**ROCESSOR; See PROCESSOR and CPU.

CP/M

CONTROL **P**ROGRAM FOR **M**ICROPROCESSORS; CP/M is the first OPERATING SYSTEM to become a standard across a large number of different vendors' COMPUTERS. CP/M is a single-USER OPERATING SYSTEM for Z80, 8080 and 8085 COMPUTERS. CP/M became popular because it was one of the first OPERATING SYSTEMS written for MICROPROCESSORS. As more vendors chose the Z80 for their PROCESSOR and CP/M for its OPERATING SYSTEM, it became a popular choice for the next vendor. CP/M was written for PROGRAMMERS or people familiar with

COMPUTER usage; as a result, first-time USERS require training in its use. There are several PROGRAMS written which camouflage the CP/M COMMANDS with USER-FRIENDLY MENUS for ease of use, however.

CP/M and CP/M-80 are synonymous. CP/M-86 is CP/M for the 8086 and 8088 COMPUTERS. Concurrent CP/M and Concurrent CP/M-86 are MULTITASKING versions of CP/M. MP/M is the MULTIUSER version of Concurrent CP/M. CP/M OPERATING SYSTEMS are products of Digital Research, Inc.

CPM

CRITICAL **P**ATH **M**ETHOD; CPM is a project management planning and control technique implemented on COMPUTERS. The critical path is the series of activities and tasks in the project that have no built-in slack time. Any task in the critical path that takes longer than expected will lengthen the total time of the project.

CPS

CHARACTERS **P**ER **S**ECOND; CPS measures the speed of a SERIAL PRINTER or the speed of an INFORMATION transfer between HARDWARE devices or over a COMMUNICATIONS CHANNEL.

CPU

CENTRAL **P**ROCESSING **U**NIT; The CPU refers to the PROCESSOR and MAIN MEMORY. It also may refer to just the PROCESSOR by itself, such as a MICROPROCESSOR. It often refers simply to the COMPUTER, in contrast to the PERIPHERAL devices which are attached to it.

crash

UNPLANNED HARDWARE OR SOFTWARE TERMINATION; A CRASH usually refers to a PROGRAM failure, called an ABEND. It may also refer to the failure of a LOGIC or MEMORY CIRCUIT causing the HARDWARE to fail. With regards to a DISK DRIVE, it may refer to the physical destruction of the DISK surface, called a HEAD CRASH.

CRC

ERROR CHECKING TECHNIQUE; CRC is a method to ensure the accurate transfer of BINARY CODE over a CHANNEL. The MESSAGES transmitted are divided into predetermined lengths. Each length of BINARY CODE is used as a dividend which is divided by a fixed divisor. The remainder of the calculation is appended onto the end of the MESSAGE transmitted. At the receiving end, the COMPUTER recalculates the remainder and matches it against the transmitted remainder. If it doesn't match, an error is detected. CRC stands for **C**yclical **R**edundancy **C**hecking.

cross assembler/compiler

PROGRAM TRANSLATOR THAT GENERATES FOREIGN MACHINE LANGUAGE; CROSS ASSEMBLERS and CROSS COMPILERS are used to generate MACHINE LANGUAGE for another COMPUTER. They are usually used to develop PROGRAMS for MICROCHIPS or MICROCOMPUTERS (which in themselves are too small to be used for PROGRAM development). The CROSS ASSEMBLER/COMPILER generates MACHINE LANGUAGE for the smaller COMPUTER.

crosstalk

INTERFERENCE FROM ADJACENT CHANNELS; CROSSTALK is a signal that inadvertently crosses from one CHANNEL to another.

CRT

CATHODE **R**AY **T**UBE; The CRT is the technical term for the VACUUM TUBE used in a TV or VIDEO TERMINAL SCREEN. CRT is often used to refer to the entire VIDEO TERMINAL, including the KEYBOARD. See VIDEO TERMINAL.

CSMA/CD

COMMUNICATIONS NETWORK ACCESS METHOD; CSMA/CD is a collision-detection method for gaining ACCESS onto a NETWORK. When a device wants to gain ACCESS onto the NETWORK, it senses whether or not another MESSAGE is being carried (transmitted) at that time, and if so, it waits a random amount of time before attempting to gain ACCESS again. If two devices attempt to gain ACCESS at exactly the same time, they both back off (detecting a possible collision) and wait a random amount of time to retry. CSMA/CD is an ACCESS METHOD used in BASEBAND LOCAL AREA NETWORKS. CSMA/CD stands for **C**arrier **S**ense **M**ultiple **A**ccess / **C**ollision **D**etection.

CTRL

ABBREVIATION FOR CONTROL KEY; See CONTROL KEY and KEYBOARD.

cursor

THE SCREEN POINTER; The CURSOR is the square or special symbol on a VIDEO SCREEN that indicates which CHARACTER on the SCREEN is being referenced. Often, when the CURSOR is at a location occupied by a CHARACTER, it causes the CHARACTER to blink. The CURSOR may also refer to a drawing device used on a DIGITIZER TABLET.

TYPICAL
CURSOR KEY
CLUSTORS

cursor keys

KEYBOARD KEYS THAT CONTROL THE CURSOR; The CURSOR KEYS are used to move the CURSOR around on the SCREEN. KEYBOARDS can contain several different combinations of CURSOR KEYS, the left and right keys being the minimum configuration. One key depression moves the CURSOR one column to the left or right. Four keys are more adequate (left/right/up/down) and there are several other options available. A HOME KEY is a special CURSOR KEY which moves the CURSOR to the top left of the SCREEN, or to the beginning of the current line.

If the KEYBOARD does not contain any CURSOR KEYS, then CONTROL KEYS might be used to move the CURSOR. A note for PERSONAL and MICROCOMPUTER USERS: Unless the SOFTWARE PACKAGE you are using has been specialized for your TERMINAL, your CURSOR KEYS may not work and CONTROL KEY combinations may be required to move the CURSOR.

cut & paste

TEXT EDITING FUNCTION TO MOVE TEXT; A portion of TEXT is marked with a specific CHARACTER at the beginning and at the end, and is moved to another location within the DOCUMENT. The CUT & PASTE function is identified in different ways in WORD PROCESSING SYSTEMS, such as: move block, move section, move column, etc.

CYBER

SERIES OF LARGE-SCALE MAINFRAMES AND SUPERCOMPUTERS MANUFACTURED BY CONTROL DATA CORPORATION.

cybernetics

THE COMPARATIVE STUDY OF ORGANIC AND MACHINE PROCESSES; CYBERNETICS explores the internal workings of both people and machines in order to understand their similarities and differences. CYBERNETICS often refers to a machine which imitates human behavior. See ARTIFICIAL INTELLIGENCE and ROBOTS.

cycle stealing

COMPUTER DESIGN TECHNIQUE; CYCLE STEALING refers to the periodic "grabbing" of MACHINE CYCLES from the main PROCESSOR, usually by some PERIPHERAL CONTROL UNIT such as a DMA (DIRECT MEMORY ACCESS) device. In this way, PROCESSING and PERIPHERAL operations can be performed concurrently or with some degree of overlap.

cyclical redundancy checking

See CRC.

cylinder

AGGREGATE OF TRACKS ON A DISK; TRACKS are concentric circles on a DISK platter. If the platter is recorded on both sides, the combination of the same TRACK on top and on the bottom is called a CYLINDER. In a multiple platter DISK PACK, the CYLINDER is the total of all the same number TRACKS on all the platters.

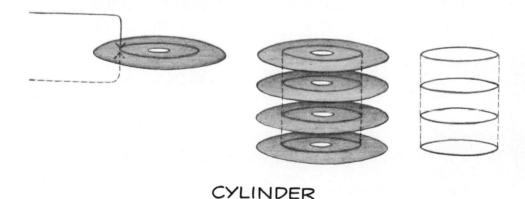

CYLINDER

DA

See **DA**TA **A**DMINISTRATOR.

DAC

See **D**IGITAL TO
ANALOG **C**ONVERTER.

DAD

DATA BASE **A**CTION
DIAGRAM; A DAD
describes the
PROCESSING performed
on DATA in a
DATA BASE.

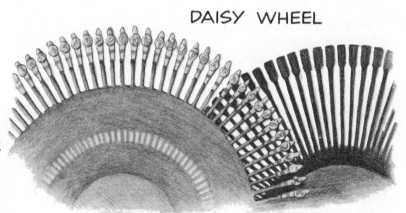

DAISY WHEEL

daisy wheel

LETTER QUALITY PRINTER MECHANISM; Shaped CHARACTER images are attached
to the end of spokes on a plastic or metal wheel. The wheel spins in one direction as it
moves serially across the paper. When it reaches the selected print location, a hammer
hits the end of the spoke, impressing the CHARACTER at the end of the selected spoke
into the ribbon and onto the paper. DAISY WHEEL PRINTERS are called SERIAL
PRINTERS and CHARACTER PRINTERS.

DASD

DIRECT **A**CCESS **S**TORAGE **D**EVICE; MAGNETIC DISK and MAGNETIC DRUM are
DASDs. DASD is pronounced /daz-dee/. See DIRECT ACCESS and DISK.

data

UNITS OF INFORMATION WHICH CAN BE PRECISELY DEFINED; Technically, DATA are raw facts and figures which are PROCESSED into INFORMATION. For example: hours worked and hourly rate are DATA; this week's gross pay is INFORMATION. Since we store both DATA and INFORMATION in our FILES and DATA BASES, the terms DATA and INFORMATION are often used synonymously. The traditional view of DATA vs INFORMATION (raw fact vs derived) is an important distinction, however, when a DATA BASE is designed.

As we integrate DATA with TEXT, GRAPHICS and voice (OFFICE AUTOMATION), the use of the term DATA has become even more specific. It implies DATA structures which have a precise definition. DATA are defined by DATA ELEMENTS, which define a unit of DATA according to name, size, type and range of values. Name, address, city, state, zip code and customer number are examples of DATA ELEMENTS. TEXT, GRAPHICS and voice FILES, are STREAM ORIENTED and are structured differently than DATA.

data administration

DATA MANAGEMENT; DATA ADMINISTRATION is the management of an organization's DATA/INFORMATION as an organizational resource. The flow of DATA/INFORMATION within an organization can be complex. The same DATA is viewed differently as it moves from department to department. For example: A customer places an order. That order becomes: a sales commission and quota fulfillment for sales, a demographic statistic for marketing, an order to keep track of in the order processing department, an effect on cash flow projection for financial officers, picking schedules for the warehouse, and production scheduling for manufacturing. USERS have their own view of this DATA and have different requirements for interrogating it and UPDATING it. Operations people need detail, management needs summaries. Before long-lasting DATA BASE designs can be achieved, the DATA and the DATA relationships must be carefully analyzed, classified and maintained. See DATA ADMINISTRATOR.

data administrator

MANAGER OF DATA; DATA ADMINISTRATORS analyze the flow of DATA and INFORMATION in an organization. They analyze USER requirements for DATA and INFORMATION across departmental lines and develop individual USER views of this DATA. DATA ADMINISTRATORS classify groups of related DATA by developing DATA MODELS. The DATA MODELS describe the DATA and their relationships with other DATA and with USERS. DATA MODELS specify common DATA that cross departmental boundaries within an organization. DATA/INFORMATION must be viewed organizationwide in order to develop the proper framework for DATA BASE design. A DATA DICTIONARY is developed which documents the analysis by the DATA ADMINISTRATOR. The DATA MODELS and DATA DICTIONARY, combined with TRANSACTION volume (analyzed by SYSTEMS ANALYSTS) are the raw materials for DATA BASE design.

data bank

ELECTRONIC DEPOSITORY OF DATA.

data base

(1) DBMS DATA BASE, (2) FILE, (3) DATA/INFORMATION BANK;

(1) Technically, a DATA BASE is an ELECTRONIC organization of DATA and INFORMATION organized and maintained by a DATA BASE MANAGEMENT SYSTEM. A DATA BASE implies integration of DATA across the entire environment that it serves. It also implies central control of DATA for consistency and accuracy with USERS having ACCESS to their authorized view of it.

(2) DATA BASE often refers to a MASTER FILE which is *not* organized and maintained by a DATA BASE MANAGEMENT SYSTEM.

(3) DATA BASE is used to refer to any ELECTRONIC depository of DATA/INFORMATION.

data base administrator

DATA BASE DESIGNER AND MANAGER; The DATA BASE ADMINISTRATOR is responsible for the physical design of the DATA structures in the DATA BASE and for the evaluation, selection and implementation of the DATA BASE MANAGEMENT SYSTEM. In smaller organizations, the DATA ADMINISTRATOR and DATA BASE ADMINISTRATOR are often one in the same; however, the DA is a DATA MANAGEMENT function and the DBA is a SYSTEMS PROGRAMMING function. The DATA BASE ADMINISTRATOR implements the DATA BASE SOFTWARE that meets the requirements outlined by the organization's DATA ADMINISTRATOR and SYSTEMS ANALYSTS.

data base designer

See DATA BASE ADMINISTRATOR.

data base machine

A COMPUTER DEDICATED TO HANDLING THE ACCESSING OF THE DATA BASE; The DATA BASE MACHINE is a separate COMPUTER which is TIGHTLY COUPLED to the main COMPUTER. It handles the storage and retrieval of DATA into and out of the DATA BASE. PROGRAMS in the PROCESSING COMPUTER transfer DATA to and from the DATA BASE MACHINE via a high-speed CHANNEL. A DATA BASE MACHINE may be a standard COMPUTER with a specialized OPERATING SYSTEM designed for it, or it may be a COMPUTER with specialized HARDWARE for DATA BASE operations. A DATA BASE MACHINE is also called a BACK END PROCESSOR. See also DATA BASE SERVER.

data base management system

SOFTWARE THAT ORGANIZES AND RETRIEVES DATA IN A DATA BASE; A DATA BASE MANAGEMENT SYSTEM makes it easier to ACCESS all varieties of DATA/INFORMATION stored in a COMPUTER. It allows USERS to request DATA the way *they* see it rather than the way the COMPUTER sees it. If a DBMS is not used, it requires more detailed PROGRAMMING to ACCESS DATA. For example, if a USER has a request for DATA that resides in different FILES (customer FILE, order FILE, and invoice FILE), the traditional APPLICATION PROGRAM would have to be written to bring in all three of those RECORDS and copy out the FIELDS required. If a DBMS is used, the PROGRAM commands the DBMS to deliver just the FIELDS requested, no matter where they reside.

The DBMS is a SOFTWARE PACKAGE which acts as an INTERFACE between the USER'S PROGRAMS and the physical DATA BASE. The DBMS allows for the organization of *non-redundant* DATA in the DATA BASE. It keeps track of all the DATA and allows each USER to have an individual view of the DATA. The USER'S view is called a SUBSCHEMA (combination of DATA ELEMENTS required by a particular USER). THE USER'S APPLICATION PROGRAM asks the DBMS to select that USER'S view and deliver it to the PROGRAM (USER). Only the DBMS knows where and how to get it. If a structural change is made to the DATA BASE (new FIELDS are added, FIELDS are enlarged, etc.), only the USER PROGRAMS that use that DATA will be affected. In a traditional FILE structure, every APPLICATION PROGRAM is affected when a structural change to the RECORD is made (since the APPLICATION PROGRAM ACCESSES the entire RECORD structure regardless of how much of the DATA is actually used in that particular PROGRAM). The DBMS acts as a buffer between the PROGRAMS and the physical structure of the DATA BASE.

Selection of a DBMS (if there are choices within a vendor's environment) can be critical. Since much of the organization's DATA will be placed into the DATA BASE, the PROCESSING time required to ACCESS the DATA BASE must be carefully evaluated. A DATA MODEL is first developed which defines the DATA and their logical relationships with other DATA. Then the TRANSACTION activity that will be PROCESSED against this DATA BASE is evaluated. The resulting selection is the DBMS that will manage a particular DATA MODEL with efficient machine performance.

A portion of the DBMS resides in MEMORY and is called upon by the APPLICATION PROGRAM each time DATA must be transferred to or from the DATA BASE. The DBMS will call upon the ACCESS METHODS in the OPERATING SYSTEM for physical DATA transfers. If the DBMS is running in a separate dedicated computer (DATA BASE MACHINE), the ACCESS METHODS are contained in a specialized OPERATING SYSTEM in the DATA BASE COMPUTER.

NOTE: The term DATA BASE is often used to refer to any storage structure or INFORMATION bank. A DBMS DATA BASE implies true DATA MANAGEMENT SOFTWARE.

MAJOR FEATURES OF A DBMS

DATA INDEPENDENCE— The APPLICATION PROGRAMS are not concerned with the location of any DATA they use. Advanced DBMSs use DATA DICTIONARIES and NON-PROCEDURAL languages, which may mean that no changes are required in the PROGRAMS when a structural change to DATA is made.

SECURITY— The DBMS can test for USER authorization at the APPLICATION PROGRAM level, SUBSCHEMA level, or FIELD level, depending on the DBMS.

ON-LINE QUERY— An INTERACTIVE QUERY capability allows USERS ACCESS to their DATA using a QUERY LANGUAGE.

APPLICATION DEVELOPMENT LANGUAGE— A HIGH-LEVEL NON-PROCEDURAL LANGUAGE developed around the DBMS may allow PROGRAMMERS and USERS to develop APPLICATION PROGRAMS faster than with CONVENTIONAL PROGRAMMING LANGUAGES.

DATA BASE DESIGN

The DATA/INFORMATION stored in a DATA BASE depends on the functions of the organization. The ultimate DATA BASE structure into which the DATA is designed (HIERARCHICAL, NETWORK, RELATIONAL, etc.) depends on the volume and frequency of the daily TRANSACTIONS and management's ad hoc requirements for INFORMATION.

Operations people need detail, management needs summaries. If detail DATA is stored in the DATA BASE, the DATA can be PROCESSED by a PROGRAM into any variety of INFORMATION desired. Yet, if large amounts of detail are maintained in the DATA BASE, ON-LINE storage costs may become a consideration. If INFORMATION is derived from the detail DATA and the detail is eliminated, it may be difficult and/or time-consuming to go back and generate a different derivation later. DATA BASE design is often a compromise between operational requirements for efficient daily TRANSACTION PROCESSING and management's requirements for ad hoc QUERIES and REPORTS.

data base manager

Same as DATA BASE MANAGEMENT SYSTEM.

data base server

COMPUTER IN A NETWORK DEDICATED TO ACCESSING DATA; A DATA BASE SERVER is a separate COMPUTER in a COMMUNICATIONS NETWORK which serves many USERS at their WORKSTATIONS. Unlike a DATA BASE MACHINE, which is TIGHTLY COUPLED to the MAIN COMPUTER, the DATA BASE SERVER is LOOSELY COUPLED in the NETWORK.

datacenter

COMPUTER OPERATIONS DEPARTMENT; The DATACENTER contains the COMPUTERS and is responsible for their daily operation. The DATA LIBRARY is the part of the DATACENTER where DISKS and TAPES are cataloged and stored. Often an INPUT/OUTPUT control section is part of the DATACENTER, which accepts and distributes work from USER departments. The DATA ENTRY department may also be under the jurisdiction of the DATACENTER. DATACENTER personnel may be responsible for the evaluation and selection of HARDWARE and SYSTEM SOFTWARE.

data communications

TRANSFER OF DATA BETWEEN REMOTE LOCATIONS; See COMMUNICATIONS.

data compression

COMPACTION OF BINARY CODE; DATA COMPRESSION is used to save storage space and transmission time. Various techniques are used; however, their principle is the same. A group of BITS is analyzed for content and converted to and represented by a smaller number of BITS. When the DATA is PROCESSED, it must be DECODED back into its original form.

data description language

LANGUAGE USED TO DEFINE DATA; A DATA DESCRIPTION LANGUAGE defines DATA ELEMENTS and their relationships, and is used to create DATA MODELS and DATA DICTIONARIES.

data dictionary

DATA BASE OF DATA; A DATA DICTIONARY can be used in different ways. It can be a high-level DOCUMENTATION SYSTEM for the DATA ADMINISTRATOR, or it can be a working PROGRAM used by the DATA BASE MANAGEMENT SYSTEM SOFTWARE, or both.

Essentially, the DATA DICTIONARY is a self-contained INFORMATION SYSTEM regarding the organization's LOGICAL and PHYSICAL DATA. It can be viewed as a DATA BASE of DATA and DATA BASES. The DATA DICTIONARY itself may or may not be organized by a DATA BASE MANAGEMENT SYSTEM.

The name, type, range of values, source, and authorization for ACCESS for each DATA ELEMENT are stored in the DATA DICTIONARY. In addition, the names of each APPLICATION PROGRAM that uses that DATA may also be stored as well. The DATA DICTIONARY SYSTEM can be used to determine the magnitude of a contemplated change to the DATA by preparing a REPORT of all the PROGRAMS that would be affected.

The DATA DICTIONARY may be used to actually drive the DATA BASE MANAGEMENT SYSTEM. The DBMS would refer to it each time it required ACCESS to the physical DATA BASE. In this way, the definitions of DATA are always current, since changes are only made to the DATA DICTIONARY.

data element

THE SMALLEST UNIT OF DATA THAT CAN BE DEFINED; Name, address, city, account number, status code, amount due, and year-to-date gross pay, are all examples of DATA ELEMENTS. A DATA ELEMENT must be precisely defined by type, size, range of values, etc. The DATA ELEMENT is technically the LOGICAL definition of DATA, whereas a FIELD refers to the PHYSICAL DATA residing in a RECORD. For example, the DATA ELEMENT, "name," defines the type of DATA stored in the "name" FIELD of 138 RECORDS. However, DATA ELEMENT and FIELD as well as DATA ITEM and VARIABLE are all used interchangeably.

data encryption standard

See DES.

data entry

ENTERING DATA INTO THE COMPUTER; DATA ENTRY can refer to the department, the people, or the PROGRAMS that enter DATA/INFORMATION into the COMPUTER. DATA ENTRY includes human typing on TERMINAL KEYBOARDS, as well as VOICE RECOGNITION and OPTICAL SCANNING. DATA ENTRY PROGRAMS are extremely important because they establish the DATA in the DATA BASE. DATA INPUT can be tested for type and range of values within the PROGRAM, but there is no way a PROGRAM can test for the "right" DATA. If the DATA is keyboarded by people, it is often necessary to verify the INPUT manually by matching a PRINTOUT of the captured DATA with the SOURCE DOCUMENT. Verification can be performed by double entry of the DATA by different DATA ENTRY operators. The COMPUTER matches the INPUT from one operator with the INPUT from the second operator. If DATA entered is immediately UPDATING the DATA BASE, then verification of the correct account number is necessary. The name of the individual or customer can be flashed on the SCREEN verifying the correct matching of the account number. See CHECK DIGIT.

data flow diagram

FLOW CHART OF MOVEMENT OF DATA WITHIN AN ORGANIZATION; The DATA FLOW DIAGRAM describes the DATA, as well as the manual and machine PROCESSING performed on the DATA.

data independence

SEPARATION OF DATA FROM PROCESSING IN A DBMS ENVIRONMENT; In conventional FILE SYSTEMS, each PROGRAM must reserve space for the entire RECORD even if DATA in only a part of that RECORD is required. The reason is that if the size of a DATA ELEMENT changes (increase address by 5 CHARACTERS, for example), the physical increase of the address FIELD in the RECORD will throw off all the references to the other FIELDS. Every PROGRAM which PROCESSES any DATA in that RECORD must be changed.

In a DATA BASE MANAGEMENT SYSTEM environment, APPLICATION PROGRAMS reserve space for only the DATA they require. They "ask" the DBMS for their unique collection of DATA (called a SUBSCHEMA). When structural changes to DATA occur, they only affect the PROGRAMS that will actually PROCESS them. A change often requires no more than one entry to the DBMS, which may set up the PROCEDURES automatically to change the PROGRAMS which are affected. If an APPLICATION DEVELOPMENT LANGUAGE designed specifically around the DBMS were used to develop the PROGRAMS, there might not be any changes whatsoever necessary in the PROGRAMS.

data item

Same as DATA ELEMENT or FIELD.

DATA LIBRARY

THE COMPUTER GLOSSARY

data library

STORAGE CENTER FOR OFF-LINE DATA; DISKS and TAPES are cataloged and stored in the DATA LIBRARY. DATA LIBRARY personnel determine when DISKS and TAPES can be re-used, or when they must be cleaned or replaced. See DATACENTER.

data management

STORAGE/RETRIEVAL AND CONTROL OF DATA; DATA MANAGEMENT may refer to any of several levels of the management of DATA. From bottom to top they are:

> DATA MANAGEMENT may refer to FILE or DATA BASE ACCESS METHODS which manage the physical storage and retrieval of DATA on a DISK.

> DATA MANAGEMENT may refer to self-contained DATA PROCESSING SYSTEMS, which allow for the creation, storage, retrieval and manipulation of FILES or DATA BASES (See DATA MANAGEMENT SYSTEM).

> DATA MANAGEMENT may refer to high-level management functions which manage DATA as an organizational resource (See DATA ADMINISTRATION).

data management system

DATA PROCESSING SYSTEM; A DATA MANAGEMENT SYSTEM is a self-contained SOFTWARE SYSTEM which allows for the creation, storage, retrieval and manipulation of FILES or DATA BASES. It may use its own FILE or DATA BASE MANAGEMENT SYSTEM as a foundation, or it may work with existing FILES or DATA BASES, or both. DATA MANAGEMENT SYSTEMS provide a HIGH-LEVEL NON-PROCEDURAL language for APPLICATION development, and thus are often described as APPLICATION GENERATORS. These languages may be MENU DRIVEN or COMMAND DRIVEN. DATA MANAGEMENT SYSTEMS provide a QUERY LANGUAGE and REPORT WRITER for retrieval. Some also provide BUSINESS GRAPHICS and FINANCIAL PLANNING. A DATA MANAGEMENT SYSTEM may be used as a DECISION SUPPORT SYSTEM if it has facilities to ad hoc manipulate DATA into a variety of forms.

A DATA MANAGEMENT SYSTEM may also INTERFACE with CONVENTIONAL PROGRAMS like COBOL and FORTRAN. The DATA MANAGEMENT SYSTEM may eliminate some, most or all CONVENTIONAL PROGRAMMING for the development of an INFORMATION SYSTEM.

A major advantage of a *fully-integrated* DATA MANAGEMENT SYSTEM, is that a *single* COMMAND language can activate and manipulate any DATA PROCESSING function.

data manipulation language

LANGUAGE WHICH DEFINES DATA BASE PROCESSING; The DATA
MANIPULATION LANGUAGE is used in an APPLICATION PROGRAM (like COBOL
or PL/I) to INTERFACE to a DATA BASE MANAGEMENT SYSTEM.

data processing

THE CAPTURING, STORING, MANIPULATING AND RETRIEVING OF
DATA/INFORMATION; DATA PROCESSING refers to DATA APPLICATIONS, (like
payroll and inventory), in contrast to TEXT APPLICATIONS, (like WORD
PROCESSING). DATA PROCESSING may also refer to the physical operations of the
DATACENTER, in contrast to SYSTEMS and PROGRAMMING functions.

data processor

PERSON OR COMPUTER INVOLVED WITH DATA PROCESSING; A DATA
PROCESSOR usually refers to any person in the COMPUTER SYSTEMS,
PROGRAMMING or OPERATIONS fields. A DATA PROCESSOR may also refer to a
COMPUTER which can EXECUTE DATA PROCESSING PROGRAMS, in contrast to
WORD PROCESSING PROGRAMS.

data rate

THE SPEED OF DATA TRANSMISSION; A DATA RATE is the measurement of the speed
of DATA transmission in a COMPUTER or COMMUNICATIONS CHANNEL.

data resource management

MANAGEMENT OF AN ORGANIZATION'S DATA AS A RESOURCE; See DATA
ADMINISTRATION.

data set

(1) FILE, (2) MODEM; With reference to COMPUTERS, a DATA SET is a FILE. With
reference to COMMUNICATIONS, a DATA SET is a MODEM.

data tablet

See DIGITIZER TABLET.

DBA

See **DATA BASE ADMINISTRATOR**.

dBASE II

DATA BASE MANAGEMENT SYSTEM WHICH RUNS UNDER THE CP/M OPERATING SYSTEM; DBASE II is a RELATIONAL DBMS which is directed by its own PASCAL-like PROGRAMMING LANGUAGE. DATA BASES can be created and manipulated INTERACTIVELY at a TERMINAL or in a DBASE II COMMAND FILE. Because of its integrated DATA handling and PROGRAMMING LANGUAGE, DBASE II is uniquely appropriate for first-time USERS who want to learn PROGRAMMING. DBASE II is a product of Ashton-Tate.

DB/DC

DATA **B**ASE/**D**ATA **C**OMMUNICATIONS; DB/DC refers to SOFTWARE which performs DATA BASE and DATA COMMUNICATION functions. Many DATA BASE MANAGEMENT SYSTEMS provide a package which handles the ON-LINE TERMINAL functions in the COMPUTER.

DBMS

See **D**ATA **B**ASE **M**ANAGEMENT **S**YSTEM.

DBS

DIRECT **B**ROADCAST **S**ATELLITE; DBS refers to a one-way broadcast service direct from a SATELLITE to a USER'S antenna (DISH). Contrast with SBS (Satellite Business Systems) which is a two-way transmission service requiring EARTH STATIONS which transmit and receive signals at USERS' premises.

DCA

UNIVAC NETWORK ARCHITECTURE; Stands for **D**istributed **C**ommunications **A**rchitecture.

DCE

DATA **C**OMMUNICATIONS **E**QUIPMENT; A DCE is a COMMUNICATIONS device which establishes, maintains and terminates transmission over a COMMUNICATIONS CHANNEL. It also may convert the signals from the TERMINAL or COMPUTER (DTE) to transmit over the CIRCUIT. A MODEM is typically the DCE device and the TERMINAL is typically the DTE device. DCE also stands for **D**ata **C**ircuit-terminating **E**quipment.

DDCMP

COMMUNICATION PROTOCOL DEVELOPED BY DIGITAL EQUIPMENT CORPORATION; Stands for **D**igital **D**ata **C**ommunications **M**essage **P**rotocol.

DDL

See **D**ATA **D**ESCRIPTION **L**ANGUAGE.

debug

CORRECT HARDWARE OR SOFTWARE; DEBUGGING usually refers to the correcting of a PROGRAM which is not working properly. DEBUG means remove the "BUGS." DEBUGGING may also refer to the correcting of newly designed ELECTRONIC CIRCUITRY in a COMPUTER or a CHIP.

DEC

DIGITAL **E**QUIPMENT **C**ORPORATION.

DECsystem

SERIES OF MAINFRAMES MANUFACTURED BY DIGITAL EQUIPMENT CORPORATION.

decentralized processing

COMPUTERS PROCESSING IN SEPARATE LOCATIONS WITHOUT COMMUNICATIONS CAPABILITY BETWEEN THEM; Contrast with DISTRIBUTED PROCESSING, which are separate COMPUTERS *with* COMMUNICATIONS capability between them.

decision making

CHOOSING AN APPROPRIATE ALTERNATIVE; The proper balance of DECISION MAKING is a critical SYSTEMS ANALYSIS & DESIGN criterion. Expert judgement is required to determine how much DECISION MAKING should be performed by people or machines. The analysis of the processing steps performed by an intelligent and intuitive human worker requires considerable experience and talent. If an improper analysis of human DECISION MAKING is undertaken, too much DECISION MAKING may be prematurely placed into the machine. DECISION MAKING performed by COMPUTERS often tends to get buried in DOCUMENTATION which is rarely reviewed, and the actual PROCESSING may even become a mystery to the organization.

From a PROGRAMMING point of view, DECISION MAKING can be performed in two ways: (1) ALGORITHMIC—A precise set of rules and conditions which never change, or (2) HEURISTIC—A set of rules which may change over time (self-modify) as conditions occur. HEURISTIC techniques are employed in the development of ARTIFICIAL INTELLIGENCE SYSTEMS, which are designed to imitate a human's thinking capabilities.

decision support system

INTEGRATED MANAGEMENT INFORMATION AND PLANNING SYSTEM; A DECISION SUPPORT SYSTEM (DSS) provides management with the ability to: (1) ad hoc interrogate its COMPUTER SYSTEMS for all varieties of INFORMATION regarding the organization, and (2) analyze the INFORMATION in various ways, and (3) predict the impact of decisions before they are made.

QUERY LANGUAGES and REPORT WRITERS let USERS interrogate the current status of their DATA and derive INFORMATION from it. DATA manipulation PROGRAMS which select and SORT DATA will arrange it into the required sequence for analysis. MODELING SYSTEMS will provide both DATA analysis and "what if?" planning.

However, any single PROGRAM that supports a manager's decision making is only a DSS tool, not a DSS. A DSS is an *integrated* set of tools which allow DATA to be passed from one function to the other. In addition, a DSS ought to be directed by a *single* COMMAND language. A QUERY LANGUAGE may gain quick ACCESS to DATA, but if the retrieved DATA requires MODELING, an INTERFACE between the QUERY PROGRAM and a MODELING PROGRAM is required. An INTERFACE between the MODELING PROGRAM and BUSINESS GRAPHICS is then required, etc. A DSS should allow for the intermixing of DATA from the outside world as well. An integrated DSS will direcly impact the management DECISION-MAKING process and can change the way decisions are made.

Faster HARDWARE and USER-FRIENDLY SOFTWARE, make the DECISION SUPPORT SYSTEM a greater potential reality in the 1980s than the MIS in the 1970s. However, like any INFORMATION SYSTEMS planning, the nature and framework of the INFORMATION required must still be analyzed carefully before the appropriate DSS can be constructed.

decision table

LIST OF DECISIONS AND THEIR CRITERIA; DECISION TABLES use a MATRIX (TABLE) FORMAT which list criteria (INPUTS) and the results (OUTPUTS) of all the possible combinations of these criteria. A DECISION TABLE can be placed in a PROGRAM and the PROGRAM LOGIC can be derived directly from the DECISION TABLE.

OUTPUTS

INPUTS	APPROVE LOAN	DENY LOAN	SEE LOAN OFFICER	SEE LOAN OFFICER
SAME JOB OVER 5 YRS	YES	NO	NO	YES
OWNS CAR	YES	NO	YES	NO
OWNS HOME	YES	NO	YES	NO
IN DEBT	NO	YES	NO	NO

DECISION TABLE

decoder

CONVERSION DEVICE; A DECODER is any HARDWARE device or SOFTWARE
PROGRAM which converts a CODED signal back into its original form.

decollator

PAPER FORMS SEPARATOR; A DECOLLATOR separates multiple-part paper forms
into separate parts, while also removing the carbon paper.

default

STANDARD SETTING OR ACTION; The DEFAULT is the action taken by SOFTWARE
or HARDWARE, unless the USER specifies otherwise. DEFAULTS can be set up for
myriads of functions. DEFAULTS in WORD PROCESSING PACKAGES define line
width, lines per page, CHARACTERS per inch, tab settings, all of which are modifiable
by the USER. DEFAULTS can also often be permanently modified by the USER to reflect
the most often desired setting or function.

DEMA

A PROFESSIONAL ORGANIZATION DEVOTED TO THE ADVANCEMENT OF DATA
ENTRY MANAGEMENT PERSONNEL; DEMA sponsors educational courses and
conferences for DATA ENTRY managers. Stands for **D**ata **E**ntry **M**anagement
Association.

demodulation

CONVERTING A MODULATED SIGNAL BACK INTO ITS ORIGINAL FORM; See
MODULATION.

DES

DATA **E**NCRYPTION **S**TANDARD; The DES is a standardized ENCRYPTION technique
which allows BINARY CODE to be "scrambled" into an undetectable stream of BITS for
transmission over a public NETWORK. The DES uses a BINARY number, offering more
than 72 quadrillion combinations, as the "key" for ENCRYPTION. The number, which
can be randomly chosen for each transmission, is used as a pattern to convert the BITS at
both ends of the transmission.

descenders

PARTS OF LOWER CASE CHARACTERS WHICH FALL BELOW THE LINE; The lower
case CHARACTERS: g, j, p, q, y, require DESCENDERS for proper printing.

DG

DATA GENERAL CORPORATION.

diagnostics

TESTS FOR DETECTING ERRORS OR MALFUNCTIONS; DIAGNOSTICS are error messages in a PROGRAMMER'S SOURCE listing, or DIAGNOSTICS may refer to a variety of HARDWARE or SOFTWARE that perform tests to detect malfunctions. DIAGNOSTICS can be placed into ROM CHIPS and always be available for a USER or technician to check out various components of the COMPUTER SYSTEM. DIAGNOSTICS may be designed to automatically check out certain components when the power is turned on.

digital

COMPUTER CONTROLLED; The fundamental technology behind COMPUTERS is DIGITAL storage and transmission (the BITS and BYTES). By converting all forms of INFORMATION into BINARY CODE, the COMPUTER SYSTEM can accept it and store it for posterity. DIGITAL CODE can be copied over and over again by a COMPUTER without losing accuracy (unlike traditional ANALOG signals such as AUDIO and VIDEO). Using DIGITAL transmission, identical copies of DATA, TEXT, pictures or voice messages, can be created 10,000 miles away as easily as within 10 feet of the COMPUTER.

Note: While there are ANALOG COMPUTERS used in various scientific and monitor and control APPLICATIONS, the vast majority of COMPUTERS are DIGITAL. The terms COMPUTER and DIGITAL have become synonymous.

digital camera

CAMERA THAT TAKES A DIGITAL PICTURE; A DIGITAL CAMERA is similar to a television VIDEO camera in that the viewing area is broken up into a mosaic of tiny dots, called PIXELS. Unlike a TV camera, which creates an ANALOG signal for each PIXEL it perceives, a DIGITAL CAMERA converts each PIXEL into BINARY CODE. See BINARY CODE and GRAPHICS.

digital PABX

PABX WHICH HANDLES BOTH VOICE AND DATA; A DIGITAL PABX is an in-house central switching COMPUTER which interconnects one telephone line to another, as well as one DATA line to another. Both telephones and TERMINALS are connected to the DIGITAL PABX NETWORK.

A DIGITAL PABX may be a traditional ANALOG voice PABX which has been adapted for DIGITAL DATA and requires MODEMS for each DATA device. Or a DIGITAL PABX may be an all-DIGITAL switching device requiring that the telephones generate

DIGITAL voice signals (See CODEC). Some DIGITAL PABXs offer the option of ANALOG or DIGITAL transmission for both voice or DATA.

While performing all the functions of a COMPUTERIZED PABX, such as least cost routing to outside NETWORKS, a DIGITAL PABX may also perform functions like PROTOCOL CONVERSION between COMPUTERS and/or TERMINALS, as well as WP FORMAT CONVERSION between different WORD PROCESSORS.

DIGITAL PABXs may serve as a LOCAL AREA NETWORK and/or may connect to other LOCAL AREA NETWORKS. They can also serve as a GATEWAY between the LOCAL AREA NETWORK and an external NETWORK, providing the necessary PROTOCOL CONVERSION.

digital recording

See MAGNETIC TAPE & DISK.

digital signal processing

THE PROCESSING OF REAL-WORLD SIGNALS IN DIGITAL FORM; DIGITAL SIGNAL PROCESSING is a catagory of techniques which are applied to the analysis of real-world shapes and signals, such as voice and pictures.

Essentially, DIGITAL SIGNAL PROCESSING converts the objects to be analyzed into DIGITAL form (BINARY CODE) using various mathematical methods, such as the fast Fourier transform. Once a signal has been reduced to numbers, its components can be isolated and analyzed more readily than in ANALOG form.

digital termination service

See DTS.

digitize

TO TURN INTO BINARY CODE (DIGITAL); DIGITIZING usually refers to the conversion of speech or pictures into BINARY CODE. See PULSE CODE MODULATION, DIGITIZER TABLET and GRAPHICS.

In actuality, all forms of INFORMATION are DIGITIZED before the COMPUTER can accept them. TERMINALS convert keystrokes into BINARY CODE and OPTICAL SCANNERS convert real letters and numbers into BINARY CODE.

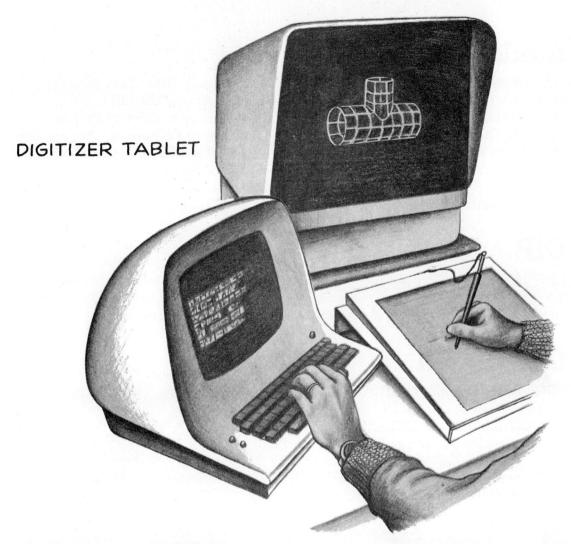

DIGITIZER TABLET

digitizer tablet

GRAPHICS INPUT DEVICE; A DIGITIZER TABLET is a flat tablet which serves as a drawing surface for GRAPHICS INPUT. DIGITIZER TABLETS can be used for sketching new images, tracing old images, selecting from MENUS or simply for moving the CURSOR around on the SCREEN. All of these functions can be performed within the same PROGRAM.

The USER makes contact with the TABLET with a device called a CURSOR (a pen-like or puck-like instrument which is connected to the TABLET by a wire). For sketching, the USER draws with the TABLET CURSOR and the SCREEN CURSOR "draws" a corresponding image. For tracing an existing image (called DIGITIZING), the SCREEN CURSOR is often not required. The DIGITIZER TABLET picks up the drawing as a series of x-y coordinates, either as a continuous stream of coordinates, or as start-stop coordinates (VECTOR GRAPHICS).

MENU selection is accomplished by a TABLET overlay or by a SCREEN display. The TABLET CURSOR selects an item by making contact with it on the overlay, or by controlling the CURSOR on the SCREEN.

diode

ELECTRONIC COMPONENT; Acting primarily as a one-way valve, there are many varieties of DIODES used in ELECTRONIC CIRCUITS, both as DISCRETE COMPONENTS and built into the CHIP. DIODES perform many different kinds of functions. They are a key element in changing AC current to DC current. They are used as temperature sensors, light sensors, and light emitters (See LED). They are used in COMMUNICATIONS to remove both ANALOG and DIGITAL signals from CARRIERS and to MODULATE signals onto CARRIERS. In DIGITAL LOGIC, they are used as one-way valves and as switches similar to TRANSISTORS.

DIP

CHIP HOUSING; A DIP is a housing commonly used to hold a CHIP. Tiny wires bond the CHIP to the metal pins which become the plugs used to insert the DIP into a socket on the PRINTED CIRCUIT BOARD. Stands for **D**ual **I**nline **P**ackage.

DIP switch

TOGGLE SWITCHES; A DIP SWITCH is a series of toggle switches built into a DIP mounted on a PRINTED CIRCUIT BOARD. DIP SWITCHES are used to set many different conditions, such as BAUD RATE or PERIPHERAL device selection. Although usually designed for the technician, USERS may occasionally have to change DIP SWITCH settings in a PERIPHERAL DEVICE on their PERSONAL COMPUTER.

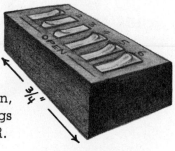

DIP SWITCH

direct access

THE ABILITY TO ACCESS A SPECIFIC STORAGE LOCATION; DISKS, DRUMS and MEMORY are examples of DIRECT ACCESS devices. Individual storage locations can be ACCESSED directly by their ADDRESS (location number of a SECTOR, TRACK or BYTE). Contrast with TAPE which is a SEQUENTIAL ACCESS device, requiring that unwanted DATA must be ACCESSED in order to get to the desired DATA. DIRECT ACCESS is synonymous with RANDOM ACCESS.

direct memory access

See DMA.

direct view storage tube

CATEGORY OF GRAPHICS TERMINAL; Just like television SCREENS, GRAPHICS
SCREENS require continuous signals to keep the image visible. Even if the picture
doesn't change, it must be transmitted from MEMORY to the SCREEN over and over
again, many times each second. The DIRECT VIEW STORAGE TUBE (DVST) is a
GRAPHICS TERMINAL which maintains the picture on the SCREEN without continuous
refreshing from the COMPUTER. However, there is no way to erase what is drawn on the
SCREEN. Any changes to the image require that the entire SCREEN is erased and
redrawn from scratch. The DIRECT VIEW STORAGE TUBE is primarily used for
VECTOR GRAPHICS.

discrete component

INDIVIDUAL ELECTRONIC COMPONENT; Elementary ELECTRONIC components
constructed as a single unit are DISCRETE COMPONENTS. Before INTEGRATED
CIRCUITS, all ELECTRONIC components, such as TRANSISTORS, RESISTORS,
DIODES and CAPACITORS were DISCRETE COMPONENTS. DISCRETE
COMPONENTS are still used in conjunction with INTEGRATED CIRCUITS, either to
augment the ICs, or because a particular type of ELECTRONIC component cannot be
microminiaturized effectively onto a CHIP.

dish

SATELLITE ANTENNA; An antenna that receives signals from a SATELLITE, looks like a
DISH, so it is often referred to as such. EARTH STATIONS, which are transmitters as
well as receivers, are in DISH form as well.

disk

DIRECT ACCESS STORAGE DEVICE; See MAGNETIC DISK & TAPE.

disk cartridge

REMOVABLE HARD DISK MODULE; DISK CARTRIDGES contain a single HARD DISK
platter which is inserted into the DRIVE as a self-contained unit.

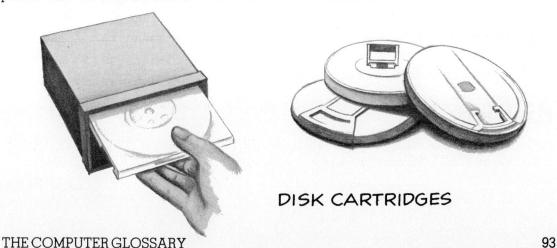

DISK CARTRIDGES

disk drive

PERIPHERAL STORAGE DEVICE; The DISK DRIVE is the unit that holds, spins, READS and WRITES MAGNETIC DISKS. The DISK DRIVE may take a FLOPPY DISK, removable DISK PACK, or DISK CARTRIDGE, or it may contain FIXED (HARD) DISKS.

disk memory

Same as DISK, *not* MEMORY.

DISK PACKS

disk pack

REMOVABLE HARD DISK MODULE; DISK PACKS contain several HARD DISK platters connected by a central spindle. The DISK PACK is kept OFF-LINE in a plastic housing with a handle. The bottom of the housing is removed and the DISK PACK is inserted into the DISK DRIVE. Then the top of the housing is removed so the ACCESS ARMS can gain entrance between the platters. The housing protects the DISK PACK against dust and contamination. DISK PACKS must be handled carefully and cannot be dropped.

diskette

Same as FLOPPY DISK.

display list

DATA WHICH DESCRIBE A COMPUTER GRAPHICS IMAGE; A DISPLAY LIST is a collection of VECTORS which make up objects in a picture. See GRAPHICS, (Vector Graphics).

distributed intelligence

PROCESSING CAPABILITY IN TERMINALS AND OTHER PERIPHERAL DEVICES; COMPUTER SYSTEMS using INTELLIGENT TERMINALS are distributing the PROCESSING workload throughout the entire SYSTEM rather than concentrating it in the main COMPUTER. The TERMINALS can perform much of the pre-PROCESSING necessary in INFORMATION SYSTEMS. The SCREEN FORMATTING, CONVERSATIONAL USER dialogue, and DATA ENTRY validation can be done in the TERMINALS instead of in the central COMPUTER.

INTELLIGENCE in other PERIPHERALS, such as DISKS and TAPES, can relieve the main COMPUTER from certain ELECTRONIC tasks.

distributed processing

SYSTEM OF COMPUTERS CONNECTED BY A COMMUNICATIONS NETWORK; Contrast with DECENTRALIZED PROCESSING where COMPUTERS are installed in remote locations without COMMUNICATIONS capability between them. Also contrast with CENTRALIZED PROCESSING where all PROCESSING is done in a central location with TERMINALS located in remote areas. DISTRIBUTED PROCESSING is a coherently designed SYSTEM where each COMPUTER SYSTEM in the NETWORK has been chosen to handle its required workload, and the COMMUNICATIONS NETWORK has been designed to support the requirements of the entire SYSTEM. However, the term is often used to refer to any collection of COMPUTERS that have COMMUNICATIONS capability between them. See SHARED RESOURCE, LOCAL AREA NETWORK and OFFICE AUTOMATION.

DL/1

IBM DATA BASE MANAGEMENT SYSTEM; DL/1 is the basic DATA handling portion of the IMS DATA BASE MANAGEMENT SYSTEM. Stands for **D**ata **L**anguage **1**.

DMA

COMPUTER DESIGN TECHNIQUE; DMA stands for **D**IRECT **M**EMORY **A**CCESS, and refers to a fast method for transferring DATA to and from MEMORY. DMA is a separate CONTROL UNIT or PROCESSOR which performs the MEMORY transfers (to and from PERIPHERALS or within MEMORY) and relieves the main PROCESSOR of the task. The DMA method may keep the PROCESSOR waiting during its operation, or may operate concurrently with the PROCESSOR. A method called CYCLE STEALING is often used, which allows for a high degree of overlap in operations.

do loop

HIGH-LEVEL PROGRAMMING LANGUAGE LOGIC STATEMENT; A DO LOOP defines a segment of PROGRAM LOGIC (LINES OF CODE) that will be repeated over and over again until some condition terminates the LOOPING. For example, "Count to 10 by 1," could be expressed as:

```
DO WHILE COUNTER < > 10          (< > = Not equal to)
STORE COUNTER + 1 TO COUNTER
ENDDO
STOP
```

document

A MEDIUM CONTAINING INFORMATION; In manual SYSTEMS, a DOCUMENT refers to any form or voucher regarding a TRANSACTION. In WORD PROCESSING, a DOCUMENT refers to the ELECTRONICALLY stored TEXT FILE, as well as the paper OUTPUT it generates.

documentation

NARRATIVE AND GRAPHICAL DESCRIPTION OF A SYSTEM; INFORMATION SYSTEM DOCUMENTATION includes:

OPERATING PROCEDURES

(1) Narrative instructions for turning the SYSTEM on and getting the PROGRAMS initiated.

(2) Narrative instructions for entering DATA at the TERMINAL accompanied with SCREEN layouts for each TERMINAL SCREEN that may be encountered.

(3) A description of error messages that can occur and the alternative methods for handling them.

(4) A description of the DEFAULTS taken in the PROGRAMS and the instructions for changing them.

SYSTEM DOCUMENTATION

(1) DATA DICTIONARY— Description of the DATA/INFORMATION stored in the FILES and DATA BASES.

(2) PROCEDURES— Narrative description of the manual PROCEDURES for obtaining SOURCE DOCUMENTS as INPUT, and distributing the REPORTS as OUTPUT. A SYSTEM FLOW CHART is a graphical picture of the DATA as it flows from SOURCE DOCUMENT to REPORT.

(3) APPLICATION PROGRAM DOCUMENTATION— Description of the INPUTS, PROCESSING and OUTPUTS for each DATA ENTRY, QUERY, UPDATE and REPORT PROGRAM. SCREEN and REPORT layouts facilitate the description of the PROGRAMS.

TECHNICAL DOCUMENTATION

(1) DATA BASE/FILE structures and ACCESS METHODS
(2) PROGRAM FLOW CHARTS
(3) PROGRAM SOURCE CODE listings
(4) Machine PROCEDURES (JCL)

The quantity and quality of PROGRAMMING DOCUMENTATION is difficult to determine for non-technical people. It depends on the PROGRAMMING LANGUAGE used as well as the conventions established in the PROGRAMMING department. See STRUCTURED PROGRAMMING.

doping

PROCESS OF ALTERING THE ELECTRICAL CONDUCTIVITY OF SEMICONDUCTOR MATERIALS; TRANSISTORS are made of SEMICONDUCTOR materials like SILICON. The actual action of the TRANSISTOR is caused by the reaction of its different components to electric charges. This reactive nature is created in the SILICON by chemically combining it with foreign elements. DOPING results in either an excess of electrons or a lack of electrons in the SILICON (called N-type or N-channel, P-type or P-channel).

DOS

DISK **O**PERATING **S**YSTEM; A DOS refers to an OPERATING SYSTEM which manages a DISK environment. DOS may also refer to an earlier category of IBM OPERATING SYSTEMS.

DOS-VSE

IBM OPERATING SYSTEM WHICH RUNS ON THE 4300 SERIES MAINFRAMES; Stands for (DOS) **V**irtual **S**torage **Ex**tended.

DOT MATRIX

dot matrix

A CHARACTER GENERATED FROM DOTS; VIDEO TERMINALS and PRINTERS use DOT MATRIX CHARACTER generation to form the CHARACTERS on the SCREEN or on paper. The CHARACTERS are formulated as patterns of tiny dots. The clarity of the CHARACTER is determined by how close the dots are spaced apart. DOT MATRIX techniques offer an infinite variety of CHARACTER styles, as well as GRAPHICS capability. See PRINTER TECHNOLOGIES.

double buffering

THE USE OF TWO BUFFERS; DOUBLE BUFFERING is a HARDWARE or SOFTWARE technique to transfer INFORMATION. INFORMATION in one BUFFER is acted on while INFORMATION in the other is transferred in or out.

double density disk

HIGH-CAPACITY FLOPPY DISK.

double sided disk

DISK WHICH IS RECORDED ON BOTH SIDES.

down

NOT FUNCTIONING; When a COMPUTER is DOWN, it usually means that the HARDWARE CIRCUITS are inoperable and some PRINTED CIRCUIT BOARD must be repaired or replaced because a CHIP or ELECTRONIC component failed to work. A COMPUTER SYSTEM can be DOWN because of a SOFTWARE failure in the SYSTEM SOFTWARE (OPERATING SYSTEM, DATA BASE MANAGEMENT SYSTEM) or in a USER'S APPLICATION PROGRAM. A COMMUNICATIONS CHANNEL is DOWN when the CHANNEL cannot transfer INFORMATION.

download

TRANSFER OF A PROGRAM OR DATA FILE FROM A CENTRAL COMPUTER TO A REMOTE COMPUTER; DOWNLOAD usually implies a transfer of an entire INFORMATION FILE or PROGRAM, rather than just a single TRANSACTION. An INTELLIGENT TERMINAL may receive its INSTRUCTIONS DOWNLOADED from the main COMPUTER.

downtime

THE TIME DURING WHICH THE COMPUTER IS NON-FUNCTIONING.

downward compatible

COMPATIBLE WITH A SMALLER OR PREVIOUS GENERATION MODEL; A COMPUTER that runs PROGRAMS which can also run on the previous generation model or on a smaller model is DOWNWARD COMPATIBLE.

DP

See **DATA PROCESSING**.

DPMA

DATA PROCESSING MANAGEMENT ASSOCIATION; Founded in 1951, the DPMA includes directors and managers of DATA PROCESSING installations, PROGRAMMERS, SYSTEMS ANALYSTS and research specialists. DPMA is the founder of the Certificate in Data Processing (CDP) examination program, now administrated by an international organization. It also offers many professional educational programs, courses, and seminars, in addition to sponsoring student organizations around the country interested in DATA PROCESSING.

DPS

PRIMARY DESIGNATION FOR HONEYWELL COMPUTERS (SUCH AS THE DPS-6, DPS-7 AND DPS-8 SERIES).

drive

PERIPHERAL STORAGE UNIT; A DRIVE refers to a TAPE DRIVE or DISK DRIVE, which is the device that holds, spins, READS and WRITES the magnetic storage medium.

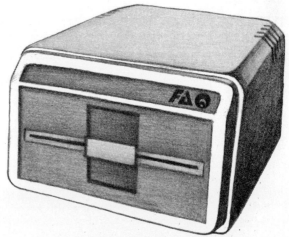

FLOPPY DISK DRIVE

drum

DIRECT ACCESS STORAGE DEVICE; See MAGNETIC DRUM.

drum plotter

GRAPHICS PLOTTER THAT HANDLES CONTINUOUS FORMS; See PLOTTER.

drum printer

LINE PRINTER THAT USES TYPE CHARACTERS ON A DRUM AS ITS PRINTING MECHANISM; See PRINTER TECHNOLOGIES.

dry plasma etching

METHOD FOR DEVELOPING A MASK ON A WAFER; The DRY PLASMA ETCHING process replaces the film and acid bath method (known as "wet" processing) which is used to create a design on a WAFER. The DRY PLASMA method shoots hot ions through a MASK directly into the CHIP surface, which evaporates the SILICON dioxide layer.

DSA

HONEYWELL NETWORK ARCHITECTURE; Stands for **D**istributed **S**ystems **A**rchitecture.

DSS

See **D**ECISION **S**UPPORT **S**YSTEM.

DTE

DATA **T**ERMINATING **E**QUIPMENT; A DTE is the source and/or destination of signals on a COMMUNICATIONS CHANNEL. A DTE is usually a TERMINAL or a COMPUTER.

DTS

DIGITAL COMMUNICATIONS SERVICE TO THE USER'S PREMISES; A DTS provides DIGITAL CHANNELS directly to the USER'S TERMINALS and COMPUTERS. Stands for **D**IGITAL **T**ERMINATION **S**ERVICE.

dumb terminal

AN INPUT/OUTPUT DEVICE; A DUMB TERMINAL is a TERMINAL without INTELLIGENCE. It is entirely dependent on the main COMPUTER for PROCESSING. DUMB TERMINALS transmit and receive DATA over a COMMUNICATIONS CHANNEL using an ASYNCHRONOUS PROTOCOL called an ASCII or TELETYPE PROTOCOL. See SMART TERMINAL and INTELLIGENT TERMINAL.

dump

TO COPY ONTO ANOTHER STORAGE MEDIUM OR TO PRINT AS IS; A DUMP usually refers to an unchanged copy or PRINTOUT of DATA or INSTRUCTIONS. A DISK or TAPE DUMP is not easily recognized without a RECORD LAYOUT that describes the organization of the material on the DISK or TAPE. See MEMORY DUMP.

DVST

See **DIRECT VIEW STORAGE TUBE**.

dynamic RAM

CATEGORY OF ELECTRONIC MEMORY; DYNAMIC RAMs are MEMORY CHIPS which require continuous regeneration. Their storage cells (BITS) must be regenerated hundreds of times per second in order to maintain their proper patterns. DYNAMIC RAMs are faster and denser than STATIC RAMs, which do not require regeneration. Unlike FIRMWARE CHIPS, such as ROMs and PROMs, both varieties of RAMs require power to hold their content. Storage cells (BITS) of DYNAMIC RAMs are usually constructed of a TRANSISTOR and a CAPACITOR.

EAM

SAME AS UNIT RECORD EQUIPMENT; Stands for **E**lectronic **A**ccounting **M**achine.

earth station

TRANSMITTER AND RECEIVER FOR SATELLITE COMMUNICATIONS; An EARTH STATION is shaped like a DISH. It is used for transmission of MICROWAVE signals to a SATELLITE and as an antenna to receive them.

EBCDIC

STANDARD DATA CODE; EBCDIC is a BINARY CODE made up of 8-BITS (BYTE) allowing 256 possible CHARACTER combinations. Developed by IBM, it is used extensively on IBM COMPUTERS, IBM PLUG COMPATIBLE devices, and other MAINFRAMES. EBCDIC stands for **E**xtended **B**inary **C**oded **D**ecimal **I**nterchange **C**ode and is pronounced /eb'-suh-dik/. EBCDIC and ASCII are the two most widely used DATA CODES.

ECL

TYPE OF MICROELECTRONIC CIRCUIT DESIGN; ECL stands for **E**mitter **C**oupled **L**ogic and is noted for its extremely fast switching speeds. ECL is a variety of BIPOLAR TRANSISTOR.

ECLIPSE

SERIES OF MINICOMPUTERS MANUFACTURED BY DATA GENERAL CORPORATION.

EARTH STATION

edit

VALIDATE OR UPDATE; EDIT PROGRAMS may be DATA ENTRY PROGRAMS that
validate the INPUT or UPDATE PROGRAMS which change FILES and DATA BASES. In
manual SYSTEMS, EDIT means change or UPDATE. See DATA ENTRY, TEXT EDITING
and UPDATE.

An EDIT INSTRUCTION refers to a special FORMAT INSTRUCTION which may insert
decimal points, commas, dollars signs, etc., into a FIELD.

edit key

FUNCTION KEY FOR EDITING PURPOSES; See FUNCTION KEY, KEYBOARD and
WORD PROCESSING.

EDP

ELECTRONIC DATA PROCESSING; EDP was the first acronym used to identify the
COMPUTER field.

EEPROM

REUSABLE MEMORY CHIP FOR PROGRAM STORAGE; INSTRUCTIONS and/or
INFORMATION are stored in the EEPROM by WRITING the BINARY code into it from
the COMPUTER. The COMPUTER can erase it and WRITE it again. EEPROMs are
valuable in portable TERMINALS and COMPUTERS, since they are a NON-VOLATILE
storage device. EEPROM is FIRMWARE and stands for Electrically Erasable
Programmable Read Only Memory.

EFT

ELECTRONIC FUNDS TRANSFER; EFT is the exchange of money via COMMUNICATIONS. EFT refers to any financial TRANSACTION which originates at a TERMINAL and transfers a sum of money from one account to another.

EIA

ELECTRONICS INDUSTRY ASSOCIATION; Founded in 1924, members include manufacturers of ELECTRONIC parts and SYSTEMS. EIA sponsors ELECTRONIC shows and seminars, and gives many awards for outstanding contributions to the ELECTRONICS industry. The EIA sets electrical and ELECTRONIC INTERFACE standards like the EIA RS-232-C, TERMINAL and MODEM INTERFACE.

EIA RS-232-C

See RS-232.

electroluminescent display

FLAT SCREEN TECHNOLOGY; ELECTROLUMINESCENT display SCREENS contain a powdered or THIN-FILM PHOSPHOR layer sandwiched between an x-axis panel and a y-axis panel. An individual dot (PIXEL) is selectable by charging an x-wire on one panel and a y-wire on the other panel. When the x-y coordinate is charged, the PHOSPHOR in that vicinity emits visible light.

electronic

THE USE OF ELECTRICITY AS INTELLIGENCE; ELECTRONICS pertain to the use of electricity in "intelligence-bearing" devices, such as telephone, radio, television, instrumentation, ANALOG and DIGITAL COMPUTERS, and TELECOMMUNICATIONS, etc. Electricity which is used as raw power for heating, lighting and motors is considered electrical, *not* ELECTRONIC. Although coined before, the magazine Electronics (first published April 1930) brought the term to popularity. The subheading of the magazine then read: Electron Tubes— Their Radio, Audio, Visio and Industrial Applications. The word ELECTRONIC was derived from the use of the electron tube (VACUUM TUBE), which was originally used as an amplifier of ELECTRONIC signals.

electronic circuit

COLLECTION OF ELECTRONIC COMPONENTS WHICH PERFORM A FUNCTION; ELECTRONIC CIRCUITS are pathways through which electricity is directed in a prescribed pattern to accomplish some task. ELECTRONIC CIRCUITS used in DIGITAL COMPUTERS deal with discrete on/off pulses (BITS). ELECTRONIC CIRCUITS used in ANALOG COMPUTERS or ANALOG devices like radio and television, deal with electrical vibrations.

A DIGITAL CIRCUIT in a COMPUTER could be viewed as a complicated mass of plumbing. The "pipes" are the CIRCUIT paths and the "valves" are the TRANSISTORS. The "water" is the electricity. Now, imagine opening a water valve and the water that flows through the valve and down a pipe will eventually reach another valve and cause it to turn on, allowing water in another pipe to flow through, which will reach another valve, and so on and so on. A RESISTOR could be viewed as a large pipe squeezing into a smaller-diameter pipe, a CAPACITOR as a storage tank, and a DIODE as a one-way valve, allowing water to flow in only one direction. See CHIP and BOOLEAN LOGIC.

electronic funds transfer

See EFT.

electronic mail

MAIL BY COMMUNICATIONS; ELECTRONIC MAIL is the ELECTRONIC transmission of letters, messages and memos through a COMMUNICATIONS NETWORK. The simplest form of ELECTRONIC MAIL is the use of FACSIMILE TERMINALS at remote locations and a standard telephone for transmission between them. The advantage of FACSIMILE is that pictures can be transmitted, as well as DATA/INFORMATION.

Using COMPUTERS a more elaborate message INFORMATION SYSTEM can be developed with VIDEO TERMINALS at each USER'S desk. USERS develop their mail on their TERMINAL (which may be stored in their own or a central message bank) and request transmission to one or several recipient USERS. This mail can be transmitted through an organization's internal NETWORK, or it can be linked to external carriers for remote transmission. The recipients can request their mail from a centrally stored message bank when they return to their offices and can then catalog their mail for future reference, or delete it. More sophisticated SYSTEMS will keep track of response desired messages and prompt the USERS periodically if they have not answered their messages.

electronic paper

COMPUTER MEMORY; See COMPUTER (The 3 C's) and MEMORY.

electronic printer

See PAGE PRINTER.

electronic publishing

DISTRIBUTION OF PUBLISHED MATERIALS ELECTRONICALLY; ELECTRONIC PUBLISHING refers to any form of INFORMATION which is stored in ELECTRONIC form and made available to the reader or subscriber via a COMMUNICATIONS CHANNEL. See VIDEOTEX.

electronic spreadsheet

SPREADSHEET SIMULATED IN THE COMPUTER'S MEMORY; ELECTRONIC SPREADSHEETS are used for planning purposes and various PROGRAMMING functions which are primarily equation oriented. Popularized by a MICROCOMPUTER SOFTWARE PACKAGE called VISICALC, ELECTRONIC SPREADSHEETS are available on all sizes of COMPUTERS. The larger the MEMORY available, the larger the amount of numbers that can be represented.

An ELECTRONIC SPREADSHEET appears to the USER at a TERMINAL as a MATRIX of cells, each cell identified with a row and column number. The SPREADSHEET can be horizontally or vertically SCROLLED using the CURSOR KEYS, since the SCREEN can only view a limited number of cells at one time. The cells are filled with either numerical DATA, or descriptions which refer to the DATA. Equations are created by the USER which tie the DATA cells together, as for example, "product A + product B + product C = total products"; or "gross revenues – expenses = net income." The total of one cell can be used as DATA for another cell so that the calculations can ripple through an entire SPREADSHEET.

Calculations can be performed based on actual DATA or forecast DATA, which then allows the SPREADSHEET to act as a "what if?" planning SYSTEM. ELECTRONIC SPREADSHEETS are used for budgets, financial statements, income tax preparation, financial and operations MODELING, and many other equation-based functions. See FINANCIAL PLANNING SYSTEM.

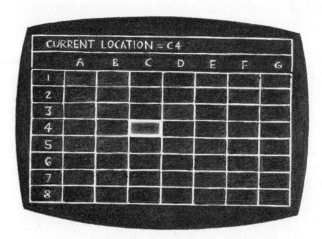

ELECTRONIC SPREADSHEET

electronic typewriter

ELECTRIC TYPEWRITER OR MEMORY TYPEWRITER; An ELECTRONIC TYPEWRITER may refer to an electric typewriter with an ELECTRONIC KEYBOARD and some limited typewriter enhancements. Or it may refer to a MEMORY TYPEWRITER which can perform a wide range of TEXT EDITING features. See MEMORY TYPEWRITER and WORD PROCESSOR.

electrophotographic

PRINTING TECHNIQUE USED IN COPYING MACHINES; See PRINTER TECHNOLOGIES.

electrosensitive

PRINTING TECHNIQUE USING SPECIAL PAPER; See PRINTER TECHNOLOGIES.

electrostatic

PRINTING TECHNIQUE USING SPECIAL PAPER; See PRINTER TECHNOLOGIES.

embedded system

SPECIALIZED COMPUTER ENVIRONMENT; An EMBEDDED SYSTEM is a COMPUTER used as a control function *embedded* within the device it is controlling. An EMBEDDED SYSTEM implies custom-built SOFTWARE which integrates SYSTEM SOFTWARE and APPLICATION SOFTWARE functions.

emulator

A COPYCAT; EMULATORS allow COMPUTERS and PERIPHERALS to perform like other models or brands. A COMPUTER can be designed to EMULATE another COMPUTER and carry out INSTRUCTIONS written for both COMPUTERS. TERMINALS can be designed to EMULATE different standard COMMUNICATIONS PROTOCOLS and therefore operate in several NETWORKS. The EMULATOR itself can be HARDWARE, SOFTWARE or a combination of the two.

encryption

CODING OF INFORMATION FOR SECURITY PURPOSES; ENCRYPTION converts the standard DIGITAL CODE into a special CODE which is transmitted over the COMMUNICATIONS CHANNEL. At the other end, the CODE is converted back into its original form. See DES.

endless loop

A PROGRAM LOOP THAT HAS NO LOGICAL END; A LOOP in a PROGRAM is a set of INSTRUCTIONS which keep repeating until a certain condition occurs and the LOOP terminates. If the condition does not occur, the LOOP will not end. When a PROGRAM is first developed, an ENDLESS LOOP may occur because the PROGRAM LOGIC is incorrect. ENDLESS LOOPS may also be set up intentionally. For example: A PROGRAM that displays an advertisement on the VIDEO TERMINAL and continues to repeat the ad over and over again. See LOOPING.

end user

PERSON WHO USES THE COMPUTER; In this book, USER refers to END USER.

engine

PROCESSOR; An ENGINE is another term for a PROCESSOR. Since a PROCESSOR simply EXECUTES INSTRUCTIONS one after the other, its EXECUTION speed determines the ultimate THROUGHPUT of the COMPUTER. A faster ENGINE or PROCESSOR simply speeds up the whole process.

entity

ANY THING AN ORGANIZATION WANTS TO DESCRIBE; An ENTITY could be a customer, order, insurance policy, aircraft or oil well. An ENTITY is described by ATTRIBUTES (DATA ELEMENTS) which are its characteristics, and/or by its relationship to other ENTITIES.

EOF

END OF FILE; When a SEQUENTIAL FILE is being READ, the PROGRAM must test for reaching the end of the FILE. The EOF designation could be a special mark recorded (WRITTEN) onto the storage medium, or the last RECORD could contain some sort of EOF CODE.

EPROM

REUSABLE MEMORY CHIP FOR PROGRAM STORAGE; INSTRUCTIONS and/or INFORMATION are stored in the EPROM by WRITING the BINARY CODE into it from the COMPUTER. The COMPUTER WRITES the EPROM, but it must be removed and placed under ultraviolet light to erase the contents. EPROM is FIRMWARE and stands for **E**rasable **P**rogrammable **R**ead **O**nly **M**emory.

ergonomics

THE STUDY OF PEOPLE AND MACHINES WORKING TOGETHER; ERGONOMICS refers to the design of machinery so that it INTERFACES effectively with people. An ERGONOMICALLY-designed device implies that the unit is based on having applied ERGONOMICS to its design. The term is used to refer to virtually any improvement over the last model!

error checking

TESTING FOR ERRORS; ERROR CHECKING may refer to various techniques which test for the valid condition of DATA. See PARITY CHECKING and CRC (Cyclical Redundancy Checking) for DIGITAL ERROR CHECKING. See DATA ENTRY for INPUT ERROR CHECKING.

esc

See **ESC**APE KEY.

escape key

KEYBOARD CONTROL KEY; The ESCAPE KEY is a standard control key which is used differently by vendors of SOFTWARE PROGRAMS. In an INTERACTIVE dialogue, it is often used to transfer control to another section of the PROGRAM. The ESCAPE CODE is also used extensively as a control CHARACTER, which acts as a start CHARACTER, followed by a sequence of additional control CODES.

ESS

ELECTRONIC **S**WITCHING **S**YSTEM DEVELOPED BY BELL LABS; An ESS is a large scale COMPUTER switching SYSTEM used by the Bell Telephone companies to switch telephone conversations in a central office.

ETHERNET

LOCAL AREA NETWORK; ETHERNET is a BASEBAND COMMUNICATIONS NETWORK which has been introduced by Xerox, Digital Equipment Corporation and Intel.

execute

TO CARRY OUT INSTRUCTIONS IN A PROGRAM; EXECUTION of a PROGRAM is the actual running of the PROGRAM in the COMPUTER.

executive

ANOTHER NAME FOR THE OPERATING SYSTEM; See OPERATING SYSTEM.

exclusive or

BOOLEAN LOGIC CONDITION; An EXCLUSIVE OR is a condition whereby only one of two INPUTS may be present in order to produce OUTPUT. If neither INPUT is present, or if both INPUTS are present, then there will be no OUTPUT.

expert system

PROBLEM-SOLVING APPLICATION AT AN EXPERT LEVEL; EXPERT SYSTEMS are KNOWLEDGE BASED SYSTEMS which contain a DATA BASE of knowledge about a particular subject (the KNOWLEDGE BASE). The degree of expertise relies on the quality of DATA obtained from human experts on the subject. EXPERT SYSTEMS are designed to perform at a human expert level; however, in practice, they will perform both well below and well above that of an individual expert. The EXPERT SYSTEM also incorporates an INFERENCE PROGRAM, which derives a conclusion based on the DATA contained in the KNOWLEDGE BASE and the DATA entered by the USER. EXPERT SYSTEMS are ARTIFICIAL INTELLIGENCE APPLICATIONS.

facilities management

MANAGEMENT OF A USER'S OWN COMPUTER INSTALLATION BY AN OUTSIDE ORGANIZATION; All operations including SYSTEMS, PROGRAMMING, and the DATACENTER can be peformed by the FACILITIES MANAGEMENT organization on the USER'S premises.

facsimile

PICTURE TRANSMISSION BETWEEN REMOTE LOCATIONS; Also called FAX or TELECOPYING. A page of paper containing any form of writing or drawing is entered into the FAX terminal in one location. The FAX terminal CODES the INPUT and transmits it to the destination FAX terminal, using a standard dial-up or leased telephone line. FACSIMILE SYSTEMS are designed using either ANALOG or DIGITAL techniques for CODING and transmission. FACSIMILE is the simplest form of ELECTRONIC MAIL that can handle picture images, as well as DATA/TEXT.

fail safe

NON-STOP OPERATION; A FAIL SAFE COMPUTER SYSTEM has built-in redundancy which will keep the SYSTEM running in the event of a HARDWARE failure. FAIL SAFE SYSTEMS can be designed using conventional COMPUTER SYSTEMS and customized SOFTWARE, or redundant CIRCUITS can be designed into the COMPUTER SYSTEM from the beginning. FAIL SAFE SYSTEMS imply extra cost, since much duplicity is required.

fail soft

ABILITY TO FAIL WITH MINIMUM DESTRUCTION; FAIL SOFT COMPUTER SYSTEMS are designed to perform a series of tasks, in the event of a failure, that will provide less destruction than without it. For example, if a power failure is detected, a battery system may keep the COMPUTER running long enough to take a MEMORY DUMP. FAIL SOFT implies failure detection, but not failure correction. See FAIL SAFE.

fax

See FACSIMILE.

FDM

FREQUENCY DIVISION MULTIPLEXING; FDM is a COMMUNICATIONS transmission method widely used to transmit multiple signals over a single CHANNEL. Each signal transmitted (DATA, voice, etc.) is MODULATED onto a CARRIER of a different FREQUENCY. The multiple signals actually travel simultaneously over the CHANNEL. Contrast with TDM (TIME DIVISION MULTIPLEXING) wherein the signals are in DIGITAL form and BITS from each signal are interleaved. See CARRIER and BROADBAND.

feasibility study

PRELIMINARY ANALYSIS OF AN INFORMATION OR COMPUTER SYSTEM; A FEASIBILITY STUDY determines if a proposed problem can be solved viably by the installation of an INFORMATION SYSTEM and/or COMPUTER SYSTEM. The operational (can it work in the environments?), economical (COST/BENEFITS ANALYSIS), and technical (can it be built?) aspects are part of a FEASIBILITY STUDY. The result of a FEASIBILITY STUDY should provide sufficient data for a go or no-go decision.

FET

FIELD EFFECT TRANSISTOR; The FET is the type of TRANSISTOR used in MOS (METAL OXIDE SEMICONDUCTOR) INTEGRATED CIRCUITS. See MOS.

fiche

SHEET OF MICROFILM; Same as MICROFICHE. Pronounced /feesh/.

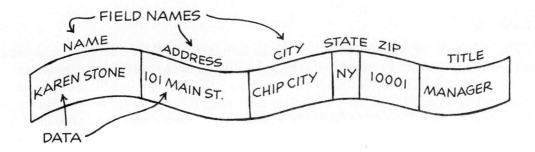

FIELDS IN A RECORD

field

A DEFINED UNIT OF DATA/INFORMATION IN A RECORD; A FIELD defines the physical storage location of a unit of DATA/INFORMATION. A FIELD is one or more BYTES in size, and a combination of FIELDS make up a RECORD. A FIELD also defines a unit of DATA/INFORMATION on a SOURCE DOCUMENT, REPORT or VIDEO SCREEN.

Since the FIELD is the smallest unit of DATA/INFORMATION that can be defined and manipulated, it is really the common denominator between USER and COMPUTER. When USERS ACCESS and manipulate their DATA using INTERACTIVE PROGRAMS like QUERY LANGUAGES and REPORT WRITERS, they often refer to their DATA by FIELD (DATA ELEMENT) name.

A DATA ELEMENT refers to the LOGICAL description of DATA; the FIELD refers to the PHYSICAL location of DATA. See DATA ELEMENT.

field effect transistor

See FET.

field engineer

HARDWARE INSTALLATION, MAINTENANCE AND SERVICE PROFESSIONAL; FIELD ENGINEERS install COMPUTER HARDWARE on customers' premises, perform routine PREVENTIVE MAINTENANCE and repair the equipment when it goes DOWN. FIELD ENGINEERS are versed in DIGITAL ELECTRONICS.

field service representative

Same as FIELD ENGINEER.

file

A COLLECTION OF RELATED RECORDS; In manual SYSTEMS, a set of related items for a particular account or individual is called a FILE, such as the FILE for customer XYZ. In DATA PROCESSING, that is considered a RECORD, while a FILE implies a collection of related RECORDS— the entire customer FILE, for example. FILES are used extensively in DATA/INFORMATION PROCESSING to mean a collection of related DATA RECORDS (DATA FILE), a collection of words and sentences (TEXT FILE), or a collection of PROGRAM statements (SOURCE PROGRAM or OBJECT PROGRAM). See FILE SYSTEM.

file (record) locking

DATA MANAGEMENT FOR MULTIPLE USERS; When multiple USERS have ACCESS to FILES and DATA BASES, FILE and/or RECORD LOCKING provides first-come, first-served management of the DATA. A RECORD is LOCKED when it is ACCESSED by one USER; all other USERS cannot ACCESS it until the first USER has finished manipulating it. If it is necessary to manipulate an entire FILE, the FILE can be LOCKED as well.

file maintenance

PERIODIC UPDATING OF A FILE; FILE MAINTENANCE pertains to the routine addition, deletion and changing of RECORDS in a FILE. For example, employees in a company are hired, leave the company and change their status (address, title, pay rate) several times throughout their tenure. Customers, vendors and inventory products are added to the organization. FILE MAINTENANCE refers to the periodic UPDATING of a FILE rather than its daily TRANSACTION PROCESSING. FILE MAINTENANCE also refers to the periodic reorganization of the DISK space in a COMPUTER SYSTEM. After many PROGRAMS have been run and RECORDS and FILES have been added and manipulated, a periodic reorganization of the DISK may be necessary. Unwanted DATA is purged and FILES which may have become physically fragmented are regrouped.

file protection

PROTECTION FROM ACCIDENTAL OVERWRITING ON A DISK OR TAPE; PHYSICAL protection is provided by some indicator either permanently attached to the medium (like a sliding switch), or placed onto the medium by the USER (such as a stick-on silver label on a FLOPPY DISK, or a plastic ring on a TAPE reel). In this case, the DISK or TAPE DRIVE will not WRITE at all onto the medium, even if it is directed to do so by the PROGRAM.

LOGICAL FILE PROTECTION is designed into the SOFTWARE, such as the OPERATING SYSTEM. FILES stored on a DISK or TAPE can be designated as READ ONLY (R/O) and PROGRAMS cannot transfer any new DATA into them (nor can they be accidently erased). In this way, both regular and READ ONLY FILES can be stored on the same DISK or TAPE.

file server

COMPUTER CONTROLLING DISKS IN A COMMUNICATIONS NETWORK; See DATA BASE SERVER and SHARED RESOURCE.

file system

NON-DATA BASE SYSTEM; A FILE SYSTEM implies the creation and manipulation of FILES using traditional methods, whereby each PROGRAM makes room for the size of the RECORD in the FILE. Contrast with a DATA BASE MANAGEMENT SYSTEM which delivers just the required DATA to each USER'S PROGRAM. A FILE SYSTEM implies no DATA INDEPENDENCE.

financial planning language

COMMAND LANGUAGE FOR FINANCIAL PLANNING SYSTEMS; FINANCIAL PLANNING LANGUAGES have been developed to work with a particular FINANCIAL PLANNING SYSTEM. Some of them are easy to use for the first-time USER, and allow for the creation of a DATA MODEL with very little attention to PROGRAMMING technique. See FINANCIAL PLANNING SYSTEM.

financial planning system

FINANCIAL MODELING SOFTWARE PACKAGE; FINANCIAL PLANNING SYSTEMS are DECISION SUPPORT SYSTEMS that allow the financial planner/manager to examine and evaluate many alternatives before making final decisons. FINANCIAL PLANNING SYSTEMS employ the use of a MODEL, which is a series of DATA ELEMENTS in equation form; for example: gross profit = gross sales - cost of goods sold. Different values can be plugged into the DATA ELEMENTS and the impact of various options can be assessed (what if?). See ELECTRONIC SPREADSHEET.

Sensitivity analysis is a feature of FINANCIAL PLANNING SYSTEMS, whereby various DATA can be assigned a range of values. When the calculations cause the DATA to exceed their range, they are highlighted for USER attention.

Another feature is goal seeking. In this case the PROGRAM calculates a desired outcome. For example: In an organization, the above equation would be replicated many times for different product lines with many variables affecting the MODEL, such as labor cost, overtime, etc. If the SYSTEM is given the minimums and maximums of the various INPUTS, it can calculate an optimum mix of INPUTS to obtain the desired OUTPUT (for example, a gross margin of 50% in our equation above).

The USER develops the MODEL and equations using the FINANCIAL PLANNING LANGUAGE designed as part of the SYSTEM.

firmware

MEMORY CHIP FOR PROGRAM STORAGE; FIRMWARE is "hard" SOFTWARE. The PROGRAM is stored in the FIRMWARE and the PROCESSOR EXECUTES the PROGRAM by extracting INSTRUCTIONS from the FIRMWARE MEMORY. FIRMWARE is used extensively in the architecture of COMPUTERS. It is also used in myriads of consumer products, such as games, toys, and appliances. EEPROMS, EPROMS, PROMS and ROMS are FIRMWARE. MICROCODE is also FIRMWARE.

fixed disk

NON-REMOVABLE DISK; FIXED DISKS are HARD DISK DRIVES with one or more DISK platters fixed inside the unit. All INFORMATION must be transferred to and from the FIXED DISK via the COMPUTER, rather than by inserting a DISK CARTRIDGE or DISK PACK. See WINCHESTER DISK.

fixed length field/record

FIELD AND RECORD STRUCTURES OF UNIFORM SIZE; FIXED LENGTH FIELDS are FIELDS that always contain the same number of BYTES, regardless of the content within them. For example: a 25-BYTE name FIELD will always take up 25 BYTES of space on a DISK, regardless of the length of the name that is stored in it. FIXED LENGTH RECORDS are RECORDS which contain the same number of FIXED LENGTH FIELDS.

fixed point

METHOD FOR STORING AND CALCULATING NUMBERS; FIXED POINT implies that all numbers have the decimal point (or BINARY point) in the same location. Contrast with FLOATING POINT.

flag

STATUS INDICATOR; A FLAG can be a HARDWARE or SOFTWARE indicator that is used to keep track of, and signal, some condition. It is usually no more than a one-BYTE FIELD in a PROGRAM.

flatbed plotter

GRAPHICS PLOTTER THAT CREATES A FIXED MAXIMUM PRINTED IMAGE; See PLOTTER.

flat file

TRADITIONAL FILE/RECORD STRUCTURE; A FLAT FILE refers to RECORDS which simply contain FIELDS of DATA. It implies there are no pointers in the RECORD to other RECORDS, or DATA in the RECORD about other RECORDS (as there are in many forms of DATA BASE structures). See RELATIONAL DATA BASE.

flat screen

THIN PANEL VIDEO SCREEN; A FLAT SCREEN is a thin panel SCREEN, in contrast to the long VACUUM TUBE (CRT) which is predominantly used. Although some FLAT CRTs have been developed, other technologies such as ELECTROLUMINESCENT DISPLAY and PLASMA DISPLAY should become predominant. LCD and LED technologies, used in DIGITAL watches, are also used for FLAT SCREENS.

flexible disk

Same as FLOPPY DISK.

flip-flop

ELECTRONIC COMPONENT; A FLIP-FLOP is an ELECTRONIC component which alternates between one state and another. When charged, it changes its present state to its opposite state (*0* to *1*, *1* to *0*). Made of several TRANSISTORS, a FLIP-FLOP is used in the design of STATIC MEMORIES and HARDWARE REGISTERS.

floating point

METHOD FOR CALCULATING NUMBERS; FLOATING POINT numbers do not line up like normal (FIXED POINT) numbers. The significant digits (no zeros on the right) are stored as a unit called the *mantissa* and the location of the point is stored separately as an *exponent*. FLOATING POINT is a method for calculating a large range of numbers quickly.

FLOATING POINT operations can be implemented in HARDWARE or in SOFTWARE. They can also be performed in a separate FLOATING POINT PROCESSOR, which is connected to the standard PROCESSOR via a CHANNEL.

MANTISSA	EXPONENT		ACTUAL VALUE
6508	0	=	6508
6508	1	=	65080
6508	-1	=	650.8

FLOATING POINT

floating point processor

FLOATING POINT HARDWARE; A FLOATING POINT PROCESSOR is an arithmetic unit which performs FLOATING POINT operations. A FLOATING POINT PROCESSOR may refer to a CPU with built-in FLOATING POINT capabilities, or to a separate unit which is attached to a standard COMPUTER CPU. ARRAY PROCESSORS are often FLOATING POINT PROCESSORS.

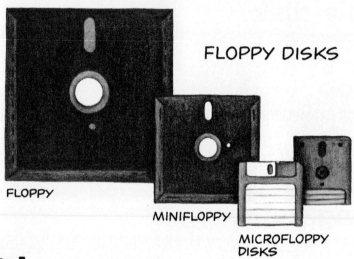

FLOPPY DISKS

FLOPPY

MINIFLOPPY

MICROFLOPPY DISKS

floppy disk

STORAGE FOR PROGRAMS AND INFORMATION; FLOPPY DISKS are a magnetic storage medium which can be recorded, erased and used over and over again. FLOPPY DISKS are a single flexible plastic DISK which are available in several standard sizes. The term FLOPPY DISK may refer to all the varieties.

Full size FLOPPY DISKS are 8" in diameter; MINIFLOPPY DISKS are 5 1/4" in diameter. They are both permanently housed in a stiff paper-like plastic envelope (usually black) and remain in the envelope at all times. When the DISK is inserted into the FLOPPY DISK DRIVE, the DISK DRIVE spindle clamps the DISK and spins it inside the envelope. An ACCESS ARM moves the READ/WRITE HEAD across the DISK surface through the openings in the DISK.

8" FLOPPY DISKS and MINIFLOPPY DISKS are available in several combinations of SINGLE SIDED or DOUBLE SIDED, HARD SECTORED or SOFT SECTORED, SINGLE DENSITY or DOUBLE DENSITY versions. The FLOPPY DISK DRIVE that records the DISK sets these standards, and the appropriate DISK must be used. For example: SINGLE SIDED-SINGLE DENSITY-SOFT SECTORED or SINGLE SIDED-DOUBLE DENSITY-HARD SECTORED are typical of many variations.

Note: FILE PROTECTION for FLOPPY and MINIFLOPPY DISKS is confusing. The FILE PROTECTION notch works exactly the opposite on each variety. The 8" FLOPPY requires that the notch is uncovered for FILE PROTECTION, while the 5 1/4" FLOPPY requires that the notch is covered.

MICROFLOPPY DISKS are available in sizes ranging from 3 to 4". They are housed in a semi-rigid or rigid plastic shell of varying design. FILE PROTECTION is usually provided by a sliding tab on the plastic housing.

The number of BYTES that can be recorded on a FLOPPY DISK depends on the FLOPPY DISK DRIVE technology (from approximately 80,000 to over 1,000,000 BYTES). FLOPPY DISKS are used extensively in PERSONAL COMPUTERS, small business COMPUTERS, WORD PROCESSING, and DATA ENTRY. See MAGNETIC DISK & TAPE.

flow chart

A GRAPHICAL PICTURE OF THE SEQUENCE OF OPERATIONS OF A PROGRAM OR AN INFORMATION SYSTEM; INFORMATION SYSTEM FLOW CHARTS show how DATA and INFORMATION on SOURCE DOCUMENTS flow through the COMPUTER SYSTEM to final distribution to USERS. PROGRAM FLOW CHARTS show the sequence of INSTRUCTIONS in a single PROGRAM (PROGRAM LOGIC). Different symbols are used for each type of FLOW CHART.

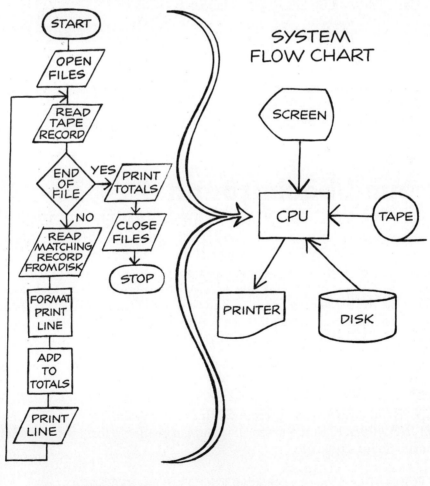

FOCUS

DATA MANAGEMENT SYSTEM WHICH RUNS ON IBM COMPUTERS; FOCUS offers a variety of DECISION SUPPORT facilities for the USER, including FINANCIAL PLANNING and statistical analyses capabilities. FOCUS is a product of Information Builders, Inc.

font

TYPE STYLE; A FONT is a particular type style. This is a sample of the Stymie light FONT. *This is a sample of Stymie medium italic.*

for next loop

HIGH-LEVEL PROGRAMMING LANGUAGE LOGIC STATEMENT; FOR NEXT LOOP defines a segment of PROGRAM LOGIC (LINES OF CODE) that will be repeated over and over again, a specific number of times. For example:

Print Hello followed by Goodbye 10 times:

```
FOR X = 1 TO 10
PRINT "Hello"
PRINT "Goodbye"
NEXT X
```

All statements between the FOR and NEXT are repeated the number of times specified in the FOR statement.

foreground/background

A TECHNIQUE FOR HANDLING ON-LINE (TRANSACTION PROCESSING) AND BATCH PROCESSING IN THE SAME COMPUTER; FOREGROUND/BACKGROUND dynamically balances the COMPUTER in favor of the USERS at the TERMINALS. The INTERACTIVE PROGRAMS are assigned the higher priority (FOREGROUND) and the BATCH PROGRAMS the lower (BACKGROUND). The BATCH PROGRAMS are PROCESSED in the available machine time between the FOREGROUND tasks and can take considerably longer to complete if there is a lot of TERMINAL activity. FOREGROUND/BACKGROUND is an OPERATING SYSTEM technique.

format

ORGANIZATION OR ARRANGEMENT; A SCREEN or REPORT FORMAT is the display or printing of INFORMATION in a prescribed human readable form with columns, spaces, commas, dollar signs, etc.

A RECORD FORMAT is the arrangement of FIELDS in the RECORD.

THE COMPUTER GLOSSARY

A DISK FORMAT is a particular arrangement for recording RECORDS on a DISK. A DISK must be FORMATTED by a special UTILITY PROGRAM before INFORMATION or PROGRAMS can be WRITTEN onto it. The DISK FORMAT PROGRAM WRITES identifying DATA onto the TRACKS for future references by the DISK OPERATING SYSTEM.

form feed key

PRINTER CONTROL KEY; The FORM FEED KEY advances the paper in the PRINTER to the top of the next page.

FORTH

HIGH-LEVEL PROGRAMMING LANGUAGE AND OPERATING SYSTEM; FORTH was created by Charles Moore in the late 1960s, as a tool for the PROGRAMMER who wants direct control of the COMPUTER. FORTH contains a resident ASSEMBLY LANGUAGE so that PROGRAMMERS can work at the machine level, as well. FORTH is noted for its extensibility; the language and the OPERATING SYSTEM can be expanded by the USER. FORTH is quite different from other languages, although its syntax somewhat resembles LISP. FORTH is used in business, SCIENTIFIC and PROCESS CONTROL APPLICATIONS, and is extensively used in ROBOTICS and arcade game PROGRAMMING. FORTH is both a COMPILER and an INTERPRETER. The primary PROGRAM LOGIC is first COMPILED and then EXECUTED under its OPERATING SYSTEM/INTERPRETER. FORTH stands for **FO**u**RTH**-generation language.

FORTRAN

HIGH-LEVEL PROGRAMMING LANGUAGE DEVELOPED FOR SOLVING SCIENTIFIC AND MATHEMATICAL PROBLEMS; FORTRAN was the first HIGH-LEVEL PROGRAMMING LANGUAGE. It was developed in 1954 by IBM, and was designed to easily express mathematical formulas for COMPUTER PROCESSING. It is still the most widely used PROGRAMMING LANGUAGE for scientific, engineering and mathematical problems. (Although occasionally, business APPLICATIONS are developed in FORTRAN as well.) FORTRAN is a COMPILER language and stands for **FOR**mula **TRAN**slator.

fourth-generation language

NON-PROCEDURAL, USER-FRIENDLY LANGUAGE; The generations of PROGRAMMING LANGUAGES are: First-generation language is MACHINE LANGUAGE (what the COMPUTER understands). Second-generation language is ASSEMBLY LANGUAGE (symbolic form for stating MACHINE LANGUAGE). Third-generation languages are HIGH-LEVEL languages, like COBOL, FORTRAN and PL/I. FOURTH-GENERATION LANGUAGES are NON-PROCEDURAL, MENU DRIVEN or COMMAND DRIVEN languages. Many products claim FOURTH-GENERATION LANGUAGE capability, including both PROCEDURAL PROGRAMMING LANGUAGES and NON-PROCEDURAL QUERY LANGUAGES, REPORT WRITERS and APPLICATION GENERATORS.

frame

SINGLE BLOCK OF DATA; A FRAME is a group of DATA which makes up a single full picture SCREEN in GRAPHICS or VIDEOTEX. A FRAME is also a group of BITS which make up an elementary BLOCK of DATA for transmission by certain COMMUNICATIONS PROTOCOLS.

frequency

VIBRATIONS PER SECOND; The FREQUENCY of a CARRIER is the number of electrical vibrations generated in one second.

frequency division multiplexing

See FDM.

frequency modulation

See FM.

front end processor

COMMUNICATIONS COMPUTER; The FRONT END PROCESSOR is a COMPUTER which connects to the COMMUNICATIONS CHANNELS on one end and the main COMPUTER on the other. SOFTWARE in the FRONT END PROCESSOR directs the transmitting and receiving of MESSAGES according to the rules of the COMMUNICATIONS PROTOCOL used in the NETWORK. The SOFTWARE detects and corrects transmission errors, assembles and disassembles MESSAGES, etc., so that only pure INFORMATION is transferred to and from the main COMPUTER (stripped of all CODES that are attached for transmission through the NETWORK). A FRONT END PROCESSOR is sometimes synonymous with a COMMUNICATIONS CONTROL UNIT, although the latter is usually not as flexible as a FRONT END PROCESSOR.

full-duplex

COMMUNICATIONS MODE; FULL-DUPLEX transmission means signals are being transmitted and received at the same time. In all DIGITAL NETWORKS, this is achieved with two pairs of wires. In ANALOG NETWORKS, this can be achieved by dividing the BANDWIDTH of the line into two FREQUENCIES, one for sending and the other for receiving. See CARRIER and FDM.

full-screen

USING THE ENTIRE SCREEN; FULL-SCREEN operations imply that the entire face of the VIDEO SCREEN is used for display. The PROGRAM may direct DATA onto any portion of the SCREEN. Contrast with TELETYPE mode, whereby new DATA entered is displayed a line at a time on the bottom of the SCREEN.

FUNCTION KEYS

function keys

COMMAND KEYS; FUNCTION KEYS are separate keys added to a TERMINAL
KEYBOARD, or a set of keys in a KEYPAD which is connected to the TERMINAL. The
depression of a FUNCTION KEY by the USER causes some function in the PROGRAM to
be performed. However, the PROGRAM must be PROGRAMMED to test the CODE
generated by the FUNCTION KEY, otherwise the FUNCTION KEY will not work.
SOFTWARE PACKAGES are sometimes developed with a special translation table which
allows customizing of the SOFTWARE to work with a particular USER'S KEYBOARD.
FUNCTION KEYS are valuable in WORD PROCESSING and GRAPHICS
APPLICATIONS where a high degree of INTERACTIVE dialogue takes place. The
FUNCTION KEY allows for a single key depression to activate some function, rather than
using a CONTROL KEY plus one or two other keys, or typing a lengthy COMMAND
CODE.

functional specifications

DOCUMENTATION FOR THE DESIGN OF AN INFORMATION SYSTEM; The
FUNCTIONAL SPECS document the DATA BASE, human and machine PROCEDURES,
and the INPUTS, PROCESSES and OUTPUTS for each DATA ENTRY, QUERY,
UPDATE, and REPORT PROGRAM in the SYSTEM. The FUNCTIONAL
SPECIFICATIONS are the blueprint for the INFORMATION SYSTEM. See
DOCUMENTATION.

gas discharge display

See PLASMA DISPLAY.

gate

COMPONENT IN ELECTRONIC CIRCUITRY; A GATE often refers to a LOGIC GATE, which is a combination of switches designed according to BOOLEAN LOGIC. A GATE is also an elementary part of a MOSFET TRANSISTOR, which acts as the bridge between one side and the other. In any event, a GATE will always refer to the concept of a gate (a device which opens and closes).

gate array

See LOGIC ARRAY.

gateway

INTERFACE BETWEEN COMMUNICATIONS NETWORKS; A GATEWAY is a COMPUTER which connects two distinctly different COMMUNICATIONS NETWORKS together. The GATEWAY will perform the PROTOCOL CONVERSIONS necessary to transmit between the NETWORKS. For example, a GATEWAY would connect a LOCAL AREA NETWORK to a national or foreign NETWORK.

gather write

See SCATTER READ/GATHER WRITE.

GCOS

OPERATING SYSTEM USED ON HONEYWELL MINICOMPUTERS AND MAINFRAMES.

general purpose computer

STANDARD DIGITAL COMPUTER; The versatility and flexibility of a DIGITAL COMPUTER is based on it being a GENERAL PURPOSE COMPUTER that is made specific by following a set of INSTRUCTIONS called a PROGRAM. Most DIGITAL COMPUTERS are GENERAL PURPOSE COMPUTERS, although some are specialized for specific APPLICATIONS.

gigabyte

ONE BILLION BYTES; See SPACE/TIME.

GIGO

GARBAGE IN GARBAGE OUT; Also Garbage In Gospel Out!

GIS

IBM QUERY AND DATA MANIPULATION LANGUAGE; Stands for Generalized Information System.

glitch

TEMPORARY HARDWARE MALFUNCTION; A GLITCH refers to any temporary or random malfunction in HARDWARE. A "BUG" refers to a permanent error in the LOGIC of the SYSTEM. Sometimes a BUG in a SOFTWARE PROGRAM may cause the HARDWARE to appear as if it had a GLITCH in it (and vice versa). At times, it can be extremely difficult to determine whether a problem lies within the HARDWARE or within the SOFTWARE.

global

AN OPERATION PERFORMED ON AN ENTIRE SET; A GLOBAL operation implies a manipulation of an entire FILE, DATA BASE, VOLUME, PROGRAM or SYSTEM.

goto

BRANCH STATEMENT IN A PROGRAM; A GOTO statement directs the COMPUTER to go to some other part of the PROGRAM. A GOTO statement is a HIGH-LEVEL PROGRAMMING LANGUAGE statement. The equivalent INSTRUCTION in a LOW-LEVEL language is called a BRANCH or JUMP.

grandfather, father, son

PREVIOUS GENERATIONS OF FILES AND DATA BASES; The SON is the current FILE or DATA BASE being worked on. A copy of the SON becomes the FATHER (BACKUP copy) for the next PROCESSING period, and the previous FATHER becomes the GRANDFATHER.

graph

PICTORIAL REPRESENTATION OF INFORMATION; See BUSINESS GRAPHICS.

graphics

PICTURE CREATION AND PROCESSING; People can design and create picture images in a COMPUTER SYSTEM with GRAPHICS SOFTWARE and INPUT devices, like DIGITIZER TABLETS and LIGHT PENS. GRAPHICS SOFTWARE can generate picture images in the COMPUTER as well, by converting numeric DATA into picture form (See BUSINESS GRAPHICS). Also, real pictures can be "photographed" into the COMPUTER SYSTEM by being SCANNED by a DIGITAL CAMERA.

Images can be generated in single color (MONOCHROME) or multiple colors depending on the type of GRAPHICS TERMINAL used. GRAPHICS OUTPUT is displayed on GRAPHICS TERMINALS or printed on PLOTTERS and GRAPHICS PRINTERS. COM units (COMPUTER OUTPUT MICROFILM) can generate extremely HIGH-RESOLUTION GRAPHICS on film directly from the COMPUTER. Specialized cameras also make instant film or 35mm slide copies directly from the TERMINAL SCREEN.

Once a picture is entered into a COMPUTER and stored on a DISK or TAPE, it can be used as a master for future reference. Copies of the picture can be modified in the COMPUTER in any of a variety of ways: colors can be changed; objects can be shortened, enlarged, squeezed, combined with other objects; etc. Real images (photographs) can be combined with designed images in an infinite variety of ways.

Pictures in a COMPUTER are really just numbers which can represent all the thousands of dots (PIXELS) in the picture (RASTER GRAPHICS technique), or just the point-to-point lines of the picture itself (VECTOR GRAPHICS technique). See Vector Graphics vs Raster Graphics below.

GRAPHICS are available in all sizes of COMPUTERS; however, the more powerful the COMPUTER, the richer the range of images that can be created. COMPUTERS specialized for GRAPHICS might utilize a FLOATING POINT PROCESSOR or an ARRAY PROCESSOR so that complex PROCESSING, like 3-dimensional rotation, can be speeded up.

COMPUTER GRAPHICS vs Television

Although small business and PERSONAL COMPUTERS can cost significantly more than a color TV set, they cannot generate animated pictures as realistically as television can, nor can they generate a still picture with the same quality. The reason is that while TV sets may cost less, they don't store the signal they receive from the broadcasting station; they simply identify and transmit the signal directly to the SCREEN. Images created in COMPUTERS are generated in MEMORY (working storage) and are transmitted from MEMORY to the SCREEN. Since the standard TV SCREEN is made up of hundreds of thousands of dots (PIXELS), there usually isn't enough MEMORY in small COMPUTERS to hold a standard TV SCREEN'S worth of PIXELS. SCREENS with fewer PIXELS are used in small COMPUTERS, which result in less realism on the SCREEN (curves and diagonal lines have a stairstep effect). However, large COMPUTER GRAPHICS SYSTEMS can generate thoroughly lifelike images on the SCREEN that even exceed the realism of a standard television set.

VECTOR GRAPHICS vs RASTER GRAPHICS

There are two methods used for generating and maintaining pictures in a COMPUTER GRAPHICS SYSTEM: VECTOR GRAPHICS and RASTER GRAPHICS.

VECTOR GRAPHICS

The first method, called VECTOR GRAPHICS, is frequently used for drawing. Each line of each object can be drawn into the COMPUTER using a DIGITIZER TABLET or LIGHT PEN, or the lines can be generated by a GRAPHICS SOFTWARE PROGRAM. Each line (called a VECTOR) has a beginning and ending point on an X-Y MATRIX. For example, a square requires 4 VECTORS, one for each side. Since a VECTOR GRAPHICS SCREEN can only draw straight lines, curves must be approximated by many short VECTORS. Therefore, a circle would require dozens of VECTORS. The picture is stored in the COMPUTER SYSTEM as a DISPLAY LIST, which is a collection of all the VECTORS making up the objects in the picture.

CAD (COMPUTER AIDED DESIGN) SYSTEMS employ VECTOR GRAPHICS because the designer develops the objects in the COMPUTER. Identification for each part of the drawing (roof, wall, side, cone, etc.) is entered by the designer into the CAD SYSTEM. Images developed in VECTOR GRAPHICS mode can be changed (shortened, lengthened, rotated) by standard GRAPHICS SOFTWARE routines because objects can be identified by their lines (VECTORS).

BUSINESS GRAPHICS SOFTWARE PACKAGES generate VECTOR GRAPHICS. In fact, most COMPUTER GRAPHICS SYSTEMS store the picture description in VECTOR GRAPHICS form. VECTOR GRAPHICS images can be transmitted from the COMPUTER directly to X-Y PLOTTERS and VECTOR GRAPHICS TERMINALS, since these devices actually "draw" the lines (VECTORS) from the coordinates they receive.

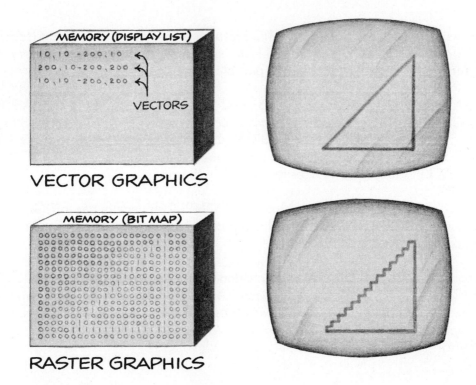

VECTOR GRAPHICS

RASTER GRAPHICS

RASTER GRAPHICS

The second method, called RASTER GRAPHICS, is the more common VIDEO display technique, and essentially is the same concept behind television. It is also the method used to "photograph" a picture into the COMPUTER.

The entire picture or SCREEN area is divided into hundreds of horizontal lines, each line containing hundreds of dots (called PIXELS). The camera records the image as a mosaic of dots (PIXELS) of varying color and brightness. The color and light intensity of each dot are converted into a continuously varying set of values for TV (ANALOG), and discrete values for COMPUTERS (DIGITAL). Since TV is moving pictures, the camera usually generates 30 picture FRAMES per second (enough to provide flicker-free animation).

In order to display the RASTER GRAPHICS picture, the DIGITAL picture is transferred into the COMPUTER'S MAIN MEMORY, or a special MEMORY reserved just for GRAPHICS. This reserved MEMORY is called the BIT MAP and there is a unit of storage reserved for every PIXEL on the SCREEN. The picture stored in the BIT MAP is continuously transmitted to the VIDEO SCREEN, dot for dot, a line at a time, over and over again. Any changes made to any portions of the BIT MAP are instantly reflected on the SCREEN. Wholesale color changes can be accomplished by performing a SEARCH AND REPLACE on a selected color, which is represented by a specific number in the BIT MAP. Animation is accomplished by continuously copying new sequences from other areas of MEMORY into the BIT MAP, one after the other.

Pictures maintained in RASTER GRAPHICS form often require more storage (MEMORY and DISK) than in VECTOR GRAPHICS form, since storage is required for every PIXEL in the entire picture area, even if it's just part of the background.

Most GRAPHICS TERMINALS used in standard COMPUTER SYSTEMS are RASTER GRAPHICS TERMINALS. In order for images created by VECTOR GRAPHICS to be displayed on a RASTER GRAPHICS SCREEN, they must be converted by SOFTWARE into the RASTER GRAPHICS BIT MAP. Except for X-Y PLOTTERS, most PRINTERS also require RASTER GRAPHICS images for GRAPHICS printing.

Note: An X-Y PLOTTER attached to a low-cost COMPUTER usually has a HIGHER RESOLUTION than the TERMINAL, and can generate better quality pictures on paper than can be viewed on the SCREEN.

Television signals are standardized within national boundaries; COMPUTER RASTER GRAPHICS are not standardized at all. Each RASTER GRAPHICS SYSTEM can employ any number of PIXELS on the SCREEN, which can generate from a handful to millions of colors, depending on the capacity of the HARDWARE and the design of the SOFTWARE.

graphics tablet
GRAPHICS INPUT DEVICE; See DIGITIZER TABLET.

graphics terminal
GRAPHICS INPUT/OUTPUT DEVICE; GRAPHICS INPUT is entered by the KEYBOARD, which may contain a series of specialized FUNCTION KEYS, dials and wheels. A LIGHT PEN is an optional GRAPHICS INPUT device. GRAPHICS SCREENS are available in four varieties: RASTER GRAPHICS, VECTOR GRAPHICS, combination RASTER GRAPHICS and VECTOR GRAPHICS, and DIRECT VIEW STORAGE TUBE.

gulp
UNSPECIFIED NUMBER OF BYTES; A GULP is a bunch of BYTES!

half-adder

ELEMENTARY ARITHMETIC CIRCUIT; The HALF-ADDER adds one BIT to another BIT and generates the result BIT and the carry BIT. The HALF-ADDER is located in the ALU (ARITHMETIC LOGIC UNIT).

half-duplex

COMMUNICATIONS MODE; HALF-DUPLEX means transmission in two directions, but in only one direction at a time. Contrast with FULL-DUPLEX, which is simultaneous transmission in both directions at the same time. A CB radio is an example of HALF-DUPLEX transmission. The transmission is only in one direction at a time. The PROTOCOL is: Speak and say "over" to signal the end of the transmission.

handset

PART OF THE TELEPHONE THAT IS HELD IN THE HAND; The HANDSET contains the speaker and the microphone.

hard copy

PRINTED ON PAPER; Contrast with SOFT COPY, which is in AUDIO or VIDEO FORMAT.

hard disk

MAGNETIC DISK MADE OF A RIGID MATERIAL; HARD DISKS come in removable DISK CARTRIDGE and DISK PACK form, as well as in FIXED DISK varieties. Contrast with FLOPPY DISK and MAGNETIC TAPE. See MAGNETIC DISK & TAPE.

hard sectored

DISK SECTOR IDENTIFICATION TECHNIQUE; SECTORS on a DISK that are HARD SECTORED are identified by some fixed mark on the DISK medium itself. HARD SECTORED FLOPPY DISKS have a hole punched in them, marking the beginning of each of the SECTORS.

hardware

THE MACHINERY; The CPU and all PERIPHERALS. Any MICROELECTRONICS device. Contrast with SOFTWARE, which are the INSTRUCTIONS that tell the COMPUTER what to do. The SOFTWARE is stored in HARDWARE devices such as DISK or TAPE, and is copied into the COMPUTER'S MEMORY (HARDWARE) when we want the COMPUTER to do work.

HARDWARE vs SOFTWARE

In operation, a COMPUTER SYSTEM is both HARDWARE and SOFTWARE. One is useless without the other, and each dictates rules for the other. The HARDWARE sets the rules for the kinds of INSTRUCTIONS it can follow and the SOFTWARE INSTRUCTIONS then tell the HARDWARE what to do.

As inseparable as HARDWARE and SOFTWARE are in operation, they are quite different when developed and evaluated on their own. HARDWARE is the world of *storage and transmission*; SOFTWARE is the world of *logic and language*.

The more MEMORY and DISK storage a COMPUTER SYSTEM has, the more work can be done. The faster the MEMORY and DISKS (and other PERIPHERAL devices) transmit DATA and INSTRUCTIONS between them, the faster the work gets done. Although there is logic involved in the design of the ELECTRONIC CIRCUITS and COMPUTER ARCHITECTURE, the logic focuses on the efficiency of the storage and transmission. A USER'S problem can be translated into a pure HARDWARE requirement, based on the size of the FILES and DATA BASES that will be created. See COMPUTER SYSTEM (Computer System Features) and STANDARDS & COMPATIBILITY.

SOFTWARE, on the other hand, is involved with a logical solution to the USER'S specific problem. The PROGRAMMER has to incorporate two sets of LOGIC into the PROGRAM. One set is a prescribed sequence of *what* to do and intermixed with that is a prescribed sequence of *how* to do it. The *what* to do is based on the USER'S problem and the *how* to do it is based on the syntax of the PROGRAMMING LANGUAGE used. The higher the level of language used, the more PROGRAMMERS can concentrate on the *what* and less on the *how*.

There are an infinite number of problems to be solved, and there are many logical solutions for solving each of them. Therefore, there are an infinite number of SOFTWARE PROGRAMS which have been, and will be, developed. Since SOFTWARE is so intrinsically linked with a USER'S problem, the criteria for the evaluation of SOFTWARE is far more complex than it is for HARDWARE.

hardwired

DESIGNED AND BUILT IN; HARDWIRED usually refers to COMPUTER CIRCUITRY, which is designed to perform a certain function and cannot be changed. It also refers to devices which are TIGHTLY COUPLED, such as one PROCESSOR HARDWIRED to another. A HARDWIRED TERMINAL is a TERMINAL directly connected to the CPU without going through a COMMUNICATIONS NETWORK.

Even SOFTWARE can be HARDWIRED. A HARDWIRED SUBROUTINE means PROGRAM LOGIC designed for a specific problem. HARDWIRED implies fixed in nature and not easily changed.

hash total

A TOTAL OF SELECTED DATA; A HASH TOTAL is a control method for ensuring the accuracy of PROCESSED DATA. A HASH TOTAL refers to a totalling of several FIELDS of DATA in a FILE, even FIELDS that may normally not be used for calculation. At various stages in the PROCESSING, the HASH TOTAL is recalculated and matched against the original. If any DATA has been lost or PROCESSED erroneously, the HASH TOTAL will not match.

HDLC

INTERNATIONAL COMMUNICATIONS PROTOCOL; HDLC is an ISO (International Standards Organization) standard which has been adopted fully or in part by many vendors. HDLC is used in the X.25 COMMUNICATIONS NETWORK. HDLC stands for **H**igh-level **D**ata **L**ink **C**ontrol.

head crash

PHYSICAL COLLISION OF A HARD DISK; A HEAD CRASH occurs when the READ/WRITE HEAD collides with the recording surface of a HARD DISK platter. HEAD CRASHES occur due to contamination by dust and dirt, or because of misalignment of the READ/WRITE HEAD or DISK PACK. The recorded content of the DISK is destroyed, and both the DISK PACK and READ/WRITE HEAD must be replaced.

header (label)

PRELIMINARY IDENTIFICATION; A HEADER RECORD or HEADER LABEL is an identification RECORD which is the first RECORD of the FILE. The name of the FILE, the date of last UPDATE, and various other status data are part of the HEADER LABEL. A HEADER is also a CHARACTER or group of BITS which marks the beginning of a DATA FRAME for certain COMMUNICATIONS PROTOCOLS. A HEADER can be any preliminary DATA used for identification purposes.

help screen

INSTRUCTIONAL INFORMATION REGARDING USE OF SOFTWARE; HELP
SCREENS are instructions about how to use the SYSTEM that can be displayed on the
SCREEN at any time. A MENU driven SYSTEM would not require HELP SCREENS,
since all the options are displayed on the MENU.

hertz

FREQUENCY RATING; The number of electrical vibrations (or cycles) in a second is
rated in HERTZ. 1 HERTZ is equal to 1 cycle per second. In 1883, Heinrich Hertz
detected electromagnetic WAVES. HERTZ is abbreviated Hz.

heuristic

A METHOD OF PROGRAMMING IN WHICH THE SOLUTION TO THE PROBLEM IS
DEVELOPED RATHER THAN FIXED; HEURISTIC PROGRAM design provides a
framework for solving the problem, rather than having a specific solution to the problem.
Contrast with ALGORITHMIC PROGRAMMING, where the steps to solving the problem
are fixed and the LOGIC (rules) will not vary. HEURISTIC PROGRAMS are used in
ARTIFICIAL INTELLIGENCE APPLICATIONS.

hexadecimal (hex)

A NUMBER BASED ON 16 DIGITS; HEXADECIMAL means *16*: (hex = 6) + (dec = 10).
PROGRAMMERS use HEXADECIMAL as a shorthand method for representing BINARY
numbers. Each 4 BITS of BINARY is converted to a single HEXADECIMAL digit.

Decimal	BINARY	HEXADECIMAL
0	0000	0
1	0001	1
2	0010	2
3	0011	3
4	0100	4
5	0101	5
6	0110	6
7	0111	7
8	1000	8
9	1001	9
10	1010	A
11	1011	B
12	1100	C
13	1101	D
14	1110	E
15	1111	F

hierarchical

COMMUNICATIONS OR DATA BASE
STRUCTURE; HIERARCHICAL structures imply
that ACCESS begins at the top and spreads
down throughout the rest of the components,
as in any hierarchy.

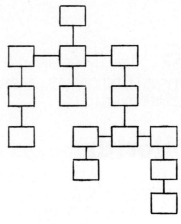

HIERARCHICAL

high-level language

PROBLEM-ORIENTED LANGUAGE; HIGH-LEVEL LANGUAGES are designed to
allow the PROGRAMMER to concentrate on the LOGIC of the problem to be solved.
They eliminate the requirement that the PROGRAMMER have an intimate knowledge of
the COMPUTER'S MACHINE LANGUAGE, although PROGRAMMING technique is
still required. COMPILERS such as ALGOL, BASIC, COBOL, FORTRAN, PASCAL
and PL/I are examples of HIGH-LEVEL LANGUAGES. HIGH-LEVEL means more
oriented toward people. Contrast with LOW-LEVEL ASSEMBLY LANGUAGES, which
are closer to the machine.

high-resolution

HIGH GRADE IMAGE QUALITY; HIGH-RESOLUTION (HI-RES) refers to a large
number of dots in a DOT MATRIX or PIXELS in a picture image.

higher than high-level language

APPLICATION ORIENTED-LANGUAGES; There are myriads of problem-solving
languages which are used on COMPUTERS. Many of them, such as REPORT WRITERS
and FINANCIAL PLANNING LANGUAGES, are designed for the specific problem they
are trying to solve. They are much easier to use than CONVENTIONAL
PROGRAMMING LANGUAGES and are thus even *higher* than standard HIGH-LEVEL
LANGUAGES. NON-PROCEDURAL languages are HIGHER THAN HIGH-LEVEL
LANGUAGES.

HIPO

PROGRAM FLOW CHARTING TECHNIQUE; HIPO is an IBM FLOW CHARTING
technique which provides a graphical method for designing and DOCUMENTING
PROGRAMS. Stands for **H**ierarchy plus **I**nput-**P**rocess-**O**utput and is pronounced /high-po/.

hi-res

ABBREVIATION OF **HI**GH **RES**OLUTION.

HIS

HONEYWELL **I**NFORMATION **S**YSTEMS (COMPUTER SYSTEMS DIVISION OF HONEYWELL, INC).

Hollerith

PUNCHED CARD CODE; Herman Hollerith developed PUNCHED CARD DATA PROCESSING for the U. S. census of 1890. HOLLERITH cards contain 80 columns (CHARACTERS) of INFORMATION, CODED as the presence or absence of holes punched in the column.

home key

CURSOR KEY; The HOME KEY directs the CURSOR to the top left portion of the VIDEO SCREEN. It may also direct the CURSOR to the leftmost positon of the current line.

host

MAIN COMPUTER; The HOST is generally the central or controlling COMPUTER in a DISTRIBUTED SYSTEM.

housekeeping

ROUTINE INITIALIZATION STEPS IN A PROGRAM; HOUSEKEEPING resets all the COUNTERS and FLAGS, may clear selected MEMORY locations, and generally sets up the PROGRAM for proper EXECUTION.

HP

HEWLETT-**P**ACKARD CORPORATION.

hybrid computer

DIGITAL COMPUTER THAT PROCESSES ANALOG SIGNALS; A HYBRID COMPUTER peforms DIGITAL PROCESSING on ANALOG INPUTS which have been converted to DIGITAL form. HYBRID COMPUTERS are used extensively in PROCESS CONTROL and ROBOTICS.

Hz

ABBREVIATION FOR **H**ERT**Z**.

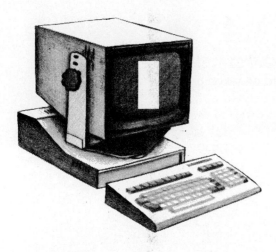

IBM

INTERNATIONAL **B**USINESS **M**ACHINES CORPORATION.

IC

INTEGRATED **C**IRCUIT; See CHIP.

icon

PICTURE REPRESENTATION; An ICON is a graphic image used to refer to some object. ICONS are displayed on VIDEO SCREENS for quick identification of objects (DATA, FILES, PERIPHERALS, functions, etc.).

IDMS

DATA BASE MANAGEMENT SYSTEM WHICH RUNS ON IBM COMPUTERS; IDMS provides a number of products which surround the IDMS DATA BASE, including a NATURAL LANGUAGE QUERY LANGUAGE. IDMS is a product of Cullinane Database Systems, Inc., and stands for **I**ntegrated **D**ata **M**anagement **S**ystem.

IEEE

INSTITUTE OF **E**LECTRICAL AND **E**LECTRONIC **E**NGINEERS; IEEE holds numerous meetings and technical conferences on all topics of engineering and COMPUTER control. Their membership includes engineers and scientists in ELECTRONICS and allied fields, in addition to 30,000 students. Founded in 1963, the IEEE has over 200,000 members. Local meetings cover current topics of interest in the ELECTRONICS field. The IEEE is involved with setting standards for the COMPUTER and COMMUNICATIONS field.

if then else

HIGH-LEVEL PROGRAMMING LANGUAGE LOGIC STATEMENT; IF THEN ELSE
defines the DATA to be compared and the actions to be taken as a result of the
comparison. If the IF condition is true, the THEN is carried out. If the IF condition is not
true, the ELSE is carried out. For example, "count to 10 by 1," could be expressed as:

```
LOOP:       IF COUNTER = 10 THEN STOP
            ELSE COUNTER = COUNTER + 1
            GOTO LOOP
```

image processing

IMAGE IDENTIFICATION AND ANALYSIS; IMAGE PROCESSING is a category of
COMPUTER GRAPHICS techniques that analyze pictures for content. IMAGE
PROCESSING techniques can identify levels of shades, colors and relationships that
cannot be perceived by the human eye. Any object or photograph can be DIGITIZED
into the COMPUTER (into RASTER GRAPHICS FORMAT) and analyzed by IMAGE
PROCESSING. IMAGE PROCESSING is used to create weather maps from satellite
pictures, although considerable PROCESSING time is required to decode the images.
IMAGE PROCESSING is used for solving myriads of identification problems, as for
example, in forensic medicine.

IMOS

OPERATING SYSTEM USED ON NCR I-9000 SERIES.

impact printer

CHARACTER AND LINE PRINTER TECHNOLOGY; Fully-formed CHARACTERS are
impacted into the ribbon and onto the paper. See PRINTER TECHNOLOGIES.

implementation

INSTALLATION OF A COMPUTER SYSTEM OR AN INFORMATION SYSTEM;
COMPUTER SYSTEM IMPLEMENTATION refers to the installation of the HARDWARE
and the SYSTEM SOFTWARE. INFORMATION SYSTEM IMPLEMENTATION refers to
the installation of the new DATA BASES and APPLICATION PROGRAMS and adoption
of new manual PROCEDURES.

IMS

IBM DATA BASE MANAGEMENT SYSTEM; IMS is an example of a HIERARCHICAL
DATA BASE. Stands for **I**nformation **M**anagement **S**ystem.

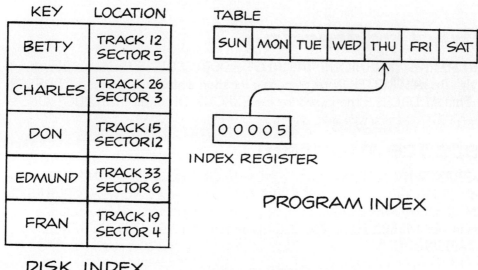

KEY   LOCATION

BETTY	TRACK 12 SECTOR 5
CHARLES	TRACK 26 SECTOR 3
DON	TRACK 15 SECTOR 12
EDMUND	TRACK 33 SECTOR 6
FRAN	TRACK 19 SECTOR 4

DISK INDEX

TABLE

| SUN | MON | TUE | WED | THU | FRI | SAT |

00005

INDEX REGISTER

PROGRAM INDEX

index

ACCESS TECHNIQUE; An INDEX is a directory of where RECORDS, FILES, PROGRAMS, etc. are stored on a DISK. INDEXES are used extensively for organization of DIRECT ACCESS storage devices. The INDEX contains the KEY (RECORD identifier), FILE or PROGRAM name, and a pointer to either an actual PHYSICAL location on the DISK or to another INDEX. An INDEX acts just like a table of contents in a book. INDEXES are stored on the DISK and copied (READ) into the COMPUTER to be searched (compared).

INDEXING is also a PROGRAMMING technique which is used to search for DATA/INFORMATION stored in a TABLE within the PROGRAM. DATA in the TABLE is referred to by SUBSCRIPTS in the PROGRAMMING LANGUAGE statements.

index register

HARDWARE REGISTER THAT PERFORMS AN INDEXING FUNCTION; An INDEX REGISTER is a storage REGISTER used to hold a value used in INDEXING DATA. A SUBSCRIPT in the PROGRAM would reference the COMPUTER'S INDEX REGISTER.

indexed addressing

PROGRAMMING TECHNIQUE; INDEXED ADDRESSING refers to referencing DATA with the use of an INDEX. See SUBSCRIPT.

indexed sequential

ACCESS METHOD; INDEXED SEQUENTIAL is a common ACCESS METHOD which organizes a FILE in a SEQUENTIAL fashion and also generates an INDEX to individual RECORDS within it. The sequence of the FILE would be the most widely used order of the FILE, for example: customer number, employee number, vendor number, etc.

indirect addressing

PROGRAMMING TECHNIQUE; INDIRECT ADDRESSING refers to referencing DATA indirectly. An INSTRUCTION references a location which contains the ADDRESS of the DATA. That ADDRESS is then used for the EXECUTION of the INSTRUCTION.

inference program

A PROGRAM WHICH DERIVES A CONCLUSION FROM CERTAIN FACTS; The INFERENCE PROGRAM is the PROCESSING portion of a KNOWLEDGE BASED SYSTEM. It contains the LOGIC for interpreting the rules in order to obtain a conclusion. An INFERENCE PROGRAM is an ARTIFICIAL INTELLIGENCE APPLICATION.

information

FORMS OF COMMUNICATION (DATA, TEXT, PICTURES, VOICE); Traditionally, INFORMATION has been viewed as the end result of PROCESSING DATA (turning DATA, raw facts and figures, into meaningful INFORMATION). As we integrate GRAPHICS, voice, and WORD PROCESSING into our organizations, the term INFORMATION is becoming more expansive. It may be helpful to view INFORMATION as having several forms. Each form is structured differently according to how it is used. DATA is INFORMATION that can be precisely defined such as account number, amount due, invoice date, etc. TEXT and voice are INFORMATION defined by STRINGS of words. Pictures are INFORMATION defined by FRAMES or DISPLAY LISTS (See GRAPHICS). See DATA.

Information Center

DEPARTMENT DEDICATED TO USER-ORIENTED COMPUTING; The INFORMATION CENTER is a separate section within the MIS department which provides tools, assistance, and training to USERS for USER-oriented and USER-controlled COMPUTER activities. Products like QUERY LANGUAGES, REPORT WRITERS, and FINANCIAL PLANNING SYSTEMS are examples of the SOFTWARE PACKAGES which are provided. INFORMATION CENTER CONSULTANTS work with USERS to make available the necessary FILES and DATA BASES from the main COMPUTER to support USER analysis of the DATA.

information management

THE MANAGEMENT OF INFORMATION; The INFORMATION SCIENCE that deals with the definitions, uses, value and distribution of INFORMATION. INFORMATION MANAGEMENT deals with all INFORMATION that is PROCESSED by an organization, whether it is INPUT to the COMPUTER or not. INFORMATION MANAGEMENT evaluates the types of INFORMATION an organization requires to function and progress effectively.

INFORMATION MANAGEMENT must be viewed separately from HARDWARE/SOFTWARE management. INFORMATION is complex because the nature of business TRANSACTIONS is complex. It must be analyzed and understood before effective COMPUTER solutions can be developed. See DATA ADMINISTRATION.

information processing

CAPTURING, STORING, MANIPULATING AND RETRIEVING INFORMATION; INFORMATION PROCESSING may mean the same as DATA PROCESSING, or it may refer to the entire MIS operation.

information resource management

See INFORMATION MANAGEMENT.

information science

THE FIELD OF INFORMATION MANAGEMENT; INFORMATION SCIENCE deals with the analysis of INFORMATION as an organizational resource. See INFORMATION MANAGEMENT.

Information Services

See INFORMATION SYSTEMS.

information system

A BUSINESS APPLICATION OF THE COMPUTER; An INFORMATION SYSTEM is made up of a DATA BASE, PROCEDURES, and COMPUTER PROGRAMS which collectively provide for the capturing, storing, manipulating and retrieving of INFORMATION. For example: A payroll INFORMATION SYSTEM contains a payroll DATA BASE, all the DATA ENTRY, QUERY, UPDATE, and REPORT PROGRAMS necessary to PROCESS payroll, and the machine PROCEDURES necessary to direct the flow of DATA from one PROGRAM to another. A DOCUMENTATION manual is also part of the INFORMATION SYSTEM describing how payroll INFORMATION is gathered and entered into the COMPUTER, and how the OUTPUTS of the SYSTEM are distributed and used.

Sometimes business INFORMATION SYSTEMS are divided into two classes: the production SYSTEM and the INFORMATION retrieval SYSTEM. The production SYSTEM is the day-to-day TRANSACTION PROCESSING SYSTEM; the INFORMATION retrieval SYSTEM (which may be in a separate COMPUTER) contains synthesized DATA derived from the production SYSTEM, which is made available to USERS at TERMINALS.

The terms INFORMATION SYSTEM and APPLICATION are synonymous.

Information Systems

FORMAL TITLE FOR A DP/MIS DEPARTMENT; INFORMATION SYSTEMS may refer to the department responsible for COMPUTER and INFORMATION activities for the entire organization. INFORMATION SYSTEMS is often synonymous with INFORMATION Services or MANAGEMENT INFORMATION SYSTEMS or MANAGEMENT INFORMATION Services.

information utility

GENERALIZED INFORMATION SERVICE WHICH MAINTAINS UP-TO-DATE INFORMATION BANKS FOR PUBLIC USE.

ink jet

PRINTER MECHANISM WHICH SPRAYS INK ONTO PAPER; See PRINTER TECHNOLOGIES.

input

DATA/INFORMATION ENTERED INTO THE COMPUTER; INPUT can refer to any INFORMATION that will be entered into the COMPUTER, the act of entering the INFORMATION, or the INFORMATION after it has been entered. Storing INFORMATION on a DISK is technically an INPUT to the COMPUTER first, and then an OUTPUT from the COMPUTER onto the DISK. See READ and WRITE.

input program

Same as DATA ENTRY PROGRAM.

inquiry program

Same as QUERY PROGRAM.

instruction

COMMAND TO THE COMPUTER; The FORMAT of a COMPUTER INSTRUCTION is: OP CODE and OPERANDS (verb and nouns). The OP CODE is the basic COMMAND, such as add or subtract, and the OPERANDS are the references to DATA. Example: Add 1 to a COUNTER. The OP CODE is "Add," and the '1' and "COUNTER" are the OPERANDS.

The OPERANDS refer to specific locations within the PROGRAM by number. The actual MACHINE LANGUAGE INSTRUCTION might look like this: ADD 123, 148-152. That means: add the 1 stored in location 123 to the number in the COUNTER (residing in locations 148 to 152) and store the result back in locations 148 to 152. ASSEMBLERS and COMPILERS determine the actual numbers (ADDRESSES) and generate all the MACHINE LANGUAGE INSTRUCTIONS in BINARY.

INSTRUCTIONS are SOFTWARE, and groups of INSTRUCTIONS which perform specific functions are called PROGRAMS. Segments of PROGRAMS are called MODULES or SUBROUTINES. See MACHINE LANGUAGE.

instruction set

SET OF INSTRUCTIONS DESIGNED AND BUILT INTO THE COMPUTER; The INSTRUCTION SET is a major component of COMPUTER ARCHITECTURE. It is the formal set of directions the COMPUTER follows in order to PROCESS INFORMATION. The INSTRUCTION SET can contain several dozen INSTRUCTIONS or several hundred, depending on the complexity of the design. The INSTRUCTION SET dictates the MACHINE LANGUAGE FORMAT for PROGRAMS to run in the COMPUTER. SOFTWARE PROGRAMS must be translated (COMPILED) into a specific COMPUTER'S MACHINE LANGUAGE in order for the COMPUTER to carry out the INSTRUCTIONS. Individual MACHINE LANGUAGE INSTRUCTIONS are generally from 1 to 4 BYTES long.

integer

A WHOLE NUMBER; 123 would be the INTEGER of 123 1/4.

integrated circuit

THE INTEGRATION OF ONE OR MORE ELECTRONIC CIRCUITS ON A CHIP; See CHIP.

integrated voice/data PABX

See DIGITAL PABX.

Intellect

NATURAL LANGUAGE QUERY LANGUAGE; INTELLECT is designed to understand a QUERY stated in a person's natural language, such as "tell me the number of employees in the personnel department." INTELLECT is a product of Artificial Intelligence, Inc.

intelligence

COMPUTER CAPABILITY; Every COMPUTER is INTELLIGENT.

intelligent terminal

TERMINAL WITH A COMPUTER IN IT; See DISTRIBUTED INTELLIGENCE.

interactive

CONVERSING WITH THE COMPUTER; An INTERACTIVE SYSTEM is an ON-LINE, CONVERSATIONAL SYSTEM. Contrast with a BATCH SYSTEM.

interactive cable TV

INTERACTIVE TELEVISION VIA CABLE TV; INTERACTIVE CABLE TV provides full television service combined with INTERACTIVE capabilities. Viewers can respond to the actual TV program being viewed and take part in the program by voting on issues or reacting to certain questions or situations. INTERACTIVE CABLE TV implies full television viewing, in contrast with VIDEOTEX and TELETEXT services, which provide limited GRAPHICS and animation. However, all services (VIDEOTEX, TELETEXT, as well as TIME-SHARING) may be provided over different INTERACTIVE CABLE TV channels. A DECODER, which contains a KEYBOARD or KEYPAD for INTERACTIVE use, is required to adapt the cable to the TV set.

interblock gap

Same as INTERRECORD GAP.

interface

INTERCONNECTION BETWEEN HARDWARE, SOFTWARE, AND PEOPLE; HARDWARE INTERFACES are physical pathways that must connect and exchange ELECTRONIC signals in a prescribed order. SOFTWARE INTERFACES are specific messages established between PROGRAMS. TERMINAL SCREENS, KEYBOARDS and JOY STICKS are examples of INTERFACES between PEOPLE and machines. See PEOPLE/MACHINE INTERFACES and STANDARDS & COMPATIBILITY (Software Interfaces).

International Standards Organization

See ISO.

interpreter

A HIGH-LEVEL PROGRAMMING LANGUAGE TRANSLATOR; INTERPRETERS
EXECUTE a PROGRAM one line at a time. The PROGRAM always remains in its
original form (SOURCE LANGUAGE) and the INTERPRETER provides the translation at
the time the PROGRAM is run.

It is convenient to write a new PROGRAM with an INTERPRETER. The INTERPRETER
allows the PROGRAMMER to EXECUTE a piece of the PROGRAM INTERACTIVELY,
rather than wait for the entire PROGRAM to be translated and tested as is required with
a COMPILER. An INTERPRETER also allows the PROGRAMMING LANGUAGE to be
used as a desktop calculator.

PROGRAMMING LANGUAGES like BASIC are often available in both INTERPRETER
and COMPILER form. It is possible to develop and test a PROGRAM in INTERPRETER
form, and later COMPILE it for faster EXECUTION in the COMPUTER. The COMPILED
version is translated once and remains in MACHINE LANGUAGE form, rather than
SOURCE LANGUAGE.

interrecord gap

SPACE GENERATED BETWEEN INFORMATION ON A MAGNETIC TAPE; The start-up
and stop-down space generated after recording a physical BLOCK of INFORMATION is
the INTERRECORD GAP (abbreviated IRG). See BLOCK.

interrupt

TRANSFER OF CONTROL TO ANOTHER PROGRAM; INTERRUPTS are HARDWARE
features which automatically transfer control to a specific control PROGRAM residing in
the COMPUTER. INTERRUPTS can be generated by the COMPUTER operator, by
USERS at TERMINALS, or by the PROGRAMS running in the COMPUTER. When
PROGRAM "A" calls for an INFORMATION transfer, an INTERRUPT is generated to
transfer control to PROGRAM "B". This is done so PROGRAM "B" can be operated upon
while PROGRAM "A" is waiting for INFORMATION.

inverted file

A FILE INDEXED ON CHARACTERISTICS; An INVERTED FILE is organized with INDEXES maintained on the characteristics of the DATA. For example: All employees who are administrators would have an administrators INDEX containing the employee numbers (KEYS) of every administrator in the FILE. When various characteristics of DATA are kept in an INVERTED FILE, the matching of selected combinations can be performed in the INDEXES, rather than searching through all the RECORDS in the FILE.

inverter

LOGIC GATE; An INVERTER reverses the INPUT to the opposite state. An INVERTER performs the BOOLEAN LOGIC function called NOT, which changes *0s* to *1s* and *1s* to *0s*.

I/O

AN INFORMATION TRANSFER BETWEEN A CPU AND A PERIPHERAL DEVICE; An I/O is an INPUT/OUTPUT. Every INFORMATION transfer is an OUTPUT from one device and an INPUT into another.

I/O bound

EXCESSIVE INPUT/OUTPUT; An I/O BOUND COMPUTER means that there is an excessive amount of INPUT/OUTPUT transfers taking place within the SYSTEM. Faster I/O CHANNELS and DISKS may be implemented to speed up an I/O BOUND COMPUTER.

I/O channel

COMPUTER CHANNEL; An I/O CHANNEL refers to the physical pathway between the COMPUTER and a PERIPHERAL device. Contrast with CHANNELS in a COMMUNICATIONS NETWORK.

IPL

INITIALIZATION OF THE COMPUTER; An IPL is the same as the BOOT function. It gets the COMPUTER started. IPL stands for Initial Program Load.

IRG

See INTERRECORD GAP.

IRM

See INFORMATION RESOURCE MANAGEMENT.

IRX

OPERATING SYSTEM USED ON LARGE MODELS OF THE NCR I-9000 SERIES.

IS

See INFORMATION **S**YSTEMS.

ISAM

INDEXED SEQUENTIAL ACCESS METHOD; Widely used DISK ACCESS METHOD which stores DATA sequentially and also maintains an INDEX of KEYS to RECORDS for DIRECT ACCESS capability.

ISO

INTERNATIONAL **S**TANDARDS **O**RGANIZATION; ISO is involved with setting COMMUNICATIONS standards worldwide. They have developed the OPEN SYSTEMS INTERCONNECTION (OSI) standards, which is a multiple layered COMMUNICATIONS PROTOCOL for DISTRIBUTED PROCESSING.

ISO/OSI

INTERNATIONAL COMMUNICATIONS PROTOCOL FOR DISTRIBUTED PROCESSING; Stands for **ISO/O**pen **S**ystems Interconnection. See OPEN SYSTEMS INTERCONNECTION.

I^2L

TYPE OF MICROELECTRONIC CIRCUIT DESIGN; I^2L stands for **I**ntegrated **I**njection **L**ogic and is a particular type of BIPOLAR TRANSISTOR design. I^2L is known for its fast switching speeds.

I-9000

SERIES OF MINICOMPUTERS MANUFACTURED BY NCR.

jaggies

STAIRSTEPPED EFFECT OF DIAGONALS AND CIRCLES; The JAGGIES are produced because of a LOW-RESOLUTION GRAPHICS SCREEN. See GRAPHICS.

HIGH RESOLUTION
GRAPHICS

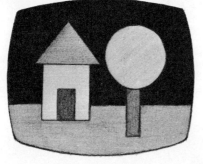 

LOW RESOLUTION
GRAPHICS

JCL

A COMMAND LANGUAGE WHICH TELLS THE COMPUTER WHICH PROGRAMS TO RUN; JOB CONTROL LANGUAGE contains descriptions and directives which are followed by the OPERATING SYSTEM (main scheduling and control PROGRAM). The JCL describes the PROGRAM characteristics, such as size of PROGRAM, FILES and DATA BASES used, running sequence, and running priority. The JCL is fed into the OPERATING SYSTEM which searches for and copies the PROGRAMS into MEMORY at their scheduled time and place. JOB CONTROL LANGUAGES can be simple for MICRO and MINICOMPUTERS or complex for MAINFRAMES.

job

THE EXECUTION OF ANY PROGRAM IN THE COMPUTER; APPLICATION PROGRAMS, UTILITY PROGRAMS and PROGRAM COMPILATIONS are all considered JOBS in COMPUTER OPERATIONS. See JCL.

job control language

See JCL.

job stream

CONSECUTIVE SERIES OF JOBS; A JOB STREAM is a series of related PROGRAMS in an APPLICATION which are run in a prescribed order. The OUTPUT of one PROGRAM is the INPUT to the next PROGRAM, and so on.

Josephson junction

CATEGORY OF MICROELECTRONIC CIRCUIT DESIGN; The JOSEPHSON JUNCTION CIRCUIT is a unique category of MICROELECTRONIC CIRCUIT which employs the use of SUPERCONDUCTORS, and also requires that its operation takes place at near-absolute zero temperatures. JOSEPHSON JUNCTION CIRCUITS are built to be immersed in a liquid helium refrigeration unit. The JOSEPHSON JUNCTION is noted for its ultra-fast switching speeds, estimated to be in the range of 5 to 20 PICOSECONDS (trillionths of a second), and is named after Brian Josephson, who developed the original theory behind it.

joy stick

VIDEO TERMINAL INPUT DEVICE; A JOY STICK is a lever that directs the movement of the CURSOR on the VIDEO SCREEN. It allows the USER to position the CURSOR anywhere on the screen more rapidly than with the standard left, right, up and down CURSOR keys on the KEYBOARD. The JOY STICK is used extensively in arcade games to move objects around on the game board.

JOY STICK

jump

GOTO INSTRUCTION; A JUMP is another term for a BRANCH or GOTO statement in a PROGRAM which directs the COMPUTER to some other place in the PROGRAM.

K

1,000 OR 1,024; K stands for KILO, which means one thousand. However, since COMPUTERS use BINARY numbers, K often refers to 1,024, not 1,000. Take the number 1 and keep multiplying it by 2 and you get 1,024. 1 - 2 - 4 - 8 - 16 - 32 - 64 - 128 - 256 - 512 - **1,024**. That means 64K of MEMORY means 65,536 BYTES of MEMORY, not 64,000 BYTES! However, if a COMPUTER person references a $25K salary, they are referring to an even $25,000.

kerning

CHARACTER SPACING; KERNING is the PROPORTIONAL SPACING of certain combinations of letters, like *WA*, *MW*, *TA*, which requires overlapping of the CHARACTERS. KERNING is performed by PHOTOTYPESETTERS and is usually not available on LETTER QUALITY or LASER PRINTERS.

key

A RECORD IDENTIFIER; Account number, product code, employee number, customer name, etc., are all examples of KEYS used to identify a RECORD in a FILE or DATA BASE. As an identifier, each KEY value must be unique to each RECORD. SORT KEYS are all the FIELDS in the RECORD which will be used to SORT the FILE. The values in the SORT KEYS do not have to be unique.

keyboard

TERMINAL INPUT KEYS; A TERMINAL KEYBOARD contains the standard typewriter keys as well as certain specialized keys, like a CONTROL KEY, ESCAPE KEY and LINE FEED KEY. In addition, a numeric KEYPAD and/or FUNCTION KEYS may be provided. If the TERMINAL uses a VIDEO SCREEN, four CURSOR KEYS are required to move the CURSOR around on the SCREEN (left, right, up and down). Note: Some KEYBOARDS only contain the left and right CURSOR KEYS. There is no standard placement for any of the keys, other than the standard QWERTY typewriter keys. Even the shift keys and the RETURN KEY are not always in the same place as on a standard typewriter. See QWERTY KEYBOARD.

The "feel" of the keys (See N-KEY ROLLOVER) and their placement on the KEYBOARD is a critical evaluation criterion for high-volume DATA ENTRY or WORD PROCESSING. KEYBOARDS should be tested and evaluated by experienced DATA ENTRY or WORD PROCESSING operators, or experienced typists, at the very least.

PRIMARY KEYBOARD KEYS AND USES

RETURN KEY—The RETURN KEY is used to end a line of INPUT. In WORD PROCESSING, the RETURN KEY is used less frequently than with standard typewriters and is only required to end a paragraph (See WORD WRAP).

CURSOR KEYS—Also called arrow keys, CURSOR KEYS move the CURSOR around on the SCREEN. They are used extensively in WORD PROCESSING and are located in a separate cluster, often arranged like points of a compass. Note: Unless a SOFTWARE PACKAGE is developed for a specific TERMINAL or can be customized for the USER'S KEYBOARD, the USER may have to direct the CURSOR with CONTROL KEYS rather than CURSOR KEYS.

FUNCTION KEYS—FUNCTION KEYS are additional keys on the KEYBOARD that are used by the PROGRAM to activate a particular function. They are quite important in WORD PROCESSING if there is a considerable amount of EDITING being performed. A SOFTWARE PROGRAM may be designed for a particular KEYBOARD with pre-assigned FUNCTION KEYS, or the PROGRAM may allow USERS to select which FUNCTION KEYS will be used. In the latter case, a special translation PROGRAM displays the functions that are in the PROGRAM on a MENU. The USER then presses the FUNCTION KEY desired for each function and the PROGRAM stores that particular FUNCTION KEY CODE as a permanent cross-reference.

CONTROL KEY—CONTROL KEY operations are usually defined by the PROGRAM that is running in the COMPUTER. The CONTROL KEY, which operates like a typewriter shift key, is pressed along with one or more additional keys to activate some function in the PROGRAM. For example: CONTROL I might be used to enter the insert mode (which is accomplished by holding down the CONTROL KEY and then pressing the I key). WORD PROCESSING SOFTWARE on MICROCOMPUTERS may require extensive CONTROL KEY operations if there are no additional FUNCTION KEYS on the KEYBOARD that can be used.

HOME KEY—The HOME KEY usually moves the CURSOR to the top left of the SCREEN; however, it may move the CURSOR only to the beginning of the current line. The HOME KEY is often located inside a CURSOR KEY cluster designed like points of a compass.

ESCAPE KEY—The ESCAPE KEY is used as a FUNCTION KEY and is usually defined by the PROGRAM that is running in the COMPUTER. It allows the USER to "escape" from (get out of) the current activity and move onto another.

LINE FEED KEY—If the TERMINAL KEYBOARD is used for COMMUNICATIONS, the LINE FEED KEY drops the CURSOR to the next line on the VIDEO SCREEN, or moves the paper in the PRINTER to the next line. If the TERMINAL KEYBOARD is used as a COMPUTER CONSOLE, the LINE FEED can be used by a PROGRAM as a FUNCTION KEY.

Backspace key—The backspace key can operate in three modes. It may work just like the left CURSOR KEY, moving the CURSOR backward over the line. It may also delete the CHARACTERS it is moving back across. And thirdly, it may act as a TELETYPEWRITER key, called the RUBOUT KEY, which is used to cancel the last CHARACTER transmitted on the TERMINAL. In this case, a duplicate of the last CHARACTER is repeated on the SCREEN (and it has also internally deleted the last CHARACTER).

Repeating keys—KEYBOARDS can be designed to repeat each CHARACTER automatically as long as the key is depressed. Without repeating keys, a separate repeat key may be available, which is pressed along with the key to be repeated. All keys, including FUNCTION KEYS, can be built as repeating keys.

Audible feedback—Keys can be designed to produce an audible sound, such as a click, beep or dink. The sound volume can also be adjusted. Some KEYBOARDS can allow for different sounds (this is important when several TERMINALS are close together). The audible feedback provides a positive feedback for each key depression made by the USER. In addition, when BUFFERED KEYBOARDS are used (allowing the USER to type faster than the PROGRAM can display the INPUT), the audible feedback provides a measure of comfort, the USER knowing that the correct number of keystrokes have been entered.

CALCULATOR KEYPAD

TELEPHONE KEYPAD

keypad

LIMITED SET OF INPUT KEYS; A KEYPAD usually refers to a set of decimal digit keys (0 thru 9) as KEYPADS on a calculator or touch-tone telephone. Additional keys, such as commas, decimal points, plus and minus, etc., may be part of the KEYPAD. A KEYPAD may refer to any limited cluster of keys designed for special purposes. KEYPAD may also refer to the KEYPAD part of a larger KEYBOARD, to a stand-alone set of keys, or to a hand-held instrument.

THE COMPUTER GLOSSARY   155

keypunch

DATA ENTRY; KEYPUNCH may refer to the act of punching CARDS on a KEYPUNCH MACHINE, or to the machine itself. Sometimes KEYPUNCH refers to typing on any TERMINAL keyboard. The KEYPUNCH department is now the DATA ENTRY department in an organization.

keypunch machine

DATA ENTRY MACHINE; A KEYPUNCH MACHINE is a KEYBOARD and CARD PUNCH machine. USER keystrokes are converted into an appropriate CODE punched into the PUNCHED CARD.

key-to-disk machine

STAND-ALONE DATA ENTRY MACHINE; A KEY-TO-DISK SYSTEM is a stand-alone DATA ENTRY SYSTEM which stores KEYBOARD INPUT on a MAGNETIC DISK for PROCESSING by another COMPUTER.

key-to-tape machine

STAND-ALONE DATA ENTRY MACHINE; A KEY-TO-TAPE SYSTEM is a stand-alone DATA ENTRY SYSTEM which stores KEYBOARD INPUT on a MAGNETIC TAPE for PROCESSING by another COMPUTER. The KEY-TO-TAPE MACHINE, introduced by Mohawk Data Sciences in the mid 1960s, was the first advancement in BATCH DATA ENTRY beyond the KEYPUNCH MACHINE.

kilo

ONE THOUSAND; See K.

knowledge base

DATA BASE OF KNOWLEDGE ABOUT A PARTICULAR SUBJECT; A KNOWLEDGE BASE contains the knowledge required for a KNOWLEDGE BASED SYSTEM. See EXPERT SYSTEM.

knowledge based system

A PROBLEM-SOLVING APPLICATION BASED ON ACCUMULATED KNOWLEDGE; A KNOWLEDGE BASED SYSTEM utilizes a DATA BASE of knowledge (KNOWLEDGE BASE) about a subject for its operation. See EXPERT SYSTEM.

KSR

TELEPRINTER WITH KEYBOARD; Stands for **K**eyboard **S**end **R**eceive. Contrast with RO TELEPRINTERS, which receive only.

THE COMPUTER GLOSSARY

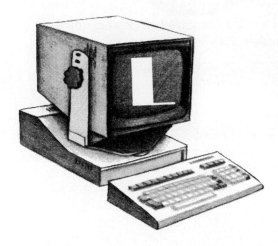

label

MNEMONIC NAME; A LABEL is a DATA, FILE or PROGRAM name. See MNEMONIC.

LAN

See **LOCAL AREA NETWORK**.

laser

LIGHT GENERATOR; LASERS are used to generate light pulses which are transmitted over glass wires (OPTICAL FIBERS). Light pulses are being used in place of electrical pulses since they are not affected by nearby electrical interferences. Unlike a light bulb, the light generated by a LASER is very uniform. LASER light can be precisely focused and is used in a wide variety of technologies, such as in ELECTROPHOTOGRAPHIC printing and OPTICAL DISK storage. LASER stands for **L**ight **A**mplification from the **S**timulated **E**mission of **R**adiation.

laser printer

See PAGE PRINTER.

LCD

DISPLAY TECHNOLOGY; LCDs are the dark digits on a pale gray background used extensively in DIGITAL watches and single and multiple line displays. LCD stands for **L**iquid **C**rystal **D**isplay. The liquid crystals are rod-shaped molecules that flow like liquid. The liquid crystal digits are sandwiched between a polarizing filter on top and a reflector on the bottom. Normally, the liquid crystals allow light to transmit through them and reflect back to the viewer (pale gray). When a segment of liquid crystal is charged, the liquid crystals change their orientation and absorb light, giving a dark appearance.

LCDs replaced the LEDs in DIGITAL watches because they require less power. Power is only required to move molecules of liquid crystal rather than to energize a substance which emits light.

leased line

DEDICATED COMMUNICATIONS CHANNEL LEASED FROM A COMMON CARRIER; LEASED LINES usually can handle greater transmission speeds than the dial-up telephone SYSTEM. LEASED LINES from the telephone company can be CONDITIONED (ELECTRONICALLY fine tuned), which can reduce transmission error rate.

LED

LIGHT EMITTING DIODE; LEDs are a particular variety of SEMICONDUCTOR DIODES which emit light when charged with electricity. LEDs usually give off a red glow, although other colors can be generated as well. LEDs were the digit displays of the earlier DIGITAL watches. Their higher power requirement caused them to give way to the LCD display, which is always visible and does not require activation by the wearer. LEDs are used for the drive-in-use lights found on FLOPPY and HARD DISK DRIVES, as well as in display panels for countless ELECTRONIC products. LED is pronounced /L-E-D/. LEDs are also used to generate light signals for transmission in OPTICAL FIBERS.

letter quality

THE PRINT QUALITY OF AN ELECTRIC TYPEWRITER; LETTER QUALITY usually refers to WORD PROCESSING PRINTERS which print CHARACTERS similar to an electric typewriter. Other PRINTER TECHNOLOGIES can generate LETTER QUALITY printing, such as PAGE PRINTERS, PHOTOTYPESETTERS, HIGH-RESOLUTION GRAPHICS PRINTERS, etc.

LF key

See LINE FEED KEY.

librarian

PERSON WHO WORKS IN THE DATA LIBRARY; See DATA LIBRARY.

light emitting diode

See LED.

light guide

LIGHT CHANNEL; A LIGHT GUIDE is a CHANNEL designed for the transmission of light, such as a cable of OPTICAL FIBERS.

LIGHT PEN

light pen

VIDEO TERMINAL INPUT DEVICE; A LIGHT PEN is a light-sensitive STYLUS connected by a wire to the VIDEO TERMINAL. The USER brings the LIGHT PEN to the desired point on the SCREEN surface and presses a button causing the LIGHT PEN to identify the location of the light on the SCREEN. LIGHT PENS are used to select options from a MENU displayed on the SCREEN or to draw images by "dragging" the CURSOR around the SCREEN on a GRAPHICS TERMINAL.

The PIXELS on the TERMINAL SCREEN are constantly being illuminated in sequence over and over again. When the LIGHT PEN senses light, the TERMINAL knows which PIXEL is being illuminated at that moment, and that location identification is sent to the PROGRAM.

lightwave

LIGHT; LIGHTWAVES are light in the infrared, visible and ultraviolet ranges.

line dot matrix

LINE PRINTER WHICH USES THE DOT MATRIX PRINTING TECHNIQUE; See PRINTER TECHNOLOGIES.

line driver

COMMUNICATIONS TRANSMITTER/RECEIVER; LINE DRIVERS are used to extend the transmission distance between TERMINALS and COMPUTERS which are directly connected. They extend the usual limitation of approximately 50 feet to several miles. A LINE DRIVER is connected at both ends of a PRIVATE LINE, and transmission is maintained in DIGITAL form.

line feed key

TERMINAL CONTROL KEY; The LINE FEED KEY advances the CURSOR on the VIDEO SCREEN to the next line, or the paper in the PRINTER to the next line.

line of code

STATEMENT(S) IN A PROGRAMMING LANGUAGE; A LINE OF CODE in ASSEMBLY LANGUAGE is usually just one COMPUTER INSTRUCTION. A LINE OF CODE in a HIGH-LEVEL LANGUAGE may represent a simple or complex series of INSTRUCTIONS to the COMPUTER. LINES OF CODE are used to measure the complexity of a PROGRAM; however, PROGRAMS must be compared within the same category of language. For example: 8 LINES OF CODE in a REPORT WRITER may be equivalent to 100 or more LINES OF CODE in a COBOL PROGRAM.

line printer

HARD COPY PERIPHERAL DEVICE; See PRINTER.

linear programming

MATHEMATICAL PROGRAMMING; LINEAR PROGRAMMING is used to obtain an optimum solution in resource allocation problems, such as production planning.

link editor

UTILITY PROGRAM WHICH ADAPTS A PROGRAM TO A COMPUTER; The LINK EDITOR adapts an APPLICATION PROGRAM which has just been COMPILED to run under a particular OPERATING SYSTEM.

liquid crystal display

See LCD.

LISP

HIGH-LEVEL PROGRAMMING LANGUAGE; LISP is a PROGRAMMING LANGUAGE used extensively in NON-NUMERIC PROGRAMMING, wherein symbolic objects, rather than numbers, are manipulated. Developed in 1960 by John McCarthy, LISP is in a category all to itself; it is very different in syntax and structure from common languages like BASIC and COBOL. For example, in LISP there is no syntactic difference between DATA and INSTRUCTIONS as there is in most other languages.

LISP is used extensively in ARTIFICIAL INTELLIGENCE APPLICATIONS, as well in areas like COMPILER creation. LISP lets PROGRAMMERS concentrate on expressing the problem-solving ALGORITHM rather than the PROGRAMMING ALGORITHM. LISP is extensible; the language itself can be modified or expanded by the USER. Many versions and varieties of LISP have been developed, including versions which perform calculations efficiently. LISP stands for **LIS**t **P**rocessing and is available as both an INTERPRETER and COMPILER.

load

TO TRANSFER INTO A COMPUTER DEVICE; LOAD the PROGRAM means copy the PROGRAM into MEMORY. LOAD the DISK means WRITE DATA onto the DISK. LOAD also refers to the act of physically mounting a TAPE on the TAPE DRIVE or inserting a DISK into the DISK DRIVE.

local area network

COMMUNICATIONS NETWORK WITHIN AN ORGANIZATION; LOCAL AREA NETWORKS (LANs) connect various HARDWARE devices (COMPUTERS, TERMINALS, DISKS, PRINTERS, etc.) together within a building or plant. LOCAL AREA NETWORKS may provide GATEWAYS to external public or private COMMUNICATIONS NETWORKS.

The difference between a LOCAL AREA NETWORK and NETWORK ARCHITECTURES (which have traditionally interconnected TERMINALS) is not just the techniques, but the philosophy behind them. LOCAL AREA NETWORKS are perceived to be the "backbone" of OFFICE AUTOMATION— a central COMMUNICATIONS NETWORK between every person and every machine so that all forms of INFORMATION can be transmitted without limitations. An important consideration for LOCAL AREA NETWORKS is their flexibility for adding and deleting various types of HARDWARE devices on the NETWORK.

LOCAL AREA NETWORKS are a major planning consideration for the 1980s. Techniques such as BASEBAND and BROADBAND BUS-type NETWORKS, DIGITAL PABXs, and combinations of both methods make up some of the alternatives for LOCAL AREA NETWORKS.

local loop

COMMUNICATIONS LINE BETWEEN A TELEPHONE USER AND THE TELEPHONE CENTRAL EXCHANGE; The LOCAL LOOP has traditionally been an ANALOG COMMUNICATIONS line; however, some LOCAL LOOPS are being adapted to DIGITAL transmission. See DTS.

log

RECORD OF COMPUTER PROCESSING; A COMPUTER LOG is a FILE into which statistics about all machine operations taking place, are stored. LOGS are used for statistical purposes and BACKUP & RECOVERY.

log-on/log-off

CONNECT/DISCONNECT BETWEEN THE USER AND THE COMPUTER SYSTEM; The LOG-ON is the PROCEDURE for USERS to identify themselves to the COMPUTER SYSTEM for authorized ACCESS to their PROGRAMS and INFORMATION. The LOG-ON usually requires an ACCESS CODE made up of a USER identification number and a password. SERVICE BUREAUS may charge their TIME-SHARING customers from the time they LOG-ON to the time they LOG-OFF the COMPUTER SYSTEM.

logic

HARDWARE AND/OR SOFTWARE EXECUTION; LOGIC may refer to HARDWARE LOGIC which is made up of ELECTRONIC CIRCUITS in PROCESSORS or PERIPHERAL CONTROL UNITS. LOGIC may refer to SOFTWARE LOGIC or PROGRAM LOGIC, which is the sequence of INSTRUCTIONS in a PROGRAM. Note: LOGIC is *not* the same as LOGICAL (See LOGICAL vs PHYSICAL). See LOGIC CHIP and PROGRAM LOGIC.

logic array

CUSTOMIZED LOGIC CHIP; LOGIC ARRAYS contain dozens of LOGIC GATES which have not been tied together. A customized CHIP is obtained by designing the final stage of the CHIP fabrication, which connects the GATES together by adhering the top metal layer. The final masking step is less costly than designing the CHIP from scratch. Same as GATE ARRAY and ULA. See CHIP.

logic chip

CHIP THAT PERFORMS PROCESSING FUNCTIONS; LOGIC CHIPS are used in PROCESSORS and CONTROL UNITS. LOGIC CHIPS are made up of LOGIC CIRCUITS. See ELECTRONIC CIRCUIT and CHIP.

logic circuit

ELECTRONIC CIRCUIT THAT PERFORMS PROCESSING FUNCTIONS; LOGIC CIRCUITS make up PROCESSORS and CONTROL UNITS. LOGIC CIRCUITS are designed as combinations of LOGIC GATES, which are BOOLEAN LOGIC building blocks. See ELECTRONIC CIRCUIT and CHIP.

logic gate

COMPONENTS IN ELECTRONIC DIGITAL CIRCUITRY; LOGIC GATES are combinations of TRANSISTORS which detect the presence or absence of pulses. LOGIC GATES in ELECTRONIC CIRCUITS follow the rules of BOOLEAN LOGIC. LOGIC GATES make up LOGIC CIRCUITS.

logic-seeking printer

PRINTER WHICH ANALYZES CONTENT; A LOGIC-SEEKING PRINTER analyzes the content of each line to be printed so blank spaces can be skipped over.

logical vs physical

THE USER'S VIEW vs THE COMPUTER'S VIEW; USER'S view and relate to their DATA LOGICALLY by DATA ELEMENT name; however, the actual FIELDS of DATA are PHYSICALLY located on TRACKS and SECTORS on a DISK. For example, a USER might want to know which customers ordered how many of a particular product this week. The USER'S LOGICAL view of this DATA is customer name and quantity. The PHYSICAL organization of this DATA might have customer name in a customer RECORD and quantity in an order RECORD, cross referenced by customer number. The actual PHYSICAL sequence of the customer RECORDS could be INDEXED while the sequence of the order RECORDS could be SEQUENTIAL.

A MESSAGE transmitted from San Francisco and reaching Boston travels over a LOGICAL CIRCUIT. The PHYSICAL CIRCUIT was San Francisco to Chicago to New York to Boston.

When a USER COMMANDS the PROGRAM to change the OUTPUT from the TERMINAL SCREEN to the PRINTER, that's a LOGICAL COMMAND. The PROGRAM will perform the PHYSICAL change of ADDRESS from device number 02 to device number 04, for example.

When a DATA BASE MANAGEMENT SYSTEM is used, the APPLICATION PROGRAM has the LOGICAL view (USER'S view) of the DATA, while the DATA BASE MANAGEMENT SYSTEM has the PHYSICAL view.

LOGICAL always implies a higher level than the PHYSICAL.

Logo

HIGH-LEVEL PROGRAMMING LANGUAGE; LOGO is a PROGRAMMING
LANGUAGE designed for the first-time USER, noted for its ease of use and its
GRAPHICS capabilities. LOGO'S GRAPHICS language is called TURTLE GRAPHICS,
which allows complex GRAPHICS images to be created with a minimum of CODING.
The TURTLE is a triangular-shaped CURSOR, which is moved around on the SCREEN
by the USER INTERACTIVELY (with LOGO COMMANDS or with the use of the
CURSOR KEYS), or by writing the COMMANDS in a LOGO PROGRAM. Stemming
originally from a National Science Foundation research project, LOGO was further
developed at Massachusetts Institute of Technology (MIT). LOGO was originally
developed on large COMPUTERS, but has been adapted to smaller PERSONAL
COMPUTERS, like the APPLE II and TI 99/4.

longitudinal redundancy checking

See LRC.

looping

PROGRAMMING LOGIC TECHNIQUE; PROGRAM LOGIC is usually designed to
PROCESS one set of DATA at a time, or handle one condition at a time. In order to
repeat the PROCESS on the next set of DATA or condition, an INSTRUCTION branches
back (points) to the first INSTRUCTION of the series. This technique is called LOOPING
and is accomplished by a JUMP, BRANCH or GOTO statement in the PROGRAM.
LOOPING is also accomplished by DO LOOPS and FOR NEXT statements in HIGH-
LEVEL LANGUAGES. In ASSEMBLY LANGUAGE, LOOPING would be used in the
expression, "Count to 10 by 1," as follows:

LOOP	ADD	"1" TO COUNTER
	COMPARE	COUNTER TO "10"
	GOTO	LOOP IF UNEQUAL
	STOP	

loosely coupled

STAND-ALONE COMPUTERS WHICH ARE INTERCONNECTED; LOOSELY
COUPLED COMPUTERS can PROCESS on their own and are not dependent on other
COMPUTERS for their routine operation. They can exchange DATA on demand by
requesting a transfer from another machine in the NETWORK. Contrast with a TIGHTLY
COUPLED COMPUTER, like a DATA BASE MACHINE or a MULTIPROCESSING
SYSTEM. These machines are completely (tightly) controlled by the machine to which
they are attached.

lo-res

ABBREVIATION OF **LO**W-**RES**OLUTION.

low-level language

PROGRAMMING LANGUAGE THAT IS VERY CLOSE TO THE MACHINE; See ASSEMBLY LANGUAGE.

low-resolution

LOW-GRADE IMAGE QUALITY; LOW-RESOLUTION (LO-RES) refers to a small number of dots in a DOT MATRIX or PIXELS in a picture image.

LPM

LINES **P**ER **M**INUTE; LPM measures the print speed of a PRINTER.

LRC

ERROR CHECKING METHOD; The LRC method creates a series of PARITY BITS for a BLOCK of DATA. It is often used in conjunction with the VRC method (which creates a PARITY BIT for each CHARACTER) for enhanced error detection. Stands for **L**ongitudinal **R**edundancy **C**hecking.

LSI

LARGE **S**CALE INTEGRATION; LSI refers to the large numbers of ELECTRONIC components built on a CHIP. LSI ranges approximately from 3,000 to 100,000 TRANSISTORS on a CHIP.

machine cycle

INTERNAL TIME CYCLE IN A COMPUTER PROCESSOR; MACHINE CYCLES govern the timing of elementary operations within the COMPUTER. They control the sequential EXECUTION of INSTRUCTIONS which take one or more MACHINE CYCLES for completion. MACHINE CYCLES are made up of several smaller states based on the COMPUTER'S CLOCK cycles.

machine language

COMPUTER'S NATIVE LANGUAGE; A PROGRAM must be in the same MACHINE LANGUAGE as the COMPUTER that is EXECUTING it. The actual MACHINE LANGUAGE is generated by SOFTWARE, not the PROGRAMMER. The PROGRAMMER writes in a PROGRAMMING LANGUAGE which is translated into MACHINE LANGUAGE by ASSEMBLERS and COMPILERS.

If a PROGRAM was developed with the use of an INTERPRETER, the PROGRAM remains in its original form all the time. It is translated by the INTERPRETER into MACHINE LANGUAGE at the time it is EXECUTING. See PROGRAMMING LANGUAGE.

machine readable

IN A FORM THAT CAN BE READ BY THE COMPUTER; PROGRAMS and INFORMATION on TAPE or DISK, in BUBBLE MEMORY or FIRMWARE are MACHINE READABLE. A PUNCHED CARD is MACHINE READABLE and can also be printed for human readability.

macro

SUBROUTINE USED BY A PROGRAM; MACROS are CANNED SUBROUTINES which
are added to the PROGRAM. When a MACRO statement is written into the PROGRAM
by the PROGRAMMER, the named MACRO SUBROUTINE replaces the MACRO
statement, or the appropriate linkage is set up to BRANCH to the MACRO
SUBROUTINE at the time of EXECUTION.

mag disk/tape

See MAGNETIC DISK & TAPE.

magnetic card

PLASTIC CARD WITH MAGNETIC TAPE STRIP; MAGNETIC CARDS require
specialized READERS which are often incorporated into POINT OF SALE TERMINALS.
Because of wear, DIGITAL DATA originally recorded onto the TAPE strip, is in a low-
density FORMAT, (less BITS per inch than on a computer TAPE or DISK). See SMART
CARD.

magnetic disk & tape

STORAGE FOR PROGRAMS AND INFORMATION; DISKS/TAPES are reusable over
and over again. DISKS/TAPES can store from several thousands of BYTES to hundreds of
millions of BYTES of INSTRUCTIONS and INFORMATION. When both media are
available, the choice of DISK vs TAPE depends on the ACCESSING requirements. TAPE
is a SEQUENTIAL ACCESS medium; DISK is a DIRECT ACCESS medium. TAPE is a
long string which must be moved forward or backward across the READ/WRITE HEAD.
Locating a PROGRAM or INFORMATION on TAPE can take minutes. DISKS rotate like
a phonograph record, the READ/WRITE HEAD (attached to an ACCESS ARM) moving
from the outer to the inner surface of the DISK, like a tone arm on a phonograph
turntable. Any surface location can be DIRECTLY ACCESSED from as slow as 1 second
(FLOPPY DISK) to as fast as 1/100th of a second (HARD DISK).

Today, INFORMATION SYSTEMS are designed for REAL-TIME (immediate) ACCESS to
INFORMATION, so DISKS have become the primary storage medium. However, since a
reel of TAPE costs considerably less than a DISK PACK or DISK CARTRIDGE, TAPE is
often used for OFF-LINE storage. DATA BASES on DISK are routinely DUMPED
(copied) to TAPE for BACKUP or historical purposes.

MAGNETIC DISK

DISKS are made of metal (HARD DISK) or flexible plastic, like TAPE (FLOPPY DISK).
Both sides are coated with a magnetic recording material. INSTRUCTIONS and
INFORMATION are recorded on circular TRACKS (circles within circles). The BITS are
written serially (one after the other) on these TRACKS. Additional BITS may be
generated by the DRIVE for self-checking and identification purposes. The innermost

HARD
DISK

FLOPPY
DISK

LARGE CAPACITY
REMOVABLE HARD DISK

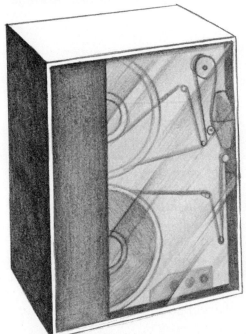

½"REEL-TO-REEL TAPE

TAPE CARTRIDGE

HARD DISK WITH
TAPE CARTRIDGE
BACKUP

DISK AND
TAPE DRIVES

TRACK is the most dense, containing the most BITS per inch on the DISK surface. TRACKS are divided into SECTORS, like pieces of a pie. SECTORS on the DISK are identified by the DISK DRIVE by either a fixed location on the DISK (HARD SECTORED) or by the recording of an identifying number on the TRACK itself (SOFT SECTORED).

Three major categories are:
1. HARD DISKS (Removable)
2. HARD DISKS (Fixed)
3. FLOPPY DISKS (Removable)

HARD DISKS provide from medium to large capacity storage with fast ACCESS to any location on the DISK. HARD DISKS come in 5 1/4", 8", or 14" diameters, as singles or as multiple platters of the same size DISK. REMOVABLE HARD DISKS are encased in MODULES called DISK PACKS and DISK CARTRIDGES. FIXED DISKS are permanently sealed and cannot be removed from the drive. FLOPPY DISKS are single flexible plastic DISKS which are encased in a stiff paper-like plastic envelope or rigid plastic shell. They contain less storage and are usually slower than their HARD DISK counterpart.

DISK storage capacities are measured in BYTES per DISK, BYTES per TRACK, and BYTES per SECTOR. DISK DRIVE speeds are rated by ACCESSES per second (average time to get to a random TRACK on the DISK).

MAGNETIC TAPE

TAPES are made of flexible plastic with only one side coated with a magnetic recording material. TAPES come in reels, CARTRIDGES or CASSETTES of all sizes, just like AUDIO TAPE. INFORMATION is usually recorded on TAPE in parallel TRACKS that run the entire length of the TAPE. 9-TRACK TAPE stores one BYTE across the width of the TAPE (8 TRACKS for the BYTE and a 9th TRACK for a PARITY BIT, which is automatically generated and used for self-checking purposes).

INSTRUCTIONS and INFORMATION are recorded as contiguous groups (BLOCKS) of BYTES separated by a space automatically generated by the TAPE DRIVE, called an INTERRECORD GAP. This allows the TAPE DRIVE to start and stop between BLOCKS of INFORMATION. TAPES are often used when large amounts of INFORMATION must be physically transported between COMPUTERS at different locations, since: (1) TAPE is less bulky to transport than HARD DISKS, and (2) there are far fewer recording standards used for TAPES than there are for DISKS (offering more compatiblity between different vendors' COMPUTERS).

TAPES are economical OFF-LINE storage; however, when they are used for archival storage they must be periodically recopied. If the TAPE is not used for several years, the magnetic BITS can contaminate each other since the TAPE surfaces are tightly coiled together. If that occurs, the INFORMATION will not be READABLE by the COMPUTER. TAPE storage capacity is measured in BPI (BITS per inch). However, because TAPE is formatted in parallel TRACKS, BPI is really equivalent to BYTES per inch. TAPE DRIVE speed is measured in inches per second (IPS).

INSTRUCTIONS and INFORMATION, converted to BINARY CODES in the COMPUTER, are WRITTEN (recorded) onto the magnetic recording surface of the DISK/TAPE as tiny magnetic spots. (A spot is a *1* BIT, a space is a *0* BIT.) WRITING is accomplished by moving the magnetic surface past an erase head and a READ/WRITE HEAD. The erase head demagnetizes the recording surface and the READ/WRITE HEAD creates a magnetic spot (BIT) by discharging an electric impulse onto the surface at the appropriate time. READING the DISK/TAPE is accomplished by passing the recorded surface over the READ/WRITE HEAD and sensing the presence or absence of the magnetized spot (BIT).

Note that BUBBLE MEMORY is also a form of magnetic recording. The BUBBLES are the BITS. However, BUBBLE MEMORY is not a moving surface medium. The BUBBLES (BITS) are moved electromagnetically inside the magnetic recording material.

magnetic drum

DIRECT ACCESS STORAGE DEVICE; A MAGNETIC DRUM is a cylinder that spins around a central hub, like a roll of paper towels. The external round cylinder is the magnetic recording surface. This recording surface is divided into TRACKS, which are circular storage channels (like rubber bands) around the DRUM. A separate READ/WRITE HEAD is fixed over each TRACK. DRUMS are used for high-speed DIRECT ACCESS storage.

main memory

THE COMPUTER'S PRIMARY WORKING STORAGE; Same as RAM. See MEMORY.

main storage

THE COMPUTER'S PRIMARY WORKING STORAGE; Same as RAM. See MEMORY.

mainframe

LARGE COMPUTER; In the beginning, all COMPUTERS were MAINFRAMES, since MAINFRAME was just another term for the cabinet that held the CPU. The term is still used to refer to the main housing that holds the CPU; however, for the most part, MAINFRAME means large COMPUTER. It also implies the required technical expertise necessary to run it.

There are small, medium and large-scale MAINFRAMES, handling as little as a hundred to several thousands of ON-LINE TERMINALS. MAINFRAMES have approximately 1 million to 64 million BYTES of MAIN MEMORY, and have the potential for ON-LINE DISK storage of up into the hundreds of billions of BYTES (GIGABYTES). Medium to large-scale MAINFRAMES use smaller COMPUTERS as FRONT END PROCESSORS to connect to their COMMUNICATIONS NETWORKS.

Small-scale MAINFRAMES and SUPERMINIS overlap in capabilities. The term used to describe the model depends on the vendor.

The original MAINFRAME vendors were Burroughs, Control Data, GE, Honeywell, IBM, NCR, RCA and Univac. All the MAINFRAME vendors (except for GE and RCA, who left the COMPUTER business) have developed at least one or more series of MINICOMPUTERS and/or MICROCOMPUTERS.

By the 21st Century, the MAINFRAME of the 1980s will be a desktop model.

maintenance

ROUTINE CHANGES TO FILES, DATA BASES AND PROGRAMS; Name and address changes, credit limit revisions, reorder point adjustments, etc., are FILE or DATA BASE MAINTENANCE. SOFTWARE MAINTENANCE is generally any change to a PROGRAM that does not entail wholesale rewriting of the entire INFORMATION SYSTEM. See PROGRAM MAINTENANCE.

management information system

See MIS.

management science

THE STUDY OF ANALYTICAL MANAGEMENT METHODS; The MANAGEMENT SCIENCES employ various statistical methods like LINEAR PROGRAMMING and SIMULATION to analyze and solve organizational problems. Synonymous with OPERATIONS RESEARCH.

management support system

See DECISION SUPPORT SYSTEM.

management system

STRUCTURE AND FUNCTION OF THE LEADERSHIP AND CONTROL OF AN ORGANIZATION; The MANAGEMENT SYSTEM is people interacting with people and machines. Together, they set the goals and objectives for the organization, outline the strategy and tactics, and develop the plans, schedules and necessary controls to run the organization.

mapping

TRANSFER OF PROGRAMS OR DATA INTO A PHYSICAL SPACE; MAPPING refers to laying out PROGRAMS or DATA onto a DISK or into MEMORY in some prescribed sequence. For example: A series of PROGRAM MODULES might be MAPPED from the DISK into MEMORY. A GRAPHICS image stored in the COMPUTER'S MEMORY (BIT MAP) is MAPPED onto the VIDEO SCREEN, whereby each PIXEL in the BIT MAP is transformed into a corresponding intensity of light on the SCREEN PIXEL. MAPPING implies that some form of transformation is taking place.

MARK IV

APPLICATION GENERATOR WHICH RUNS ON IBM COMPUTERS; MARK IV was one of the first PROGRAM GENERATORS which used fill-in-the-blank forms for descriptions of the DATA and the PROCESSING (similar to RPG). MARK IV and MARK V (ON-LINE version) are compatible products of Informatics General Corporation.

mark sense

DATA ENTRY MEDIUM; The MARK SENSE method converts pencil strokes into DIGITAL CODE for the COMPUTER. The form must be laid out with boundaries for each pencil stroke which represents a yes/no, digit or letter answer. A MARK SENSE READER detects the presence or absence of the marks and converts them into the appropriate CODE.

mask

PATTERN OF BITS USED AS A FILTER; A MASK is a STRING of BITS or CHARACTERS used to control the retention or elimination of BITS or CHARACTERS in another STRING. See MASKING.

masking

THE USE OF A MASK FOR CONTROL OR RECOGNITION; MASKING uses a MASK of BITS or CHARACTERS to filter out selected BITS or CHARACTERS from a STRING of DATA for control or recognition purposes. For example: An EDIT MASK is a STRING of CHARACTERS which is used to control the placement of special CHARACTERS, like dollar signs, decimal points, and commas in a DATA FIELD. Each CHARACTER in the DATA FIELD is filtered through the EDIT MASK by EXECUTING a special EDIT INSTRUCTION available in the COMPUTER.

MASKS are frequently used to recognize various BIT patterns that may be present in DATA. A MASK of *0s* and *1s* is used to filter out the corresponding presence or absence of BITS in the DATA in question. Special BOOLEAN LOGIC INSTRUCTIONS EXECUTE the MASK as a filter.

Various internal control functions in the COMPUTER (such as INTERRUPTS) are
selected by a BIT position in some internal HARDWARE REGISTER acting as an on/off
switch. A MASKING operation would set the switches to their appropriate positions.

See PHOTOMASKING for image transfer operations, such as those used in the
fabrication of the CHIP.

mass storage

VERY LARGE CAPACITY ON-LINE PERIPHERAL STORAGE; MASS STORAGE
devices are very large capacity MAGNETIC DISK or TAPE storage units. However, the
term is often used to refer to any type of external DISK or TAPE storage unit, in contrast
with the COMPUTER'S internal MEMORY.

master control program

See OPERATING SYSTEM.

master file

A FILE CONTAINING DESCRIPTIVE DATA AND SUMMARY/STATUS INFORMATION;
A customer FILE, employee FILE, vendor FILE and inventory FILE are examples of
MASTER FILES. Contrast with TRANSACTION FILE. When a DATA BASE
MANAGEMENT SYSTEM is used, the DATA contained in the MASTER FILE is stored in
the DATA BASE.

matrix

AN ARRAY OF ROWS AND COLUMNS; See X-Y MATRIX.

matrix printer

See DOT MATRIX and PRINTER.

medium scale integration

See MSI.

meg

ABREVIATION FOR MEGABYTE OR MEGABIT.

megabyte

ONE MILLION BYTES; One Million CHARACTERS. See SPACE/TIME.

membrane keyboard

FLAT KEYBOARD; A MEMBRANE KEYBOARD is constructed of two thin plastic sheets (called membranes), which are coated with a CIRCUIT made of electrically conductive ink. On top of the membranes is a flat printed KEYBOARD panel, and sandwiched between the two membranes is a thin sheet (called the spacer) with holes corresponding to each key on the printed panel. When a USER presses a key location on the flat panel, the top membrane is pushed through the hole in the spacer, making contact with the bottom membrane. MEMBRANE KEYBOARDS are a way of producing an economical, flat, sealed KEYBOARD.

memory

THE COMPUTER'S WORKING STORAGE; MEMORY (which is constructed of CHIPS) is the primary work space in a COMPUTER. All PROCESSING takes place in MEMORY. INSTRUCTIONS are copied into MEMORY from a PERIPHERAL device and the COMPUTER extracts them one at a time for EXECUTION. By following the directions of the INSTRUCTIONS in MEMORY, the COMPUTER is directed to INPUT DATA into the MEMORY from selected PERIPHERAL devices (DISKS, TERMINALS, etc.).

Once the DATA has been laid out in MEMORY, it can be PROCESSED (**calculated**, **compared** and **copied**). See COMPUTER (The 3 C's).

MEMORY can be viewed as an ELECTRONIC checkerboard. Each square of the checkerboard holds one CHARACTER (BYTE) of INFORMATION or INSTRUCTION and has its own ADDRESS, like a post office box. Each square (BYTE) can be ADDRESSED separately from the rest of the squares. Because of this ADDRESSING capability, the COMPUTER can break apart PROGRAMS into INSTRUCTIONS and RECORDS into FIELDS, all of which are stored as contiguous STRINGS on DISK.

MEMORY is the most important resource of the COMPUTER. It determines the complexity of as well as the number of different PROGRAMS that can be EXECUTED concurrently. The MAIN MEMORY of the COMPUTER (RAM) can accept new INSTRUCTIONS or INFORMATION from a PERIPHERAL device. Other MEMORIES, such as ROMs or PROMs, store INSTRUCTIONS and INFORMATION permanently. Other terms synonymous with the COMPUTER'S working MEMORY (RAM) are:

> CORE
> CORE STORAGE
> MAIN MEMORY
> MAIN STORAGE
> PRIMARY STORAGE
> READ/WRITE MEMORY

Note: DISKS are often referred to as DISK MEMORY. DISKS are **not** MEMORY and do not function like MEMORY.

memory bank

A PHYSICAL SECTION OF COMPUTER MEMORY; COMPUTERS with multiple MEMORY BANKS may be designed to enable INFORMATION transfers to take place simultaneously.

memory chip

CHIP THAT STORES INFORMATION AND INSTRUCTIONS; MEMORY CHIPS are made up of thousands of storage cells. The major categories of MEMORY CHIPS are RAMs and ROMs. See CHIP.

memory dump

A DISPLAY OR PRINTOUT OF THE CONTENTS OF MEMORY; When a PROGRAM ends abnormally (ABENDS), a MEMORY DUMP is usually taken to examine the status of the PROGRAM. The portion of the MEMORY that the PROGRAM occupied is displayed on the SCREEN or printed. The PROGRAMMER looks into the PROGRAM BUFFERS to figure out what DATA was being worked on when it failed. Other COUNTERS, SWITCHES and FLAGS in the PROGRAM can be inspected as well. See CHECKPOINT/RESTART.

memory protection

THE DIVISION OF MEMORY INTO PRIVATE SEGMENTS; MEMORY PROTECTION prevents one PROGRAM from accidentally destroying another PROGRAM which is running in the same MEMORY. MEMORY PROTECTION allows PROGRAMS to create a protective boundary around them while they are running. The MEMORY a PROGRAM occupies is assigned to that PROGRAM. If a PROGRAM attempts to manipulate DATA outside of its boundary, an illegal operation is detected by the HARDWARE.

MEMORY PROTECTION is implemented in HARDWARE by assigning a number (MEMORY KEY) to each physical BLOCK of MEMORY (perhaps each 2,048 BYTE segment). Each PROGRAM brought into MEMORY is assigned a number and each physical BLOCK it occupies is marked with that number. Before the COMPUTER EXECUTES each INSTRUCTION, it matches the MEMORY KEY in the PROGRAM with the MEMORY BLOCK being referenced. If it doesn't match, it causes an INTERRUPT to occur.

memory sniffing

REAL-TIME MEMORY DIAGNOSIS; MEMORY SNIFFING refers to the continuous testing of MEMORY during PROCESSING. The PROCESSOR uses CYCLE STEALING techniques to test each BYTE of MEMORY for failure. An entire MEMORY BANK can be "sniffed" (tested) every few minutes.

memory typewriter

WORD PROCESSING TYPEWRITER; A MEMORY TYPEWRITER contains a COMPUTER which allows for EDITING of a TEXT DOCUMENT in its MEMORY. In addition, a limited number of pages of TEXT can be stored in its MEMORY for recall at a later time. MEMORY TYPEWRITERS with DISK or other external storage perform as full-function WORD PROCESSORS without a VIDEO display. They usually have a one or two line LCD or LED display and provide a partial view of the DOCUMENT. MEMORY TYPEWRITERS are often used to enhance the productivity of straight typing or typing from dictation. See WORD PROCESSING.

menu

A LIST OF AVAILABLE OPTIONS IN AN INTERACTIVE PROGRAM; MENUS display all options available to the USER at the TERMINAL. Usually one key depression will select the appropriate alternative from the MENU. MENU DRIVEN SYSTEMS are easy to use for the first-time USER. Contrast with COMMAND DRIVEN SYSTEMS, which require that the USER know a language or a series of special CODES. Sometimes, a MENU will display the COMMANDS that should be entered.

menu driven

USING MENUS AS THE PRIMARY INTERACTIVE METHOD.

mesh

NETWORK STRUCTURE: A MESH structure is a net-like COMMUNICATIONS NETWORK. The term NETWORK is used for any COMMUNICATIONS NETWORK, regardless of its structure. When its stucture is truly net-like, MESH is used to avoid having to reference a NETWORK COMMUNICATIONS NETWORK.

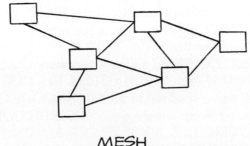

MESH

message

A COMMUNICATIONS TRANSMISSION; A MESSAGE is COMMUNICATIONS terminology for DATA being transmitted over a NETWORK. It is analogous to a JOB in a COMPUTER. The PROGRAM becomes a JOB when it is running in the machine. DATA/INFORMATION become MESSAGES when they are transmitting in a COMMUNICATIONS NETWORK.

message switch

A COMPUTER USED TO SWITCH INFORMATION FROM ONE POINT TO ANOTHER; COMPUTERS have always been ideal MESSAGE SWITCHES because of their INPUT/OUTPUT and compare capabilities. A MESSAGE is sent to the COMPUTER which determines its destination and then routes the MESSAGE to the appropriate CHANNEL. The COMPUTER can also perform the functions of a central answering machine using DIGITAL voice storage.

metal oxide semiconductor

See MOS.

MICR

MAGNETIC INK CHARACTER RECOGNITION; MICR is the special encoded CHARACTERS on bank checks and deposit slips. MICR devices READ this encoding and convert it into DIGITAL DATA for the COMPUTER.

micro

Same as MICROCOMPUTER.

microchip

MINIATURIZED ELECTRONIC CIRCUITS; See CHIP.

microcode

MACHINE INSTRUCTION TRANSLATION; MICROCODE is an architectural design feature in COMPUTERS which enables additional INSTRUCTIONS to be developed and added more easily. The MICROCODE is a translation layer between the machine INSTRUCTIONS and the machine itself. The MICROCODE (stored in a FIRMWARE CHIP) contains the INSTRUCTIONS and all the elementary CIRCUIT operations that must be performed to EXECUTE each INSTRUCTION. New INSTRUCTIONS are designed in MICROCODE and are added to the MICROCODE CHIP. Thus, only a CHIP replacement is required to implement a new INSTRUCTION, rather than a redesign of ELECTRONIC CIRCUITS. MICROPROGRAMMING is the process of developing the MICROCODE INSTRUCTIONS.

microcomputer

SMALL SCALE COMPUTER; MICROCOMPUTERS were the first COMPUTERS to use a single MICROPROCESSOR CHIP as the PROCESSOR. PERSONAL COMPUTERS and small business COMPUTERS are MICROCOMPUTERS. 8-BIT MICROCOMPUTERS usually support only one USER TERMINAL and have a maximum of 64K of MEMORY. 16-BIT MICROCOMPUTERS may support several USER TERMINALS and usually have a maximum of 1 million BYTES of MEMORY.

As the POWER of MICROCOMPUTERS increases, they can be used in two ways. They can be used either as a central COMPUTER (providing PROCESSING for several USER TERMINALS), or as a more powerful single COMPUTER for an individual USER.

microelectronics

MINIATURIZATION OF ELECTRONIC CIRCUITS; See CHIP.

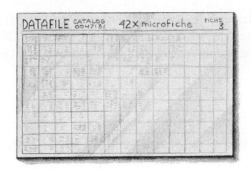

FICHE

ROLL FILM

microfiche - microfilm

MINIATURIZED DOCUMENTS ON FILM; A MICROFICHE, pronounced /my-cro-feesh/, is a 4 x 6″ sheet of film which holds several hundred DOCUMENT pages in microminiaturized form. MICROFILM is a continuous film strip, which can hold several thousand DOCUMENT pages.

MICROFICHE and MICROFILM are generated by SOURCE DOCUMENT MICROFILM units which take pictures of paper DOCUMENTS, or by COM (COMPUTER OUTPUT MICROFILM) units, which take OUTPUT directly from the COMPUTER. MICROFICHE and MICROFILM are magnified for human visibility by specialized READERS, some of which can automatically locate a particular page using various INDEXING techniques.

microfloppy disk

VARIETY OF SMALL FLOPPY DISKS; See FLOPPY DISK.

microform

MEDIUM WHICH CONTAINS MINIATURIZED IMAGES; MICROFICHE and MICROFILM are typical examples of MICROFORMS.

micromainframe

MAINFRAME PROCESSOR MICROMINIATURIZED ONTO ONE OR MORE MICROCHIPS.

micromini

MINICOMPUTER PROCESSOR MICROMINIATURIZED ONTO ONE OR MORE MICROCHIPS.

micron

UNIT OF MEASUREMENT; A MICRON is the same as 1 millionth of a meter, which is approximately 1/25,000 of an inch. The tiny components of a TRANSISTOR on a CHIP are measured in MICRONS. During the 1980s, we should reach the sub-MICRON level, whereby elements are measured in ANGSTROMS.

microprocessor

TINY PROCESSOR ON A SINGLE CHIP; A MICROPROCESSOR is the PROCESSOR used in MICROCOMPUTERS. The MICROPROCESSOR requires a power supply and MEMORY to be a complete COMPUTER. MICROPROCESSORS are also used in MINICOMPUTERS, MAINFRAMES and PERIPHERAL devices, as well as in virtually all industrial and consumer products which use a COMPUTER.

The first MICROPROCESSOR, the 4004, was developed by Ted Hoff, Jr., of Intel Corporation in 1971. (Abbreviated μp.)

microprogramming

THE PROGRAMMING OF MICROCODE; See MICROCODE.

microsecond

ONE-MILLIONTH OF A SECOND; See SPACE/TIME.

microwave

SUPER HIGH FREQUENCY RADIO WAVE; MICROWAVE COMMUNICATIONS refers to a wide variety of COMMUNICATIONS uses in the super high FREQUENCY ranges. They include line-of-sight transmission, whereby transmitters and receivers beam a straight line at each other, as well as transmissions between earth and COMMUNICATIONS SATELLITES.

millisecond

ONE-THOUSANDTH OF A SECOND; See SPACE/TIME.

minicomputer

SMALL- TO MEDIUM-SCALE COMPUTER; MINICOMPUTERS are the midrange between MICROCOMPUTERS and MAINFRAMES offering a wide variety of capabilities. Larger MINICOMPUTERS are often called SUPERMINIS, which overlap in capabilities with small-scale MAINFRAMES. MINICOMPUTER SYSTEMS can support from a handful of USER TERMINALS up to several hundred simultaneously.

minifloppy

FLOPPY DISK; A MINIFLOPPY is a 5 1/4" FLOPPY DISK used extensively in COMPUTER SYSTEMS. See FLOPPY DISK and MAGNETIC DISK & TAPE.

MIPS

INSTRUCTION EXECUTION RATE OF A CPU; Stands for **M**illion **I**nstructions **P**er **S**econd.

MIS

MANAGEMENT **I**NFORMATION **S**YSTEM; An MIS is an INFORMATION SYSTEM which has integrated all the DATA for the departments it serves. An MIS implies an INFORMATION SYSTEM that provides operations and management with all levels of DATA required. See DECISION SUPPORT SYSTEM.

MIS is also the formal name used for the INFORMATION PROCESSING department in an organization. MIS may also stand for **M**anagement **I**nformation **S**ervices.

mnemonic

A SYMBOLIC NAME ASSIGNED TO PROGRAMS AND DATA; A MNEMONIC is an alphanumeric name, usually beginning with a letter rather than a number, which is used to reference FIELDS, FILES, and SUBROUTINES in a PROGRAM. For example: *prupdpgm* could refer to the payroll UPDATE PROGRAM; *cstmstfile* might mean customer MASTER FILE; *custno* could refer to the customer number FIELD in the RECORD; *ytdgrspay* for the year-to-date gross pay FIELD.

PROGRAMMING LANGUAGES are collections of MNEMONIC COMMANDS and DATA references: *mult hrsworkd,payrte* for multiply hours worked by pay rate.

QUERY LANGUAGES and REPORT WRITERS allow USERS to reference their DATA by MNEMONICS: *Disp name addr if baldue gt 3000*, means display name and address for every item with a balance due greater than 3000.

model

MATHEMATICAL REPRESENTATION OF A DEVICE OR PROCESS; MODELS, which can be manipulated by COMPUTERS, are sets of equations which represent some condition or set of operations in the real world. A MODEL differs from an ordinary list of descriptions, in that it also describes the interrelationships of all the components. MODELS are used for analysis and planning purposes. For example: DATA MODELS, which indicate how DATA is perceived by different departments, can be used to forecast likely bottlenecks if USERS request certain kinds of INFORMATION.

Business MODELS, which represent operations such as in marketing, distribution, and manufacturing, are a series of equations into which variables can be plugged, in order to test the outcome of different decisions before they are made. See FINANCIAL PLANNING SYSTEM.

Scientific MODELS employ intricate mathematics for the replication of real-world objects. Whereas business MODELS are easily expressed in equation form (gross revenues – expenses = net income), scientific MODELS require elaborate formulas to represent objects such as airplanes, rivers and planets.

modeling

SIMULATING A CONDITION WITH THE USE OF A MODEL; MODELING simulates a condition or activity by performing a set of equations on a set of DATA. See MODEL, SCIENTIFIC APPLICATIONS, FINANCIAL PLANNING SYSTEM and ELECTRONIC SPREADSHEET.

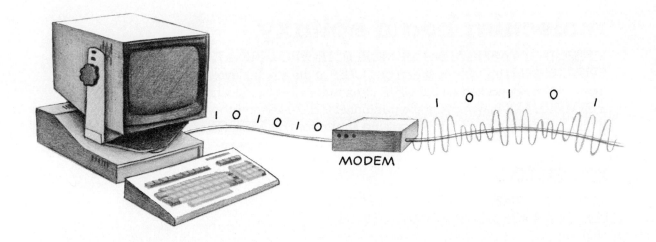

modem

A DEVICE WHICH ADAPTS A TERMINAL OR COMPUTER TO A VOICE (OR ANALOG) COMMUNICATIONS NETWORK; The MODEM converts the DIGITAL pulses from a TERMINAL or COMPUTER to AUDIO tones which can be transmitted by the telephone SYSTEM. It also converts AUDIO tones back into DIGITAL pulses at the other end. A MODEM is a DIGITAL TO ANALOG, ANALOG TO DIGITAL CONVERTER. Stands for **mo**dulator-**dem**odulator. MODEMS are available in several different transmission speeds measured in BITS per second (BPS) or BAUD RATE. MODEMS are also required to adapt TERMINALS and COMPUTERS to BROADBAND LOCAL AREA NETWORKS. A MODEM is called a DATASET by Bell Telephone.

modular programming

THE DEVELOPMENT OF PROGRAMS IN MODULES; MODULAR PROGRAMMING imposes considerable structure in the PROGRAM design which enables changes to be implemented much faster. It also allows different PROGRAMMERS to develop individual MODULES and test them separately. The MODULES are then merged together and tested as a single unit. See STRUCTURED PROGRAMMING.

modulation

THE MIXING OF A SIGNAL ONTO A CARRIER; MODULATION is the process of intermixing a voice or DATA signal onto a CARRIER for transmission in a NETWORK. See CARRIER, MODEM and FDM.

module

HARDWARE OR SOFTWARE COMPONENT; SOFTWARE MODULES are self-contained segments of a PROGRAM. HARDWARE MODULES are self-contained SYSTEMS that are part of a larger SYSTEM. See MODULAR PROGRAMMING.

molecular beam epitaxy

METHOD OF FABRICATING MICROELECTRONIC CIRCUITS; MOLECULAR BEAM EPITAXY builds up the tiny layers of a CHIP at the atomic level. Layers as thin as two atoms can be deposited on the CHIP in extremely precise locations. MOLECULAR BEAM EPITAXY may replace the traditional CHIP-making process, which creates layers by implanting materials into an existing substrate. See CHIP (The Making of a Chip).

monitor

(1) VIDEO SCREEN, (2) CONTROL PROGRAM, (3) HARDWARE/SOFTWARE PERFORMANCE MEASUREMENT DEVICE;

(1) A MONITOR is an OUTPUT device only and does not have a KEYBOARD. The MONITOR also does not contain a television tuner and will not accept a VIDEO signal created for a television CHANNEL. If there is a choice, a MONITOR usually provides a far better picture than on a television set. MONITORS are available in MONOCHROME or color, and generally connect to the COMPUTER via a single cable with a phono plug. MONITORS commonly used to connect to PERSONAL COMPUTERS require a COMPOSITE VIDEO signal; however, for enhanced color images, an RGB MONITOR is also made which requires a special RGB VIDEO OUTPUT (separate red, green and blue color signals) from the COMPUTER. RGB VIDEO can be adapted to a variety of PERSONAL COMPUTERS.

(2) A MONITOR is a control PROGRAM which is usually resident in FIRMWARE in a MICROCOMPUTER. The MONITOR is often available as soon as the COMPUTER is turned on, and provides the USER with a series of functions for operations and PROGRAMMING, such as MEMORY DUMPS, DIAGNOSTICS, and BAUD RATE settings. The MONITOR also contains a BOOTSTRAP PROGRAM to copy in the OPERATING SYSTEM.

(3) A MONITOR also may refer to a SYSTEM of performance measurement which can be implemented in HARDWARE or SOFTWARE.

monochrome

SINGLE COLOR; MONOCHROME VIDEO SCREENS are a single color display, primarily using either white, green or amber (on a dark background).

Monte Carlo method

TRIAL AND ERROR METHOD TO SOLVE A PROBLEM; Using random numbers, the MONTE CARLO METHOD repeatedly calculates the equations to obtain an optimum solution.

MOS

CATEGORY OF MICROELECTRONIC CIRCUIT DESIGN; MOS is one of two major categories of designing and fabricating LOGIC and MEMORY CHIPS (the other is BIPOLAR). MOS stands for **M**ETAL **O**XIDE **S**EMICONDUCTOR and is pronounced /moss/. MOS technology derives its name from its use of metal, oxide and SEMICONDUCTOR layers. There are several varieties of MOS technologies including PMOS, NMOS and CMOS. See CHIP.

MOSFET

TRANSISTOR USED IN MOS INTEGRATED CIRCUITS; Stands for **M**ETAL **O**XIDE **S**EMICONDUCTOR **F**IELD **E**FFECT **T**RANSISTOR. See MOS.

motherboard

COMMON CONNECTION CHANNEL BETWEEN HARDWARE DEVICES IN A MICROCOMPUTER; The MOTHERBOARD is the BUS between the PROCESSOR, the MEMORY and each of the PERIPHERAL CONTROL UNITS. PRINTED CIRCUIT BOARDS are inserted into the connectors of the MOTHERBOARD.

MOUSE

mouse

TERMINAL INPUT DEVICE; A MOUSE is a palm-sized object that is rolled across a USER'S desktop in order to move the CURSOR on the VIDEO SCREEN. The MOUSE contains a ball-bearing on its bottom and is connected to the TERMINAL by a wire. As it is moved across a surface, directional signals from the MOUSE are sent to the TERMINAL which moves the SCREEN CURSOR in the corresponding direction. The MOUSE has one or more buttons on it which perform as FUNCTION KEYS.

MPE

OPERATING SYSTEM WHICH RUNS ON THE HEWLETT-PACKARD HP-3000 SERIES OF MINICOMPUTERS; Stands for **M**ulti**P**rogramming **E**xecutive.

MPU

MICRO**P**ROCESSOR **U**NIT; Same as MICROPROCESSOR.

MS

MILLI**S**ECOND; A MILLISECOND is a thousandth of a second. See SPACE/TIME.

MSI

MEDIUM **S**CALE **I**NTEGRATION; MSI refers to the relatively small number of ELECTRONIC components (TRANSISTORS, etc.) that are built onto a single CHIP. MSI ranges approximately from 100 to 3,000 TRANSISTORS on a CHIP.

MTBF

MEAN **T**IME **B**ETWEEN **F**AILURE; MTBF is the average time a component works without failure.

multiplexing

THE TRANSMISSION OF MULTIPLE SIGNALS OVER A SINGLE CHANNEL; See FDM (FREQUENCY DIVISION MULTIPLEXING) and TDM (TIME DIVISION MULTIPLEXING).

multiplexor

COMMUNICATIONS HARDWARE DEVICE; MULTIPLEXORS bring together several low-speed COMMUNICATIONS CHANNELS and transform them into one high-speed CHANNEL; they perform the reverse operation at the other end. MULTIPLEXING in DIGITAL NETWORKS is performed by a technique called TDM (TIME DIVISION MULTIPLEXING). FDM (FREQUENCY DIVISION MULTIPLEXING) is used for transmission in ANALOG NETWORKS.

multiplexor channel

COMPUTER CHANNEL FOR MULTIPLE LOW-SPEED DEVICES; A MULTIPLEXOR CHANNEL interchanges signals between the CPU and several low-speed PERIPHERAL devices, such as PRINTERS and TERMINALS.

multiprocessing

TWO OR MORE COMPUTERS PROCESSING TOGETHER; MULTIPROCESSING COMPUTERS are tied together with a high-speed CHANNEL and share the general workload between them. In the event one fails, the other takes over. MULTIPROCESSING may also be implemented by building two or more CPUs within the same COMPUTER. In the future, more COMPUTERS will be built with MULTIPROCESSING capability, both for FAIL SAFE operation and increased PROCESSING capabilities.

multiprogramming

TWO OR MORE PROGRAMS RUNNING IN ONE COMPUTER AT THE SAME TIME; MULTIPROGRAMMING is controlled through the OPERATING SYSTEM which LOADS (copies into MEMORY) the PROGRAMS and keeps track of them until finished. The number of PROGRAMS that can be MULTIPROGRAMMED effectively depends on a combination of the amount of MEMORY available, the speed of the CPU, the quantity and speeds of the PERIPHERAL resources attached to it, as well as the efficiency of the OPERATING SYSTEM.

multitasking

TWO OR MORE SEGMENTS WITHIN A PROGRAM RUNNING IN ONE COMPUTER AT THE SAME TIME; Technically, MULTITASKING is MULTIPROGRAMMING within a single PROGRAM, whereby different sections of the PROGRAM are constructed as independent TASKS. However, MULTITASKING is often used synonymously with MULTIPROGRAMMING.

multithreading

OVERLAPPED PROCESSING; MULTITHREADING refers to the PROCESSING of TRANSACTIONS concurrently with other TRANSACTIONS. It implies that TRANSACTIONS can be worked on in parallel, and that one TRANSACTION (or COMMUNICATIONS MESSAGE) does not have to be completely PROCESSED before another is started. REENTRANT CODE is used in MULTITHREADING PROGRAMS.

multiuser

MULTIPLE TERMINALS; A MULTIUSER COMPUTER SYSTEM contains two or more USER TERMINALS which can be used concurrently.

MVS

OPERATING SYSTEM USED ON LARGE IBM MAINFRAMES; Stands for **M**ultiple **V**irtual **S**torage.

NAK

COMMUNICATIONS CODE; The NAK is a **n**egative **ack**nowledgement CODE which is used to indicate that a MESSAGE was not received, or that a TERMINAL does not wish to transmit.

nanosecond

ONE-BILLIONTH OF A SECOND. See SPACE/TIME.

native language

COMPUTER'S MACHINE LANGUAGE.

native mode

RUNNING A PROGRAM WRITTEN FOR THE COMPUTER IT IS RUNNING ON; When a COMPUTER EXECUTES a PROGRAM that was originally written for that same COMPUTER model, it is running in NATIVE MODE. Contrast with EMULATORS and SIMULATORS, which allow COMPUTERS to EXECUTE PROGRAMS originally written to be EXECUTED in a different COMPUTER.

natural language

A PERSON'S NATIVE LANGUAGE; Any COMPUTER language that lets the USER express the request or problem in everyday human language is called a NATURAL LANGUAGE. A NATURAL LANGUAGE QUERY LANGUAGE allows the USER to request DATA in any manner. For example: "show me," "get me," "locate," "display," "look for," etc.

NC

See **N**UMERICAL **C**ONTROL.

NET 1000

See AIS/NET 1000.

network

COMMUNICATIONS PATHWAYS BETWEEN TERMINALS AND COMPUTERS OR BETWEEN COMPUTERS; The NETWORK can be a mixture of different forms of COMMUNICATIONS CHANNELS.

network architecture

DESIGN OF A COMMUNICATIONS SYSTEM; The NETWORK ARCHITECTURE includes the choice of HARDWARE, SOFTWARE, and PROTOCOLS chosen in a COMMUNICATIONS NETWORK. The NETWORK ARCHITECTURE defines the method for NETWORK control; for example, whether or not COMPUTERS can act independently, or whether they are controlled by other COMPUTERS which are constantly monitoring the NETWORK. NETWORK ARCHITECTURES should incorporate built-in flexibility for future changes. IBM's SNA, Digital Equipment Corporation's DNA, and Univac's DCA are examples of NETWORK ARCHITECTURES.

network data base

DATA BASE ORGANIZATION METHOD; NETWORK DATA BASES allow for DATA relationships to be expressed in a net-like form. A single DATA ELEMENT can point to multiple DATA ELEMENTS, and can itself be pointed to by other DATA ELEMENTS. Both NETWORK DATA BASES and HIERARCHICAL DATA BASES imply a fixed pathway for "navigating" through the DATA BASE (to speed up PROCESSING).

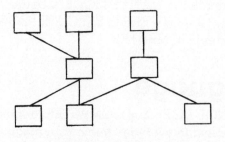

NETWORK

nibble

HALF A BYTE; A NIBBLE is 4 BITS. See BYTE.

N-key rollover

KEYBOARD DESIGN FOR FAST TYPING; N-KEY ROLLOVER allows a typist to press a series of keys in fast sequence. Each subsequent key can be pressed without having to raise the finger off the last key.

NMOS

TYPE OF MICROELECTRONIC CIRCUIT DESIGN; NMOS INTEGRATED CIRCUITS are widely used for PROCESSORS (LOGIC CHIPS) and MEMORIES. NMOS TRANSISTORS are faster than PMOS and more TRANSISTORS can be built onto a single CHIP. NMOS TRANSISTORS are also used in the CMOS technology. Stands for **N**-Channel **MOS** and is pronounced /en-moss/.

node

COMPUTER SYSTEM USED AS A JUNCTION OR CONNECTION POINT; A NODE would INTERFACE USER TERMINALS and COMPUTERS into a COMMUNICATIONS NETWORK. A NODE could be a switching point between several COMMUNICATION CHANNELS.

noise

EXTRANEOUS SIGNAL; NOISE is any extraneous signal that invades the transmission of electrical pulses or vibrations (FREQUENCIES). NOISE can come from strong electrical or magnetic signals in nearby lines, from poorly fitting electrical contacts, and from power line spikes.

NOMAD

DATA MANAGEMENT SYSTEM WHICH RUNS ON IBM COMPUTERS; NOMAD was one of the first RELATIONAL DATA BASE SYSTEMS which incorporated a NON-PROCEDURAL language for DATA manipulation. NOMAD is a product of National CSS and is available on their TIME-SHARING service.

non-impact printer

PRINTER THAT DOES NOT USE A CONVENTIONAL RIBBON AND CHARACTER HAMMER FOR PRINTING; See PRINTER TECHNOLOGIES.

non-numeric programming

PROGRAMMING THAT DEALS WITH SYMBOLIC OBJECTS RATHER THAN NUMBERS; NON-NUMERIC PROGRAMMING generally refers to the manipulation of symbolic objects, like words, things, people, and board game pieces, rather than performing numerical calculations.

non-procedural language

A LANGUAGE WHICH DOES NOT REQUIRE PROGRAMMING TECHNIQUE; NON-PROCEDURAL LANGUAGES allow a USER or PROGRAMMER to express a request to the COMPUTER in English-like statements, which specify *what* is to be done rather than *how* it is to be done. QUERY LANGUAGES, REPORT WRITERS and FINANCIAL PLANNING LANGUAGES are examples of NON-PROCEDURAL LANGUAGES. See PROCEDURAL LANGUAGES.

non-volatile memory

MEMORY WHICH HOLDS ITS CONTENT WITHOUT POWER; ROMs, PROMs, EPROMs, and EEPROMs (FIRMWARE) are examples of NON-VOLATILE MEMORIES.

NOS

OPERATING SYSTEM USED ON CDC'S CYBER SERIES LARGE-SCALE MAINFRAMES; Stands for **N**etwork **O**perating **S**ystem.

not

BOOLEAN LOGIC CONDITION; See AND, OR & NOT.

NOVA

SERIES OF MINICOMPUTERS MANUFACTURED BY DATA GENERAL CORPORATION.

ns

NANOSECOND; A NANOSECOND is a billionth of a second. See SPACE/TIME.

number crunching

LARGE NUMBERS OF CALCULATIONS; A NUMBER CRUNCHING operation implies extremely large amounts of calculations, usually referring to SCIENTIFIC APPLICATIONS, in contrast with business uses.

numerical control

MACHINE TOOL CONTROL; NUMERICAL CONTROL is used in manufacturing to automate operations, like milling, turning, punching and drilling. NC devices are machines, like drills and lathes, which operate automatically by following INSTRUCTIONS in an NC PROGRAM. Earlier NC machines were HARDWIRED and follow INSTRUCTIONS directly from PAPER TAPE or MAGNETIC TAPE. They were PROGRAMMED in a very LOW-LEVEL machine-like language.

Today, NC machines are controlled by their own MICROCOMPUTERS. HIGH-LEVEL NC PROGRAMMING LANGUAGES, like APT and COMPACT II, take much of the tedium out of PROGRAMMING by generating the appropriate tool path (the physical motions of the machine) required to perform a machine operation.

The term NUMERICAL CONTROL was formed in the 1950s when the INSTRUCTIONS to the machine tool were numeric CODES. Just like the COMPUTER industry, SYMBOLIC LANGUAGES were soon developed; however, the original term remained.

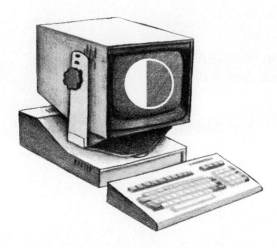

OA

See **O**FFICE **A**UTOMATION.

object code

INSTRUCTIONS WHICH CAN BE EXECUTED BY THE COMPUTER; OBJECT CODE is the OUTPUT of ASSEMBLERS and COMPILERS. Same as MACHINE LANGUAGE.

object computer

THE COMPUTER THAT WILL EXECUTE THE PROGRAM; Sometimes PROGRAMS are developed on one COMPUTER to be run (EXECUTED) on another COMPUTER. The COMPUTER they are intended for is the OBJECT COMPUTER.

OCR

OPTICAL **C**HARACTER **R**ECOGNITION; An OCR device is an OPTICAL SCANNER that recognizes actual CHARACTER images. Many different forms of typewriter or COMPUTER-printed CHARACTERS are recognizable, as well as certain qualities of hand-printing. The CHARACTERS are converted into DIGITAL CODE by the OCR machine. See MICR.

octal

A NUMBER BASED ON 8 DIGITS; OCTAL means *8*. PROGRAMMERS use OCTAL as a shorthand method for representing BINARY numbers. Each 3 BITS of BINARY are converted to a single OCTAL digit.

Decimal	BINARY	OCTAL
0	000	0
1	001	1
2	010	2
3	011	3
4	100	4
5	101	5
6	110	6
7	111	7
8	1000	10
9	1001	11

OEM

ORGANIZATIONS THAT DEVELOP CUSTOMIZED COMPUTER SYSTEMS; OEMs buy components from different HARDWARE and SOFTWARE vendors and package a complete SYSTEM for resale. Some OEMs are SOFTWARE development organizations that purchase the HARDWARE from a vendor, develop SOFTWARE for it (either generalized packages or customized for the end USER), and sell the entire SYSTEM as a TURNKEY product. Stands for **O**riginal **E**quipment **M**anufacturer (which is the opposite of what it means!).

off-line

NOT CONNECTED TO THE COMPUTER; A TERMINAL is OFF-LINE if it is not LOGGED-ON to the COMPUTER. Any PERIPHERAL device is OFF-LINE if it is not turned on and directly cabled to the COMPUTER. DISKS and TAPES in the DATA LIBRARY are OFF-LINE, as well. OFF-LINE also may refer to BATCH PROCESSING operations. Contrast with ON-LINE.

office automation

THE INTEGRATION OF ALL INFORMATION FUNCTIONS IN THE OFFICE; OFFICE AUTOMATION (OA) is an integration of several forms of INFORMATION PROCESSING, including DATA PROCESSING, WORD PROCESSING, ELECTRONIC MAIL, and GRAPHICS, as well as the human voice.

The backbone of OFFICE AUTOMATION is a LOCAL AREA NETWORK (within the same building or plant) which serves as a COMMUNICATIONS pathway between all USERS and COMPUTERS. USERS can create, store and retrieve any form of INFORMATION (message, mail, DATA, voice, etc.) and transmit it to any other USER within the organization.

All traditional office functions, such as dictation, typing, filing, copying, TWX and TELEX operation, MICROFILM and RECORDS MANAGEMENT, telephone and telephone switchboard operations, are candidates for integration into an OFFICE AUTOMATION SYSTEM.

OFFICE AUTOMATION is often used to refer to the WORD PROCESSING operation. Although WORD PROCESSING is often the first approach taken toward OFFICE AUTOMATION, OFFICE AUTOMATION implies many new ways of looking at work in the office. While it is viewed as a solution to bottlenecks and backlogs in office operations, its implementation will change the way people perform their jobs.

The irony of the so-called "Office of the Future" is that once we have all the technology to implement it properly, we probably won't need the office. If a person can gain ACCESS to all the INFORMATION that is required to do a job from a TERMINAL, and if VIDEO TELECONFERENCING allows us to see the people we're talking to, then the physical design of the office is bound to change dramatically.

on-line

CONNECTED AND AVALIABLE; ON-LINE SYSTEMS refer to TERMINALS and DATA BASES (DISKS) that are connected to the COMPUTER and are ready for use. If an INFORMATION SYSTEM is designed to immediately respond to a USER'S request, it is often called an ON-LINE REAL-TIME SYSTEM.

ON-LINE SYSTEMS are also called INTERACTIVE SYSTEMS, which implies a conversation between the USER and the COMPUTER.

The maximum amount of ON-LINE DISK storage that is available in a COMPUTER SYSTEM is an important evaluation criterion. It determines the maximum amount of INFORMATION that is immediately available to the USER at any time.

Contrast with BATCH PROCESSING and OFF-LINE.

op code

See OPERATION CODE.

open systems interconnection

INTERNATIONAL COMMUNICATIONS REFERENCE MODEL; The OPEN SYSTEMS INTERCONNECTION (OSI) is a COMMUNICATIONS standard defined by the International Standards Organization (ISO). It is a seven-layer COMMUNICATIONS PROTOCOL intended as a standard for the future development of COMMUNICATIONS SYSTEMS. The first three layers of the OSI are the same as the traditional COMMUNICATIONS NETWORKS commonly in use. The fourth layer, typically treated as one layer by most vendors, is further subdivided by the OSI into four layers (See COMMUNICATIONS PROTOCOL).

operand

PART OF A MACHINE INSTRUCTION WHICH REFERENCES DATA OR PERIPHERAL DEVICES; A and B are the OPERANDS of the INSTRUCTION: Add A to B. DRIVE, TRACK and SECTOR references are the OPERANDS of the INSTRUCTION: READ DISK DRIVE A TRACK 9 SECTOR 30. See OPERATION CODE and INSTRUCTION.

operating system

MASTER CONTROL PROGRAM WHICH RUNS THE COMPUTER; The OPERATING SYSTEM (OS) is the first PROGRAM copied into the COMPUTER'S MEMORY from a DISK or TAPE after the COMPUTER is first turned on. It is the primary SYSTEM SOFTWARE PROGRAM and acts as a "master scheduler" and "traffic cop." Some portion of the OPERATING SYSTEM resides in MEMORY at all times. Also called an EXECUTIVE or SUPERVISOR, the OPERATING SYSTEM performs the following functions:

> Responds to INTERACTIVE directions by the USER, or from a predefined set of COMMANDS (called JCL in the IBM world), and copies the requested APPLICATION PROGRAMS into MEMORY for EXECUTION at the appropriate time.

> Controls the concurrent EXECUTION of the APPLICATION PROGRAMS (TIME-SHARING or MULTIPROGRAMMING).

> Handles the INPUT/OUTPUT requests of the APPLICATION PROGRAMS (ACCESS METHODS). The OPERATING SYSTEM ACCESS METHODS create the DISK/TAPE FORMATS, and therefore "set the standards" for media (DISK/TAPE) compatibility. See STANDARDS & COMPATIBILITY.

OPERATING SYSTEMS are generally supplied by the HARDWARE vendor, although they may have been developed by a separate SOFTWARE vendor. In smaller PERSONAL COMPUTERS, the OPERATING SYSTEM is often stored in a ROM CHIP (FIRMWARE) and is immediately available when the COMPUTER is turned on.

The OPERATING SYSTEM is an important component of the COMPUTER SYSTEM. It links a USER'S PROGRAM to the machine by converting a LOGICAL request from the PROGRAM (for example: store this RECORD on the DISK) to a PHYSICAL set of COMMANDS, which activate the mechanics of the DISK DRIVE and transfer the DATA. That's how COMPUTERS with different DISK DRIVES can run the same USER PROGRAM.

An OPERATING SYSTEM is not always used, however. In many specialized APPLICATIONS, as for example, when COMPUTER CHIPS are used in appliances, games, or toys, the PROGRAM written for the CHIP combines both APPLICATION PROGRAM and OPERATING SYSTEM INSTRUCTIONS. There is often no need (nor the room) for the excess number of INSTRUCTIONS which are contained in a common OPERATING SYSTEM in the above cases.

CP/M, MS-DOS, UNIX, MVS and VM are examples of widely referenced OPERATING SYSTEMS (from MICROCOMPUTERS to MAINFRAMES).

operation code

THE COMMAND PART OF A MACHINE INSTRUCTION; The OPERATION CODE is the verb part of the INSTRUCTION which tells the COMPUTER which function to perform, such as: add, subtract, move and BRANCH. The noun parts of the INSTRUCTION are called OPERANDS. (Abbreviated OP-CODE.)

operations

See DATACENTER.

operations research

See MANAGEMENT SCIENCE.

operator

PERSON WHO OPERATES THE COMPUTER; COMPUTER OPERATORS perform various DATACENTER activities, such as mounting DISKS and TAPES, aligning paper in the PRINTER, and generally operating the COMPUTER. OPERATORS interact with the OPERATING SYSTEM (MASTER CONTROL PROGRAM) and must be conversant with its COMMAND language. OPERATORS also may write the JOB description language (called JCL in the IBM world), which defines the PROGRAMS to be run for the OPERATING SYSTEM.

OPERATORS who are part of the DATACENTER are involved with medium- to large-scale COMPUTER SYSTEMS.

optical character recognition

SEE OCR and OPTICAL SCANNER.

optical disk

PERIPHERAL STORAGE DISK FOR PROGRAMS AND INFORMATION; OPTICAL DISK technologies (similar to VIDEODISC) are emerging as a potential for COMPUTER storage devices because they have greater storage capacities than MAGNETIC DISKS. The VIDEODISC is a READ ONLY device; however, OPTICAL DISKS are being developed that can be recorded and erased, as well. OPTICAL DISKS may eventually be used as the storage device for large ELECTRONIC filing SYSTEMS.

optical fiber

GLASS WIRE; OPTICAL FIBERS are thin strands of glass designed for the transmission of light. Electrical pulses (BITS) are converted to light pulses (by LASERS or LEDs) and transfer through OPTICAL FIBERS, like blips of light. Light pulses are not subject to interference as are electric pulses. Many forms of DIGITAL transmission are being converted to OPTICAL FIBERS, including telephone COMMUNICATIONS CHANNELS and the CHANNELS between PERIPHERAL devices and the COMPUTER.

optical recognition

See OCR and OPTICAL SCANNER.

optical scanner

HARDWARE DEVICE THAT RECOGNIZES ACTUAL IMAGES; Images on paper, film and other media can be OPTICALLY SCANNED and converted into DIGITAL form. Many varieties of OPTICAL SCANNERS are used for the recognition of CHARACTERS, BAR CODES and GRAPHICS.

CHARACTERS (OCR FONTS or others) are converted into their corresponding DIGITAL CODE; for example, a printed ABC is converted into three BYTES for A, B and C. BAR CODES are converted into their respective number. However, with GRAPHICS images OPTICAL SCANNER devices are not recognition devices. Rather, they are encoding devices which simply record the picture image as a mosaic of light and dark intensities. See GRAPHICS (Raster Graphics).

OPTICAL SCANNERS view their images through a grid. In order for a CHARACTER to be actually recognized (OCR FONT, BAR CODE), an analysis of light and dark images on the grid is made.

or

BOOLEAN LOGIC CONDITION; See AND, OR & NOT.

OS

OPERATING SYSTEM; OS is an abbreviation for OPERATING SYSTEM. OS may also refer to an earlier IBM OPERATING SYSTEM.

OS/3

OPERATING SYSTEM USED ON UNIVAC SYSTEM 80 AND SERIES 90.

OS/8

OPERATING SYSTEM USED ON DEC PDP-8 SERIES MINICOMPUTERS.

OS 1100

OPERATING SYSTEM USED ON UNIVAC SERIES 1100 MAINFRAMES.

OSI

See **O**PEN **S**YSTEMS **I**NTERCONNECTION.

output

COMPUTER GENERATED INFORMATION; OUTPUT refers to any COMPUTER generated INFORMATION in the form of HARD COPY, SOFT COPY or MACHINE READABLE form (such as DISK or TAPE).

output devices

PERIPHERAL DEVICES THAT RECEIVE OUPUT FROM THE COMPUTER; Examples of OUTPUT devices are VIDEO TERMINALS, TELEPRINTERS, MONITORS, PRINTERS, CARD PUNCHES and COM units. DISK and TAPE DRIVES are OUTPUT devices as well as storage devices, since their INPUT is the COMPUTER'S OUTPUT.

overlay

SECONDARY PROGRAM SEGMENT; PROGRAMS can be designed as a series of PROGRAM segments that will be called into MEMORY by the PROGRAM at the appropriate times. The OVERLAY segment is copied on top of existing INSTRUCTIONS in MEMORY (which would have to be recopied back into MEMORY from the DISK or TAPE if required again). This method allows a PROGRAM to run in a COMPUTER with less MEMORY than the total PROGRAM size. See VIRTUAL STORAGE (for a more integrated approach to expand the MEMORY size of a COMPUTER).

PABX

CENTRAL TELEPHONE SWITCHING MACHINE; A PABX is an in-house telephone switching machine which ELECTRONICALLY interconnects one telephone extension to another, as well as to the outside telephone SYSTEM.

Modern PABXs are controlled by COMPUTERS which perform various telephone management functions, such as least cost routing for outside calls, call forwarding and conference calling, as well as elaborate accounting of the telephone calls handled. PABX stands for **P**rivate **A**utomatic **B**ranch e**X**change and is used synonymously with PBX. When PABXs are adapted or designed for DIGITAL traffic as well as voice traffic, they are called DIGITAL PABXs.

pack/unpack

COMMANDS WHICH COMPRESS DATA; PACK and UNPACK refer to INSTRUCTIONS which will compress DATA into less storage space. PACK and UNPACK may refer specifically to the PACKED DECIMAL mode in a COMPUTER. In this case, PACK will convert decimal numbers into PACKED DECIMAL form, and UNPACK will convert PACKED DECIMAL form back into decimal numbers.

package

Same as PROGRAM or SOFTWARE PACKAGE.

packaged software

See SOFTWARE PACKAGE.

packed decimal

STORAGE MODE FOR DECIMAL NUMBERS; In order to conserve storage space, the PACKED DECIMAL mode allows for the storage of twice as many decimal digits in a single BYTE. Since decimal digits range from 0 thru 9, there is a maximum of 10 combinations required. A single BYTE can hold 256 different combinations, far more than is necessary for a single decimal digit. PACKED DECIMAL allows a different decimal digit to be stored in each 4 BITS of the BYTE, thereby halving the storage space required.

packet switching

A TECHNIQUE FOR HANDLING VARIABLE TRAFFIC IN A COMMUNICATIONS NETWORK; PACKET SWITCHING breaks apart all MESSAGES to be transmitted into fixed length units called *packets*. The packets are routed to their destination through the most expedient route, and all the packets in a single MESSAGE may not travel the same route. The destination COMPUTER reassembles the packets into their appropriate sequence. This method is used to efficiently handle MESSAGES of different lengths and priorities in a single NETWORK. X.25 is an international standard for a PACKET SWITCHING NETWORK. See COMMUNICATIONS PROTOCOL.

packing density

THE NUMBER OF BITS OR TRACKS PER SURFACE AREA; The PACKING DENSITY determines the amount of storage available on or in a storage unit, such as a MAGNETIC DISK.

padding

CHARACTERS USED TO FILL A FIELD OR BLOCK; DATA is often structured in fixed length units called FIELDS, RECORDS and BLOCKS. If DATA takes up less space than its designated unit of storage, the remainder of the space must be filled with some PADDING CHARACTER such as a blank.

paddle

GAME INPUT DEVICE; A PADDLE is used to move some object on the SCREEN in a back and forth direction. PADDLES are used to hit balls, move missiles, and steer objects (like automobiles or rockets). The PADDLE usually has one or more buttons which can be used to start and stop the game or fire a missile. Objects that move in all directions are often moved more easily with a JOY STICK than with a PADDLE.

page

VIDEOTEX FRAME OR VIRTUAL STORAGE PROGRAM SEGMENT; See VIDEOTEX and VIRTUAL STORAGE.

page printer

HIGH SPEED COMPUTER PRINTER THAT PRINTS A PAGE AT A TIME; PRINTER OUTPUT is diverted to the PAGE PRINTER (either ON-LINE to the COMPUTER or via MAGNETIC TAPE) and is an alternative to PRINTER OUTPUT produced by slower LINE PRINTERS. PAGE PRINTERS employ copying machine techniques (ELECTROPHOTOGRAPHIC) and print onto 8 1/2" x 11" paper. Multiple copies are all original printings. Some PAGE PRINTER features include printing both sides of the paper and generating collated pages. Many different type styles and sizes can be printed, as well as GRAPHICS images, eliminating the need for pre-printed stock paper forms.

PAGE PRINTERS, also called LASER PRINTERS and ELECTRONIC PRINTERS, were first developed for high-volume operations. This technology is being incorporated into desktop units which will compete with the traditional LETTER QUALITY devices, like DAISY WHEEL machines.

pagination

THE LAYOUT OF A DOCUMENT; PAGINATION refers to the FORMAT of a printed page. PAGINATION includes the number of lines per inch, the number of CHARACTERS per inch, spacing between CHARACTERS, page numbers, etc. PAGINATION is performed by WORD PROCESSORS, as well as by specialized SOFTWARE (for the publishing industry) which combines both TEXT and GRAPHICS into a finished page for printing.

paging

THE TRANSFER OF PROGRAM SEGMENTS IN AND OUT OF MEMORY; See VIRTUAL STORAGE.

paper tape

STORAGE FOR PROGRAMS AND INFORMATION; "Punched" PAPER TAPE is a rather slow, low-capacity storage medium which uses patterns of holes punched in the PAPER TAPE as its CODING method. PAPER TAPE is SEQUENTIAL ACCESS storage.

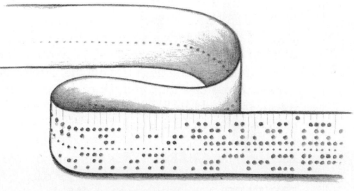

PAPER TAPE

parallel interface

MULTI-LINE CHANNEL CONNECTION; PARALLEL INTERFACES connect multi-line CHANNELS. For example: one BYTE transferred over a PARALLEL INTERFACE CHANNEL would require eight lines (pathways), one for each BIT. The same BYTE transferred over a SERIAL CHANNEL would require only one line. PARALLEL INTERFACES usually connect DISKS and TAPES to the COMPUTER, and SERIAL INTERFACES connect PRINTERS and COMMUNICATIONS CHANNELS. See SERIAL INTERFACE.

parallel processing

CONCURRENT PROCESSING; PARALLEL PROCESSING refers to a variety of techniques which cause simultaneous operations within the COMPUTER. See MULTIPROCESSING, PIPELINE PROCESSING, ARRAY PROCESSOR and DMA.

parameter

ANY VARIABLE VALUE; PARAMETERS are used to define a range of characteristics for a PROGRAM. They can be used to define ranges and FORMATS of INPUT and OUTPUT, limitations, exceptions— that is, virtually anything. The concept is that the PARAMETER can be changed by the USER each time the PROGRAM is run.

parameter-driven

PROGRAM WITH BUILT-IN FLEXIBILITY; A PARAMETER-DRIVEN PROGRAM implies the ability to change or modify the INPUT, PROCESSING, and/or OUTPUT in some way. The flexibility is based on the items chosen to be the PARAMETERS.

parity

ERROR DETECTION TECHNIQUE; The PARITY method is a way of checking for accurate transmission of DIGITAL INFORMATION, either internally within the COMPUTER SYSTEM, or externally through a COMMUNICATIONS NETWORK. The PARITY method adds a single BIT to each BYTE (CHARACTER), based on the total number of *0s* and *1s* that the BYTE contains. The PARITY BIT is carried with that BYTE as it travels from one device to another. In an even-PARITY SYSTEM, the PARITY BIT is made a *1* when the total number of the rest of the BITS in the BYTE are odd (to make it even). In an odd-PARITY SYSTEM, the PARITY BIT is made a *1* when the total number of BITS in the BYTE are even (to make it odd).

Each time the CHARACTER is transmitted from one device to another, the receiving device recalculates the PARITY BIT for each CHARACTER and matches it against the PARITY BIT that was transmitted. If it doesn't match, an error in transmission has been uncovered. (The PARITY BIT is the 9th BIT in EBCDIC CODE or the 8th BIT in ASCII CODE.)

parsing

ANALYSIS OF A LANGUAGE STATEMENT; PARSING is breaking apart a sentence
into its meaningful components. PARSING is performed by all free-form language
PROGRAMS (like HIGH-LEVEL PROGRAMMING LANGUAGES, QUERY
LANGUAGES and REPORT WRITERS) to decipher what the USER or PROGRAMMER
has requested. For example, in the QUERY LANGUAGE statement: sum salary for title
= boss; the PARSING must identify *sum* as the COMMAND, *salary* as the FIELD to be
totalled, and *title* as the FIELD to be compared to boss.

partition

RESERVED PORTION OF MEMORY; Some OPERATING SYSTEMS require that the
COMPUTER'S internal MEMORY be divided into several PARTITIONS. Usually one
PROGRAM can run in a single PARTITION at one time.

Pascal

HIGH-LEVEL PROGRAMMING LANGUAGE; PASCAL is a PROGRAMMING
LANGUAGE which is noted for its simplicity and STRUCTURED PROGRAMMING
design. PASCAL is available as both a COMPILER and an INTERPRETER, and was
developed by Niklaus Wirth (Swiss). PASCAL became available in the early 1970s and
gained popularity in universities and colleges in Europe and the United States. PASCAL
is named after the French mathematician, Blaise Pascal (mid 17th century), who
designed and built the first calculator, the "Pascaline."

patch

TEMPORARY FIX TO A PROGRAM; A PATCH implies a temporary, ad hoc change in
an APPLICATION PROGRAM, or a quick fix to a PROGRAM that doesn't work.
Eventually, too many PATCHES in a PROGRAM render it inefficient from a
PROCESSING standpoint, and/or very difficult to understand by either the original or
another PROGRAMMER.

PBX

CENTRAL TELEPHONE SWITCHING MACHINE; A PBX was originally a manually
operated in-house telephone switching machine, which would allow for the
interconnection of one line to another. The PBX gave way to the automatic PABX, which
is ELECTRONICALLY controlled; however, PBX is still used synonymously with PABX.
PBX stands for **P**rivate **B**ranch e**X**change.

PC

(1) **P**RINTED **C**IRCUIT, (2) **P**ERSONAL **C**OMPUTER.

PC board

See **P**RINTED **C**IRCUIT BOARD.

PCB

See **P**RINTED **C**IRCUIT **B**OARD.

PC-DOS

IBM VERSION OF THE MS-DOS OPERATING SYSTEM; PC-DOS runs on the IBM PERSONAL COMPUTER.

PCM

(1) **P**LUG **C**OMPATIBLE **M**ANUFACTURER, (2) **P**ULSE **C**ODE **M**ODULATION.

p-code

See UCSD P-SYSTEM.

PDP

SERIES OF MINICOMPUTERS MANUFACTURED BY DIGITAL EQUIPMENT CORPORATION.

peek/poke

INSTRUCTIONS TO LOOK AT/ALTER A BYTE OF MEMORY; A PEEK INSTRUCTION displays the MEMORY LOCATION specified in the PEEK. A POKE changes the MEMORY LOCATION specified in the POKE to the CHARACTER specified in the POKE.

pen plotter

See PLOTTER.

people/machine interface

THE METHOD OF INTERACTION BETWEEN A PERSON AND A COMPUTER; Until recently, PEOPLE/MACHINE INTERFACES were an afterthought. Today, it is recognized as one of the most important INFORMATION SYSTEM design criteria. There are two forms of this INTERFACE: (1) the visual form, which appears on a VIDEO SCREEN or a printed REPORT, and (2) the INTERACTIVE form, which is the conversation between the USER and the COMPUTER at the TERMINAL.

The visual form can include any mixture of letters, numbers, symbols and pictures. On TERMINAL SCREENS, the use of color or shadings, arrows and blinking lights, etc., all help to make the visual FORMAT more pleasing and comfortable. Instead of REPORTS printed on plain paper, PAGE PRINTERS or PHOTOTYPESETTERS can generate attractive REPORTS. Color or black and white BUSINESS GRAPHICS is a more effective method for presenting large amounts of DATA than rows and columns of numbers. Managers can absorb much more INFORMATION in the form of pictures rather than numbers, and relationships can be identified with graphs that would go unnoticed in the form of numbers.

The INTERACTIVE form requires creativity and imagination to make it simple to use. USER dialogues must enable first-time USERS to converse with the COMPUTER. USER-FRIENDLY SYSTEMS provide MENUS showing USERS all their alternatives, or they have HELP SCREENS which can be displayed at any time. There are many HARDWARE devices which can be incorporated into a TERMINAL to make the PEOPLE/MACHINE INTERFACE more comfortable. TOUCH SENSITIVE SCREENS allow USERS to point directly to a display MENU, or to objects on a SCREEN. At the very least, a full set of FUNCTION KEYS should be available on the KEYBOARD. In lieu of, or in addition to the KEYBOARD, TERMINALS can employ a JOY STICK, MOUSE, LIGHT PEN, or DIGITIZER TABLET for direction and INPUT.

peripheral

ANY INPUT, OUTPUT OR STORAGE DEVICE CONNECTED TO THE COMPUTER; DISKS, TAPES, TERMINALS, PRINTERS, OCR, MICR, and COM devices are examples.

perpendicular recording

See VERTICAL RECORDING.

personal computer

A COMPUTER USED FOR HOME OR PERSONAL USE; PERSONAL COMPUTERS are MICROCOMPUTERS which can be purchased off-the-shelf in a wide variety of COMPUTER and retail stores. The PERSONAL COMPUTER is functionally the same as the larger MINICOMPUTERS and MAINFRAMES. The difference lies in the amount of INFORMATION they can deal with, and the speed in which they can PROCESS this INFORMATION.

With the addition of a MODEM and a COMMUNICATIONS PROGRAM, PERSONAL COMPUTERS can function as TERMINALS to the outside world. They can be used to retrieve INFORMATION from any of the INFORMATION or TIME-SHARING services which are available (such as The Source and CompuServ, etc.) The advantage of the PERSONAL COMPUTER over a DUMB TERMINAL is that the COMPUTER can store the INFORMATION that is retrieved and analyze or manipulate it at a later time.

There are a wide variety of PERSONAL COMPUTERS on the market, costing from under $100 to several thousands. The COMPUTER CHIP in the $100 COMPUTER may be the very same COMPUTER CHIP in the $4,000 COMPUTER; however, the major cost no longer lies with the PROCESSOR as it did years ago. The PERIPHERAL devices cost more than the COMPUTER. FLOPPY DISKS, HIGH-RESOLUTION SCREENS, and touch-typist quality KEYBOARDS contribute significantly to the total cost. Large MEMORY banks also cost much more than the PROCESSOR itself.

PERSONAL COMPUTERS can be used for education (CAI), entertainment (games), home or hobby record keeping (DATA MANAGEMENT SYSTEM), writing (WORD PROCESSING), personal financial planning (ELECTRONIC SPREADSHEET), and ELECTRONIC MAIL, etc. In addition, they can be used to help you learn how to participate in the INTERACTIVE COMPUTER world. SOFTWARE products for PERSONAL COMPUTERS and larger MAINFRAME environments appear very similar on the TERMINAL SCREEN. Finally, you could take a stab at PROGRAMMING. Start out with a language like LOGO or BASIC. You can also do PROGRAMMING on an ELECTRONIC SPREADSHEET. You may surprise yourself. See COMPUTER SYSTEM.

phoneme

SPEECH UTTERANCE; PHONEMES are distinct sounds that make up human speech. See SPEECH SYNTHESIS.

phosphor

MATERIAL USED IN VIDEO CRTS; PHOSPHOR is a rare earth material used to coat the inside face of CRTs. It has the quality of emitting visible light when bombarded by electrons.

photocomposition

ELECTRONIC CREATION OF PRINTED MATERIALS; PHOTOCOMPOSITION refers to the ELECTRONIC composition of a page of TEXT and/or GRAPHICS for printing. It includes the PAGINATION, PHOTOTYPESETTING, and/or PAGE PRINTING required to produce a camera-ready or finished printed product.

photomask

A PLATE DESIGNED WITH AN OPAQUE AND TRANSLUSCENT IMAGE; A PHOTOMASK is used as a light filter to transfer a design onto a film or onto a material coated with film.

photomasking

PROCESS OF TRANSFERRING A DESIGN ONTO ANOTHER MATERIAL; PHOTOMASKING uses a PHOTOMASK which contains a design of opaque and transluscent areas. Light passes through the PHOTOMASK and transfers the design on the PHOTOMASK to another material. PHOTOMASKING is used to transfer the designs of ELECTRONIC CIRCUITS onto a SILICON WAFER.

phototypesetter

TYPOGRAPHER-QUALITY TEXT GENERATOR; A PHOTOTYPESETTER is a device which converts TEXT into professional quality printing. Virtually all books, including this one, have been typeset on a PHOTOTYPESETTER. INPUT is raw TEXT (words, sentences, paragraphs) either from the KEYBOARD or directly from a WORD PROCESSOR; OUTPUT is a paper-like or transparent film which is processed into a camera-ready master for printing. More advanced industrial devices will generate actual plates for printing.

The PHOTOTYPESETTER can generate CHARACTERS from various FONT tables at the same time. For example: this book was set using Stymie light, Stymie medium italic, and Stymie bold FONTS. The PHOTOTYPESETTER, working from a translation table, changed the FONTS and the type size from CODES embedded within the TEXT by the author. PHOTOTYPESETTERS conveniently handle KERNING, which is the extra compaction of combinations of letters like *WA* and *AV*.

PHOTOTYPESETTERS employ various light technologies for the creation of the CHARACTERS. Older machines use a spinning film strip which is used as a PHOTOMASK. Light passing through the film strip is enlarged by lenses to the appropriate type size, exposing the film. Current generation machines create images on CRTs which are used to expose the film. In time LASERS will generate the image directly onto the film.

pica

(1) 10 CHARACTERS PER INCH (TYPEWRITER), (2) 1/6 OF AN INCH (TYPOGRAPHY).

picosecond

ONE-TRILLIONTH OF A SECOND; Pronounced /pee-co-second/. See SPACE/TIME.

picture element

See PIXEL.

pie chart

GRAPHICAL REPRESENTATION OF INFORMATION; See BUSINESS GRAPHICS.

PILOT

CAI AUTHOR LANGUAGE; PILOT is a HIGH-LEVEL PROGRAMMING LANGUAGE designed to generate CAI PROGRAMS. PILOT is designed to make it easy to develop INTERACTIVE question-and-answer types of COURSEWARE. A special version of PILOT which incorporates TURTLE GRAPHICS (see LOGO) has been adapted to the Atari PERSONAL COMPUTER. PILOT stands for **P**rogrammed **I**nquiry **L**earning **O**r **T**eaching.

pipeline processing

OVERLAPPED PROCESSING; PIPELINE PROCESSING implies that certain internal COMPUTER operations are overlapped to achieve a higher PROCESSING speed. For example, while one INSTRUCTION is being EXECUTED, the COMPUTER might be extracting the next INSTRUCTION from MEMORY.

pixel

PICTURE ELEMENT; A PIXEL is the smallest part of a VIDEO SCREEN. A COMPUTER VIDEO SCREEN is broken up into thousands of tiny dots. A PIXEL is one or more dots which are treated as a unit. The PIXEL can represent as little as one dot for MONOCHROME SCREENS, three dots (red-green-blue) for color SCREENS, or clusters of these dots.

For MONOCHROME SCREENS, the PIXEL (normally dark) is energized to different light intensities, creating a range from dark to light. For color, each red, green and blue dot is energized to different intensities, creating a range of colors perceived as the mixture of these three dots. Black is all dots off, white is all dots on, and grays are even intensities of each color.

An economical way to generate GRAPHICS uses SCREENS in which the PIXEL is either on or off and cannot be varied. If the PIXEL is either on or off, only one BIT is required to represent that PIXEL in MEMORY. The most elaborate GRAPHICS may require as many as eight BITS to represent each red, green and blue dot. That's 256 shades per dot, or a total of 16,777,216 different color combinations! Stands for **pix** (picture) **el**ement.

PL/I

HIGH-LEVEL PROGRAMMING LANGUAGE DEVELOPED BY IBM; PL/I was introduced in 1964, the year IBM announced the System/360 series. It was developed as a general-purpose PROGRAMMING LANGUAGE, incorporating features from both COBOL and FORTRAN. PL/I is used primarily on large MAINFRAMES. PL/I stands for **P**rogramming **L**anguage 1.

planning system

See FINANCIAL PLANNING SYSTEM.

plasma display

FLAT SCREEN TECHNOLOGY; PLASMA DISPLAY SCREENS contain an inert ionized gas sandwiched between an x-axis panel and a y-axis panel. An individual dot (PIXEL) is selectable by charging an x-wire on one panel and a y-wire on the other panel. When the x-y coordinate is charged, the gas in that vicinity glows a bright orange color. A PLASMA DISPLAY is also called a GAS DISCHARGE DISPLAY.

PLATO

EDUCATIONAL SYSTEM DEVELOPED BY CONTROL DATA CORPORATION (CDC); PLATO was the first educational SYSTEM to incorporate the use of GRAPHICS with specially developed TOUCH SENSITIVE SCREENS for INTERACTIVE use. PLATO USERS can develop their own COURSEWARE to teach virtually any variety of subject, or they can use CDC COURSEWARE as well. PLATO is available on CDC's TIME-SHARING COMPUTERS and requires a special PLATO TERMINAL for use. PLATO has also been adapted by CDC to a MICROCOMPUTER for customer use.

plot

DRAWING COMMAND; A PLOT INSTRUCTION in a PROGRAMMING LANGUAGE can create a single VECTOR or a complete circle or box, depending on the language.

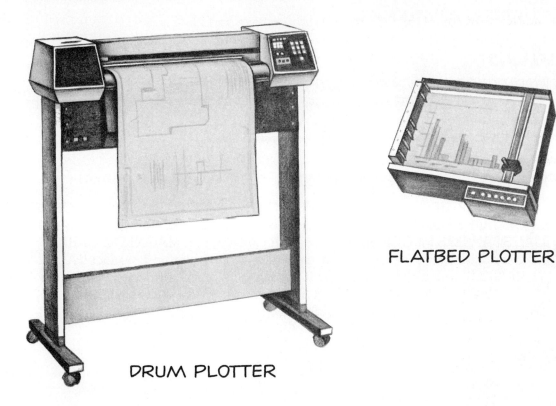

FLATBED PLOTTER

DRUM PLOTTER

plotter

GRAPHICS OUTPUT DEVICE; PLOTTERS are drawing machines that draw lines with ink pens. PLOTTERS require that the picture image is CODED in VECTOR GRAPHICS format (point-to-point). FLATBED PLOTTERS limit the overall size of the drawing to the fixed height and width of the "bed," onto which the paper is placed for drawing. FLATBED PLOTTERS draw by moving the pen in both horizontal and vertical axes. DRUM PLOTTERS limit the size to one side only (size of the drum), but not the other, since the paper is continuously moved like a standard PRINTER. DRUM PLOTTERS draw by moving the pen along one axis and the paper along the other. See PRINTER.

PLP

NORTH AMERICAN VIDEOTEX PROTOCOL; PLP is the AT&T standard VIDEOTEX
PROTOCOL for North America. PLP stands for **P**resentation **L**evel **P**rotocol.

plug compatible

HARDWARE THAT IS DESIGNED TO PERFORM EXACTLY LIKE ANOTHER
VENDOR'S PRODUCT; Both PERIPHERALS and CPUs can be PLUG COMPATIBLE.
PCM stands for **PLUG C**OMPATIBLE **M**anufacturer or **PLUG C**OMPATIBLE
MAINFRAME.

PM

See **P**REVENTIVE **M**AINTENANCE.

PMOS

TYPE OF MICROELECTRONIC CIRCUIT DESIGN; PMOS TRANSISTORS were used in
the first MICROPROCESSORS and are used in CMOS fabrication as well. PMOS CHIPS
are widely used in low-cost products like CALCULATORS and DIGITAL watches.
Stands for **P**-Channel **MOS** and is pronounced /pee-moss/.

point of sale system

AUTOMATIC CAPTURE OF RETAIL TRANSACTIONS AT THE TIME AND PLACE OF
SALE; POINT OF SALE (POS) SYSTEMS use specialized TERMINALS with features like
OPTICAL SCANNERS for OCR FONTS and BAR CODES, and MAGNETIC CARD
READERS for credit cards (which automatically pick up customer and product DATA).
POS TERMINALS, which often contain built-in cash registers for convenience, may be
directly ON-LINE to a central COMPUTER SYSTEM for immediate customer credit
checking and/or TRANSACTION PROCESSING.

poke

See PEEK/POKE.

polling

REPEATED INTERROGATION; POLLING is the continuous interrogation by one
COMPUTER of another TERMINAL or COMPUTER to determine if that device wishes to
transmit. POLLING uses SOFTWARE in the COMPUTER or in the COMMUNICATIONS
FRONT END to repeatedly send out the requests. If a TERMINAL or COMPUTER is
ready to transmit, it sends back an acknowledgement CODE (ACK) and the transmission
sequence begins.

An alternate technique is an INTERRUPT-driven SYSTEM, wherein the TERMINAL
signals the COMPUTER when MESSAGES are ready to be transmitted.

pop

See PUSH/POP.

port

COMMUNICATIONS CHANNEL INTERFACE; The number of PORTS in the COMPUTER or COMMUNICATIONS CONTROL UNIT determines the number of physical COMMUNICATIONS CHANNELS that can be connected.

porting

ADAPTING SYSTEM SOFTWARE TO A PARTICULAR COMPUTER; PORTING refers to the customization of a SYSTEM SOFTWARE product (such as an OPERATING SYSTEM) to run on a particular COMPUTER.

POS

See **P**OINT **OF S**ALE SYSTEM.

power

See COMPUTER POWER.

Prestel

BRITISH VIDEOTEX SERVICE; PRESTEL is a commercial VIDEOTEX service of British Telecom (formerly part of the British Post Office). PRESTEL services are offered in the United States through British Videotex and Teletext (BVT).

preventive maintenance

ROUTINE CHECKING OF HARDWARE TO PREVENT DOWNTIME; PREVENTIVE MAINTENANCE (PM) is performed by a FIELD ENGINEER on a regularly scheduled basis.

primary storage

THE COMPUTER'S INTERNAL MEMORY; Same as RAM. Contrast with SECONDARY STORAGE (DISK and TAPE).

print server

COMPUTER CONTROLLING A SERIES OF PRINTERS; A PRINT SERVER is a COMPUTER and PRINTER in a SHARED RESOURCE NETWORK. The PRINT SERVER manages the printing of the FILES transmitted by the USERS on the NETWORK.

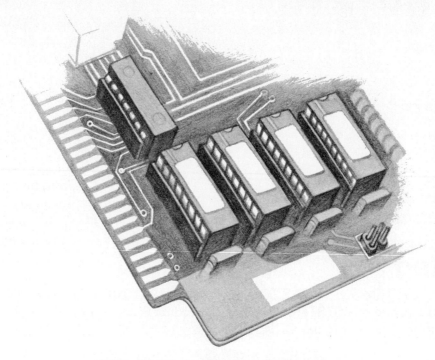

PRINTED CIRCUIT BOARD

printed circuit board

FLAT BOARD WHICH HOLDS CHIPS AND OTHER ELECTRONIC COMPONENTS;
The PRINTED CIRCUIT BOARD contains many slots for CHIPS, as well as connections
for a variety of ELECTRONIC components. The back side of the PC BOARD is printed
with electically conductive pathways between the components. The PC BOARD of the
1960s connected elementary components together. The PC BOARD of the 1980s connects
CHIPS together, each CHIP containing thousands of elementary components.

printer

DEVICE THAT CONVERTS COMPUTER OUTPUT INTO PRINTED IMAGES; The major
categories of PRINTERS are:

SERIAL PRINTERS print a CHARACTER at a time at approximately 10-400
CHARACTERS per second (CPS), equivalent to 6-240 lines per minute (LPM),
based on 100 CHARACTERS per line. SERIAL PRINTERS primarily use DOT
MATRIX and CHARACTER PRINTER technologies. Often SERIAL PRINTERS are
referred to as CHARACTER PRINTERS regardless of the PRINTING
TECHNOLOGY employed.

LINE PRINTERS print a line at a time at approximately 100-3,000 LPM and are
the standard PRINTERS found in the DATACENTER. LINE PRINTERS use DRUM,
CHAIN, TRAIN, and BAND technologies.

PAGE PRINTERS (also called LASER PRINTERS and ELECTRONIC PRINTERS)
print a page at at time at approximately 1,000-20,000 LPM and primarily employ
copying machine techniques (ELECTROPHOTOGRAPHIC).

THE COMPUTER GLOSSARY

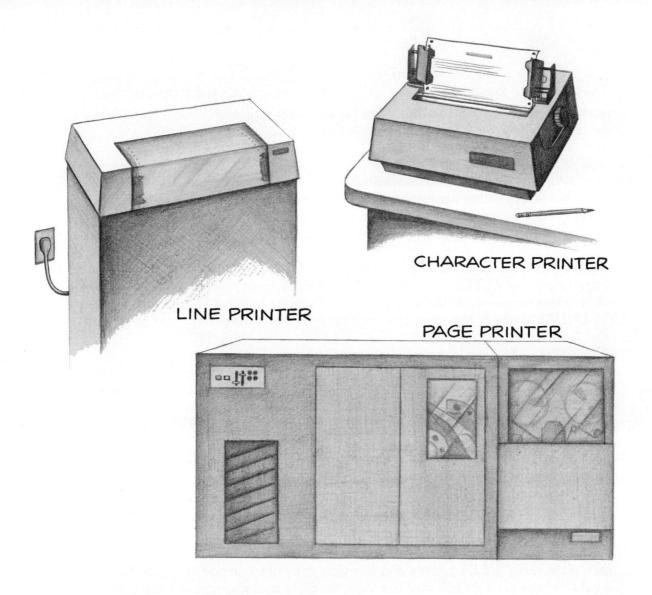

LINE PRINTER

CHARACTER PRINTER

PAGE PRINTER

GRAPHICS PRINTERS use IMPACT SERIAL DOT MATRIX, IMPACT LINE DOT MATRIX, ELECTROSTATIC, THERMAL, INK JET AND ELECTROPHOTOGRAPHIC technologies.

COLOR GRAPHICS PRINTERS use IMPACT DOT MATRIX (multiple color ribbons), ELECTROPHOTOGRAPHIC (multiple color plates), and INK JET (multiple color inks) technologies.

printer technologies

IMPACT PRINTERS

BAND, CHAIN AND TRAIN PRINTERS— A continuous loop of several CHARACTER sets connected together spins horizontally around a set of hammers. When the desired CHARACTER is in front of the selected print location, that particular hammer hits the BAND, CHAIN, or TRAIN, forcing the shaped CHARACTER image into the ribbon and onto the paper. Since the CHAIN, BAND, or TRAIN moves so fast, it appears to print a line at a time. A BAND is a solid loop, while the CHAIN is individual CHARACTER images (type slugs) chained together. The TRAIN is individual CHARACTER images (type slugs) revolving in a track, one pushing the other.

DRUM PRINTER— A rotating DRUM (cylinder) contains the CHARACTER set carved around it for each print location, like an odometer. When the desired CHARACTER for the selected print location has revolved around to the hammer line, the appropriate hammer hits the paper from behind, forcing it against the ribbon which is between the paper and the DRUM. Since the DRUM rotates so fast, it appears to print a line at a time.

CHARACTER PRINTERS— CHARACTER PRINTERS are similar to Selectric typewriters, printing one CHARACTER at a time. A DAISY WHEEL or similar mechanism is moved serially across the paper. At the selected print location, a hammer hits the shaped CHARACTER image on the wheel into the ribbon and onto the paper.

DOT MATRIX— A vertical set of printing devices moves serially across the paper, formulating CHARACTERS by printing patterns of dots onto the paper. The clarity of the CHARACTER is determined by how close the dots print together. The DOT MATRIX technique is used in IMPACT PRINTERS, which use dot hammers or wires that impact a ribbon and transfer ink onto paper, as well as in NON-IMPACT PRINTERS.

LINE DOT MATRIX— A stationary or oscillating line of dot printing devices generate images by printing the appropriate dots onto the paper a line at a time.

NON-IMPACT PRINTERS

ELECTROPHOTOGRAPHIC (copying machine technique)— A plate is charged with a high voltage and a LASER paints a negative light copy of the image to be printed onto the plate. Where the light falls onto the plate, the plate is discharged. A toner (ink) is allowed to adhere to the charged portion of the plate. The plate then fuses the image onto the paper by pressure or heat. Some ELECTROPHOTOGRAPHIC SYSTEMS use a positive approach wherein the toner is attracted to the LASER-produced latent image.

ELECTROSENSITIVE— Dots are charged onto specially coated silver-colored paper, usually in a serial fashion. The charge removes the aluminum coating, leaving a black image.

ELECTROSTATIC— Dots are charged onto specially coated paper usually a line at a time. An ink adheres to the charges, which become embedded into the paper by pressure or by heat.

INK JET— Continuous streams of ink are sprayed onto paper, or droplets of ink generate a DOT MATRIX image, usually in a serial fashion.

THERMAL— Dots are burned onto specially coated paper which turns black or blue when heat is applied to it. Moving heat elements form a DOT MATRIX image across the paper.

printout

PRINTER **OUT**PUT.

privacy

RESTRICTION OF ACCESS TO DATA; PRIVACY pertains to the distribution of DATA to people and organizations. SECURITY issues pertain to *unauthorized* ACCESS to DATA; PRIVACY issues pertain to the *authorized* distribution of DATA (who has a right to know?).

private line

(1) DEDICATED LINE LEASED FROM A COMMON CARRIER, (2) LINE OWNED AND INSTALLED BY THE USER.

problem-oriented language

LANGUAGE DESIGNED TO REFERENCE A PARTICULAR PROBLEM; PROGRAMMING LANGUAGES, like COBOL and FORTRAN, were designed for particular classes of problems, such as business and scientific. Many other PROBLEM-ORIENTED LANGUAGES are designed for even more specific APPLICATIONS, such as FINANCIAL PLANNING LANGUAGES and REPORT WRITERS.

procedural language

A LANGUAGE REQUIRING THE USE OF PROGRAMMING DISCIPLINE; PROGRAMMERS, writing in PROCEDURAL LANGUAGES, must develop a proper order of actions in order to solve the problem, based on a knowledge of DATA/INFORMATION PROCESSING operations and PROGRAMMING techniques, such as LOOPING. All CONVENTIONAL PROGRAMMING LANGUAGES are PROCEDURAL LANGUAGES.

Contrast with NON-PROCEDURAL LANGUAGE which generates the necessary PROGRAM LOGIC for the COMPUTER directly from a USER'S description of the problem.

procedure

A SERIES OF STEPS TO ACCOMPLISH A PARTICULAR TASK; Manual PROCEDURES are directions for people. A PROCEDURE FILE is a list of steps or COMMANDS to be EXECUTED in a specific order by SOFTWARE (See JCL). The PROCEDURE division in a COBOL PROGRAM is the section that describes the PROCESSING.

process

TO MANIPULATE INFORMATION; PROCESSING means any action taken on INFORMATION in a COMPUTER. PROCESSING can change the content or form of the INFORMATION, or it may simply transfer it from one source to another without change. PROCESSING can mean: (1) any work done by the COMPUTER SYSTEM, or (2) just the work done internally on the INFORMATION by the COMPUTER. For example: INFORMATION is READ from a DATA BASE (I/O), FORMATTED in the COMPUTER (PROCESSING), and printed (I/O). PROCESSING in this context is separate from the INPUT/OUTPUT operations. When COMPUTER operation performance is evaluated, the measurement of the PROCESSING time is separate and distinct from the I/O time.

process-bound

EXCESSIVE PROCESSING; A PROCESS-BOUND COMPUTER means that there is an excessive amount of PROCESSING taking place, and implies an imbalance between INPUT/OUTPUT operations and PROCESSING. A faster PROCESSOR will increase the THROUGHPUT of a PROCESS-BOUND COMPUTER.

process control

CONTROL OF MANUFACTURING PROCESSES BY COMPUTER; PROCESS CONTROL SYSTEMS monitor and control continuous industrial operations, such as oil refining, chemical processing and electrical generation. PROCESS CONTROL SYSTEMS employ HYBRID COMPUTER SYSTEMS, which convert real-world (ANALOG) signals into DIGITAL form for PROCESSING by the COMPUTER. See CAM and ANALOG TO DIGITAL CONVERTER.

processing

See CENTRALIZED PROCESSING, DISTRIBUTED PROCESSING, BATCH PROCESSING, TRANSACTION PROCESSING, MULTIPROCESSING and COMPUTER (The 3 C's).

processor

COMPUTER PORTION OF THE CPU; THE PROCESSOR is technically the COMPUTER in the CPU, although PROCESSOR and CPU are often used synonymously. It is made up of the CONTROL UNIT and the ALU (Arithmetic Logic Unit). The PROCESSOR requires a power supply and MEMORY to perform COMPUTER functions. A MICROPROCESSOR is a PROCESSOR on a single CHIP.

SOFTWARE SYSTEMS are sometimes called PROCESSORS. For example, ASSEMBLERS and COMPILERS are language PROCESSORS. SOFTWARE which performs WORD PROCESSING is called a WORD PROCESSOR.

program

A GROUP OF INSTRUCTIONS WHICH TELLS THE COMPUTER HOW TO PERFORM A SPECIFIC FUNCTION; A PROGRAM is a collection of three things: (1) INSTRUCTIONS, (2) BUFFERS, and (3) CONSTANTS. The INSTRUCTIONS are the PROGRAM LOGIC (which tells the COMPUTER what to do). The BUFFERS are empty spaces reserved in the PROGRAM which temporarily store the INFORMATION called for by the PROGRAM. The CONSTANTS are fixed values stored for PROCESSING in the PROGRAM, such as a tax table, or a calendar of days and months.

After the INFORMATION is transferred into the BUFFERS from a PERIPHERAL device or from another PROGRAM, the actual PROCESSING is performed by **calculating**, **comparing** and **copying** the INFORMATION in these BUFFERS. See COMPUTER (The 3 C's).

See SOURCE PROGRAM and OBJECT PROGRAM.

program generator

PROGRAM THAT GENERATES A PROGRAM; A PROGRAM GENERATOR generates conventional LINES OF CODE for a particular PROGRAMMING LANGUAGE from a series of descriptions. The PROGRAM GENERATOR is designed to make it easier to write a PROGRAM. It is one or more levels higher (closer to people) than the PROGRAMMING LANGUAGE it generates.

program logic

PARTICULAR SEQUENCE OF INSTRUCTIONS IN A PROGRAM; There are many solutions to a problem. The PROGRAM LOGIC is the particular solution to a particular problem as designed and written into the PROGRAM by the PROGRAMMER.

program maintenance

CHANGES IN PROGRAM LOGIC, BUFFER SIZE, OR CONSTANTS WITHIN A PROGRAM; PROGRAM LOGIC is changed when the PROGRAM is going to PROCESS differently. BUFFERS are enlarged or shortened when a DATA FIELD has changed size. CONSTANTS are changed when their fixed values have changed, such as for an interest rate.

program step

MACHINE LANGUAGE OR ASSEMBLY LANGUAGE INSTRUCTION; A PROGRAM STEP is an elementary INSTRUCTION.

programmable

CAPABLE OF BEING PROGRAMMED; A PROGRAMMABLE machine is a general-purpose device which follows a set of INSTRUCTIONS.

programmable calculator

CALCULATOR THAT CAN BE PROGRAMMED; A PROGRAMMABLE CALCULATOR is a limited function COMPUTER. The primary difference is that the PROGRAMMABLE CALCULATOR only works on numbers, not on ALPHANUMERIC DATA.

programmer

PERSON WHO DESIGNS THE LOGIC FOR AND WRITES THE LINES OF CODE OF A COMPUTER PROGRAM; PROGRAMMER generally refers to APPLICATION PROGRAMMER, the person who writes specific USER PROGRAMS.

programmer analyst

PERSON WHO ANALYZES AND DESIGNS INFORMATION SYSTEMS AND WRITES THE COMPUTER PROGRAMS AS WELL; PROGRAMMER ANALYSTS perform SYSTEMS ANALYST and PROGRAMMER functions.

programming

DEVELOPING A COMPUTER PROGRAM; The steps in PROGRAMMING are: (1) developing the PROGRAM LOGIC to solve the particular problem, (2) writing the PROGRAM LOGIC in the form of a specific PROGRAMMING LANGUAGE (CODING the PROGRAM), (3) TESTING and DEBUGGING the PROGRAM, and (4) preparing the necessary DOCUMENTATION. The PROGRAM LOGIC is the most difficult part of PROGRAMMING.

programming language

A LANGUAGE USED BY A PROGRAMMER TO DEVELOP INSTRUCTIONS FOR THE COMPUTER; The PROGRAMMING LANGUAGE is translated into MACHINE LANGUAGE by language SOFTWARE called ASSEMBLERS, COMPILERS and INTERPRETERS. Each PROGRAMMING LANGUAGE has its own grammer and syntax, like human languages. There are many dialects of the same language; however, unlike human languages in which different dialects can be understood, PROGRAMMING LANGUAGE dialects cannot. There are certain universal language standards endorsed by the American National Standards Institute, such as ANSI COBOL and ANSI FORTRAN, which are implemented by many vendors. COMPUTER SYSTEM vendors generally develop (or have developed for them) several different PROGRAMMING LANGUAGES for their COMPUTERS.

PROM

PERMANENT MEMORY CHIP FOR PROGRAM STORAGE; INSTRUCTIONS and/or INFORMATION are stored in the PROM through the use of a PROM PROGRAMMER. PROM is FIRMWARE and stands for **P**rogrammable **R**ead **O**nly **M**emory.

PROM blaster (blower)

Same as PROM PROGRAMMER.

PROM programmer

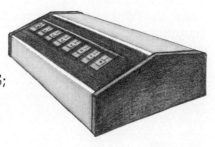

DEVICE THAT PERMANENTLY WRITES PROM CHIPS; The PROM PROGRAMMER is a machine which copies a PROGRAM in MACHINE LANGUAGE form onto one or more PROM CHIPS at the same time. The BITS in the PROM are permanently altered and cannot be reversed.

PROM PROGRAMMER

prompts

MESSAGES FROM THE COMPUTER INSTRUCTING THE USER HOW TO USE THE SYSTEM; For example: "Type ? for Help," or "Enter employee name," etc.

proportional spacing

CHARACTERS TAKING UP DIFFERENT PROPORTIONS OF SPACE; PROPORTIONAL SPACING prints or displays the CHARACTER in the space required by the CHARACTER itself, and takes up less space than with uniform spacing. For example, an *I* takes up less space than an *M*. WORD PROCESSING PRINTERS and PHOTOTYPESETTERS can generate PROPORTIONAL SPACING. PHOTOTYPESETTERS go one step beyond PROPORTIONAL SPACING with KERNING (where combinations like WA and FA are compacted even further).

protocol

See COMMUNICATIONS PROTOCOL.

prototyping

USER-INVOLVED SYSTEM DEVELOPMENT; PROTOTYPING is an alternative method to the traditional SYSTEM DEVELOPMENT METHODOLOGY. In the traditional approach, the FUNCTIONAL SPECS, which are the blueprint and design of the INFORMATION SYSTEM, must be finalized and frozen before the SYSTEM can be built. This places a large burden on managers to know what INFORMATION they want now and in the future. While the analytically-oriented person may have a clear picture of INFORMATION requirements, the average manager does not.

PROTOTYPING offers an alternative approach. Using a DATA MANAGEMENT SYSTEM, SYSTEMS ANALYSTS together with the USERS, can be formulating and developing the new SYSTEM at the same time. DATA BASES can be created and manipulated at a TERMINAL, with the USER monitoring the progess all the way. Once a USER sees something tangible on the SCREEN or on paper, it is much easier to figure out what's missing or what the next question ought to be. If PROTOTYPING is carefully done, the end result can be a working SYSTEM. Even if the final SYSTEM must be redone from scratch (using conventional languages for machine efficiency) the PROTOTYPING has served to provide specifications for a SYSTEM which will really work. In addition, and perhaps most important, the USER will have learned the real requirements for an INFORMATION and DECISION SUPPORT SYSTEM.

p-System

See UCSD P-SYSTEM.

PTT

POSTAL, TELEGRAPH & TELEPHONE; PTT is the acronym for the national governmental agency responsible for combined postal, telegraph and telephone services in many European countries.

pulse code modulation

DIGITAL SPEECH CONVERSION METHOD; PULSE CODE MODULATION (PCM) is a technique that samples an AUDIO WAVE and converts it into DIGITAL form (BINARY CODE).

punched card

STORAGE FOR INSTRUCTIONS AND INFORMATION; PUNCHED CARDS store INSTRUCTIONS and INFORMATION in the form of patterns of punched holes in the card. PUNCHED CARDS usually store 80 or 96 CHARACTERS. The holes are punched into the PUNCHED CARD by a KEYPUNCH machine or a CARD PUNCH PERIPHERAL device attached to the COMPUTER. PUNCHED CARDS are READ into the COMPUTER by a CARD READER PERIPHERAL device.

push/pop

ENTER/REMOVE AN ITEM FROM A STACK; PUSH enters a new item onto a STACK, which pushes the rest of the items down the STACK. POP removes the top item on the STACK, moving the rest of the items in the STACK up one level.

QBE

IBM QUERY LANGUAGE; QBE displays the RECORD type requested by the USER as a set of columns on the VIDEO SCREEN. The USER enters the criteria for selection under the column of the FIELD desired and the PROGRAM searches for the DATA. QBE stands for **Q**uery **B**y **E**xample.

query

FILE/DATA BASE INTERROGATION; A QUERY PROGRAM allows the USER to ACCESS INFORMATION in a FILE or DATA BASE and display the INFORMATION on a TERMINAL, or alternatively, print the INFORMATION on a PRINTER. A QUERY implies a single response or a simple listing of selected DATA; a REPORT implies a more elaborate and planned layout of DATA. QUERY is plain— REPORT is fancy.

query by example

See QBE.

query language

GENERALIZED LANGUAGE TO INTERROGATE A DATA BASE; Like PROGRAMMING LANGUAGES, QUERY LANGUAGES have their own grammar, syntax and rules. QUERY LANGUAGES offer USERS fairly flexible ways of ACCESSING their DATA BASE without having to pre-determine every conceivable interrogation request beforehand. QUERY LANGUAGES are usually featured as part of a DATA or DATA BASE MANAGEMENT SYSTEM. An example of a QUERY LANGUAGE request is: Display name address for title = professor.

When an APPLICATION PROGRAMMER develops a customized QUERY PROGRAM, it can be designed specifically for a particular USER'S requirements: Enter first 5 digits of customer number— What order do you want? However, any unusual interrogation request will require a PROGRAMMING change in the USER'S QUERY PROGRAM before the USER will be able to ACCESS the INFORMATION.

queue

TEMPORARY STORAGE FOR INFORMATION; QUEUES are any storage space reserved to temporarily hold INFORMATION, either in MEMORY or on DISK. MESSAGE QUEUES temporarily store INFORMATION from local or remote TERMINALS until the PROGRAMS can PROCESS them. PRINT QUEUES store the PROGRAM OUTPUT on DISK until a PRINTER is available to print it. QUEUE is pronounced /Q/. See SPOOLING.

qwerty keyboard

STANDARD TYPEWRITER KEYBOARD FOR THE ENGLISH LANGUAGE; The QWERTY KEYBOARD was defined for mechanical typewriters. The placement of the keys was designed to eliminate jamming, based on the most common combinations of letters in the English Language. Q, w, e, r, t and y are the first six letters starting at the top left of the first alphabetic row of the KEYBOARD.

STANDARD TYPEWRITER KEYBOARD

radio frequency

See RF.

RAM

COMPUTER MEMORY; RAM stands for **R**andom **A**ccess **M**emory, because INFORMATION can be transferred into and out of any single BYTE of MEMORY, independent of the rest. The storage cells (BITS) of a RAM CHIP require power to retain their content. If the power fails, the contents are lost. Contrast with FIRMWARE (MEMORY CHIPS which hold their content when the power is off). See MEMORY.

RAMIS II

DATA MANAGEMENT AND DECISION SUPPORT SYSTEM WHICH RUNS ON IBM COMPUTERS; The earlier version of RAMIS II was one of the first NON-PROCEDURAL DATA MANAGEMENT SYSTEMS. RAMIS II is a product of Mathematica Products Group.

random access

Same as DIRECT ACCESS.

random number generation

PROGRAMMING LANGUAGE FUNCTION WHICH GENERATES A RANDOM NUMBER; RANDOM NUMBERS can be generated from many sources. The randomness of the number can be derived from a REAL-TIME CLOCK, or by methods such as timing the duration between depressions of USER keystrokes.

raster graphics

COMPUTER GRAPHICS CODING TECHNIQUE; The RASTER GRAPHICS technique represents a picture as thousands of dots which make up a viewing area. RASTER GRAPHICS is similar to television, except that there is no national standard as there is in TV. See GRAPHICS (Raster Graphics).

RCS

REMOTE **C**OMPUTER **S**ERVICE; RCS is synonymous with remote TIME-SHARING services.

read

INPUT TO THE COMPUTER; A READ generally refers to the transfer of a copy of INFORMATION from a DISK, TAPE, or BUBBLE MEMORY device into the COMPUTER'S MEMORY. READING does not destroy the content of the device being READ. It's just like reading a book or playing a tape on a home tape recorder. The content still remains in its original place.

Internal MEMORY (RAM and ROM) is READ as well when INSTRUCTIONS and INFORMATION are being copied out of it, either to the PROCESSOR or to another place in the RAM.

read error

THE CONTENT OF A STORAGE DEVICE CANNOT BE ELECTRONICALLY IDENTIFIED; If the magnetic recording surface of a DISK or TAPE is contaminated with dust or dirt, or is physically damaged, the BITS may become unreadable. If there is a malfunction of one of the ELECTRONIC components in a storage CHIP, the contents may be unreadable.

read only

STORAGE DEVICES WITH PERMANENT CONTENT; ROMs, PROMs and VIDEODISCS are examples of READ ONLY devices.

reader

PERIPHERAL DEVICE; A READER is usually an INPUT device, such as a PUNCHED CARD READER, MAGNETIC CARD READER or OCR READER. However, a MICROFICHE or MICROFILM READER is an OUTPUT device.

read/write head

THE DEVICE THAT RECORDS AND SENSES MAGNETIC SPOTS ON A MAGNETIC DISK, DRUM OR TAPE; The magnetic recording surface is moved past the READ/WRITE HEAD and the spots (BITS) are recorded (WRITTEN) by discharging an electrical impulse at the appropriate time. The presence of a BIT is sensed (READ) by the BIT acting as a bridge, inducing current across the READ/WRITE HEAD.

read/write memory

Same as RAM.

real-time

IMMEDIATE PROCESSING; REAL-TIME COMPUTER SYSTEMS are designed to respond immediately to USER TRANSACTIONS. The term REAL-TIME is a scientific term meaning *no delay*— instantaneous response. Therefore, INTERACTIVE business APPLICATIONS would technically not be REAL-TIME (people think about what to enter). However, REAL-TIME SYSTEMS are often used to describe ON-LINE INTERACTIVE APPLICATIONS. Contrast with BATCH PROCESSING.

real-time clock

See CLOCK.

record

A GROUP OF RELATED DATA FIELDS; A RECORD is a collection of DATA and INFORMATION about a subject, such as an employee, customer, vendor or product, etc. A collection of RECORDS is called a FILE (or DATA BASE). 10,000 active employees in an organization implies 10,000 physical RECORDS in a FILE or DATA BASE. MASTER RECORDS contain semi-permanent DATA, such as for employees and customers; TRANSACTION records contain event DATA such as orders, title changes, inventory additions, etc.

record layout

FORMAT OF A RECORD; The RECORD LAYOUT describes each FIELD in the RECORD and the number of BYTES in each FIELD.

record locking

See FILE (RECORD) LOCKING.

records management

MANAGEMENT OF AN ORGANIZATION'S DOCUMENTS; RECORDS MANAGEMENT is concerned with the creation, retention and scheduled destruction of an organization's paper and film DOCUMENTS. COMPUTER-generated REPORTS and DOCUMENTS fall into the RECORDS MANAGEMENT domain, but traditional DATA PROCESSING FILES do not.

reentrant code

PROGRAM LOGIC THAT CAN BE SHARED BY MULTIPLE USERS; A single copy of a PROGRAM or SUBROUTINE written in REENTRANT CODE can be shared by any number of USERS simultaneously. Essentially, the REENTRANT routine does not keep track of anything for any USER on the SYSTEM. The PROGRAM LOGIC in the REENTRANT PROGRAM does not set any internal switches or indicators. Each USER sharing the REENTRANT CODE requires a separate PROGRAM to keep track of where the USER is in the REENTRANT PROGRAM. It would be similar to each of several people baking their own cake from a single recipe hanging on a wall. Each person could keep track of where they are on the master recipe by jotting down the step number on their own sheet of paper. REENTRANT CODE is used to design MULTITHREADING operations.

register

HARDWARE COUNTERS AND BUFFERS IN THE PROCESSER THAT KEEP TRACK OF VARIOUS ACTIVITIES; For example: The INSTRUCTION REGISTER keeps track of which INSTRUCTION is being EXECUTED. If a PROGRAM CRASHES, the HARDWARE REGISTERS can be read out to help the PROGRAMMER DEBUG the PROGRAM. The REGISTERS would show the PROGRAMMER which INSTRUCTION and DATA were being worked on at the time of the CRASH.

relational data base

DATA BASE ORGANIZATION METHOD; RELATIONAL DATA BASE organizes DATA into ARRAYS of rows and columns (the rows are the RECORDS and the columns are the FIELDS). Physically, this is the same as the traditional FLAT FILE; however, there are specific rules for their creation which make up the RELATIONAL concept.

The objective of RELATIONAL DATA BASE, introduced in 1970 by Edgar Codd, was to make ad hoc requests for DATA more easily accommodated than with traditional HIERARCHICAL or NETWORK DATA BASE structures. One of the major features of RELATIONAL DATA BASE is the ability to generate a new FILE with DATA from two RELATIONAL FILES.

relative address

ADDRESS IN RELOCATABLE CODE; The RELATIVE ADDRESS is an ADDRESS which is relative to the first location of the PROGRAM itself. The RELATIVE ADDRESS is added to the BASE ADDRESS to derive the ABSOLUTE ADDRESS. See BASE/DISPLACEMENT METHOD.

relocatable code

MACHINE LANGUAGE PROGRAMS THAT CAN RESIDE IN ANY PORTION OF MEMORY; RELOCATABLE CODE are INSTRUCTIONS that are not fixed to any particular MEMORY ADDRESS.

remote batch

Same as REMOTE JOB ENTRY.

remote job entry

See RJE.

report

A COLLECTION OF FACTS AND FIGURES; A REPORT is a specifically designed layout of DATA and INFORMATION printed on paper or alternatively filmed on MICROFILM. A REPORT may contain any number of derived totals based on the DATA and INFORMATION contained in FILES and DATA BASES. Contrast with QUERY, which is a simple interrogation or listing of DATA/INFORMATION.

report generator

Same as REPORT WRITER.

report writer

A GENERALIZED PROGRAM TO CREATE AND PRINT OR DISPLAY REPORTS; A REPORT WRITER allows USERS to create REPORTS by describing the REPORT rather than PROGRAMMING the REPORT. REPORT WRITERS can be MENU DRIVEN, allowing first-time USERS to prepare customized REPORTS with minimal training. REPORT WRITERS may be stand-alone SOFTWARE PACKAGES which can ACCESS existing FILES or DATA BASES, or they may be part of a DATA BASE MANAGEMENT SYSTEM.

resistor

ELECTRONIC COMPONENT; RESISTORS resist the flow of current in an ELECTRONIC CIRCUIT.

response time

THE TIME IT TAKES FOR THE COMPUTER TO ANSWER A QUESTION OR ACCEPT A LINE OF INPUT.

restart

RESUMING COMPUTER OPERATION AFTER A PLANNED OR UNPLANNED TERMINATION; See CHECKPOINT/RESTART.

return key

KEYBOARD KEY WHICH ENDS A LINE; The RETURN KEY is used to end a line of INPUT or end a line or paragraph in WORD PROCESSING. See KEYBOARD.

reverse polish notation

METHOD FOR EXPRESSING CALCULATIONS; REVERSE POLISH NOTATION (RPN) is used in calculators and certain PROGRAMMING LANGUAGES (like FORTH). In RPN, the numbers precede the operation. For example: 2 + 2 would be expressed 2 2 + in RPN. 10 - 3 / 4 would be 10 3 - 4 /. REVERSE POLISH NOTATION uses the STACK method for manipulating numbers.

RF

RADIO **F**REQUENCY; RF refers to the range of FREQUENCIES (electromagnetic radiation) above the AUDIO range and below visible light. All broadcast transmission, as well as MICROWAVE, falls into this range, which is between 30,000 and 300,000,000,000 vibrations per second (30KHz-300GHz).

RGB monitor

HIGH-QUALITY COLOR VIDEO MONITOR; The RGB MONITOR generates a higher-quality color display than the standard COMPOSITE VIDEO color MONITOR. It requires a special RGB VIDEO signal from the COMPUTER, which generates separate red, green, and blue signals for the MONITOR.

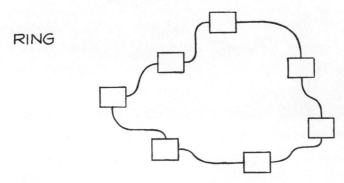

RING

ring network

COMMUNICATIONS NETWORK WHERE TERMINALS AND COMPUTERS ARE CONNECTED IN A CIRCULAR FASHION.

RJE

BATCH TRANSMISSION OF INFORMATION; RJE (**R**emote **J**ob **E**ntry) is the transmission of bulk INFORMATION from a remote TERMINAL or COMPUTER. The COMPUTER PROCESSES the TRANSACTIONS and often transmits the results back to the RJE site for printing. RJE HARDWARE at remote sites can employ TELEPRINTERS with DISK or TAPE storage, or complete MICRO or MINICOMPUTER SYSTEMS.

RO

TELEPRINTER WITHOUT KEYBOARD; Stands for **R**eceive **O**nly. RO TELEPRINTERS are used as remote PRINTERS. Contrast with KSR TELEPRINTERS.

robot

PROGRAMMABLE MULTI-FUNCTION DEVICE; ROBOTS are stand-alone HYBRID COMPUTER SYSTEMS which perform physical and computational activities. ROBOTS use ANALOG sensors for recognizing objects in the real world and DIGITAL COMPUTERS for their direction. ANALOG TO DIGITAL CONVERTERS convert temperature, motion, pressure, sound and images into BINARY CODE for the ROBOT'S COMPUTER. The OUTPUTS of the COMPUTERS direct the physical actions of the arms and joints by pulsing their motors.

ROBOTS can be designed similar to human form, although most industrial ROBOTS don't resemble people at all. They have one or more arms and joints designed for specific activities.

ROBOTS are used extensively in manufacturing; however, office and consumer APPLICATIONS are being developed. The advantage of a ROBOT is that it is a multiple-motion device, capable of performing many different tasks like a person can. ROBOTS are being integrated into the manufacturing process to perform many functions such as welding, riveting, scraping and painting.

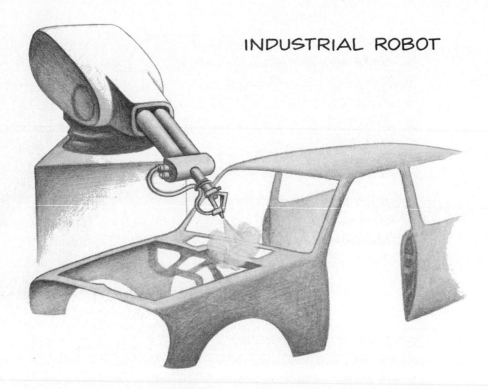

ROBOTS are also being designed with ARTIFICIAL INTELLIGENCE so they can respond more effectively to unstructured situations. For example: some specialized ROBOTS can identify objects in a pile, select the objects in the appropriate sequence and assemble them into a unit.

robotics

THE ART AND SCIENCE OF THE CREATION AND USE OF ROBOTS.

roll in/roll out

INPUT/OUTPUT; ROLL IN copies INSTRUCTIONS or INFORMATION into MEMORY, ROLL OUT copies INSTRUCTIONS or INFORMATION out of MEMORY.

ROM

PERMANENT MEMORY CHIP FOR PROGRAM STORAGE; INSTRUCTIONS and/or INFORMATION are stored in the ROM at the time of their manufacture and cannot be altered. ROM is FIRMWARE and stands for **R**ead **O**nly **M**emory. ROMs and PROMs are used in the plug-in MODULES for calculators, game COMPUTERS, and certain PERSONAL COMPUTERS. ROMs are often used to hold the OPERATING SYSTEM and/or PROGRAMMING LANGUAGE in small COMPUTERS.

RPG

REPORT **P**ROGRAM **G**ENERATOR; RPG, developed by IBM in 1964, was one of the first PROGRAM GENERATORS specifically designed for business REPORTS. RPG II, introduced in 1970, was an advanced version widely used to develop business APPLICATIONS for small COMPUTER SYSTEMS.

RPN

See **R**EVERSE **P**OLISH **N**OTATION.

RPQ

REQUEST FOR **P**RICE **Q**UOTATION; A document requesting a price for the HARDWARE or SOFTWARE that is outlined in the RPQ.

RSTS/E

OPERATING SYSTEM USED ON DEC PDP-11 SERIES OF MINICOMPUTERS.

RSX-11

OPERATING SYSTEM USED ON DEC PDP-11 AND VAX-11 SERIES MINICOMPUTERS.

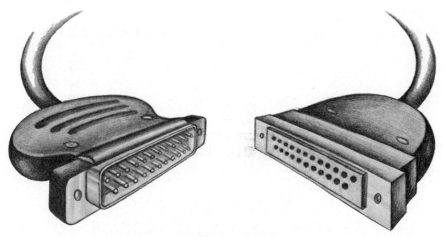

RS-232
PLUG AND SOCKET

RS-232

COMMUNICATIONS INTERFACE STANDARD; RS-232 is a widely used TERMINAL and MODEM INTERFACE.

RT-11
OPERATING SYSTEM USED ON DEC PDP-11 SERIES MINICOMPUTERS.

rubout key
TERMINAL CONTROL KEY; The RUBOUT KEY deletes the last CHARACTER that was entered on the KEYBOARD.

satellite

See COMMUNICATIONS SATELLITE.

SBS

SATELLITE COMMUNICATIONS SERVICE PROVIDED BY **S**ATELLITE **B**USINESS **S**YSTEMS; SBS customers use rooftop antennas to transmit and receive INFORMATION.

scatter read/gather write

INPUT/OUTPUT TECHNIQUE; SCATTER READ READS a BLOCK of DATA (from a PERIPHERAL storage device) and splits it into two or more separate areas in MEMORY. GATHER WRITE combines DATA from two or more areas in MEMORY and WRITES the gathered DATA as a BLOCK to a PERIPHERAL storage device.

schema

A MODEL OF THE DATA IN A DATA BASE; The SCHEMA is the definition of the entire DATA BASE. The SUBSCHEMA is an individual USER'S view (partial view) of the DATA BASE. See DATA BASE MANAGEMENT SYSTEM.

scientific applications

REAL-WORLD SIMULATION USING MATHEMATICS; SCIENTIFIC APPLICATIONS turn the real world into a number (mathematical MODEL) and then simulate the actions of the MODEL over time through the manipulation of these numbers by mathematical formulas. For example: An airplane can be described mathematically and its flight characteristics simulated in the COMPUTER. Rivers, lakes, and mountains can be simulated as well— virtually anything that has known characteristics. Laboratory experiments converted to COMPUTER MODELS can be INTERACTIVELY examined and evaluated by students without having to perform the actual experiments which might be too costly or impractical to do.

scientific computer

COMPUTER WHICH IS SPECIALIZED FOR NUMERICAL PROCESSING; SCIENTIFIC COMPUTERS imply fast mathematical capabilities. See ARRAY PROCESSOR and FLOATING POINT PROCESSOR.

scrambling

MAKING DATA UNDECIPHERABLE; See ENCRYPTION and DES.

screen

THE DISPLAY PORTION OF A VIDEO TERMINAL; The SCREEN is the CRT or display portion of a VIDEO TERMINAL. See FLAT SCREEN.

scrolling

BROWSING THROUGH INFORMATION AT A VIDEO TERMINAL; SCROLLING is the continuous movement of INFORMATION, either vertically or horizontally on a VIDEO SCREEN, as if the INFORMATION were on paper being rolled behind it.

SDLC

IBM COMMUNICATIONS PROTOCOL; SDLC is the primary PROTOCOL supported under SNA. Stands for **S**ynchronous **D**ata **L**ink **C**ontrol.

SE

See **S**YSTEMS **E**NGINEER.

search & replace

TEXT EDITING FUNCTION TO CHANGE TEXT; The SEARCH & REPLACE function is a common TEXT EDITING function in WORD PROCESSING. A STRING of TEXT is SEARCHED for and REPLACED with a different STRING of TEXT.

secondary storage

EXTERNAL STORAGE; SECONDARY STORAGE refers to DISKS and TAPES, in contrast with the COMPUTER'S internal storage (MEMORY).

sector

A SECTION OF A TRACK ON MAGNETIC DISK OR DRUM; A SECTOR is a subdivision of a TRACK and is usually the smallest unit of storage READ or WRITTEN by the DISK DRIVE at one time. See MAGNETIC DISK & TAPE.

security

PROTECTION OF INFORMATION AGAINST UNAUTHORIZED USE; PROGRAMS and DATA can be SECURED by issuing identification numbers and passwords to all authorized USERS of the SYSTEM. However, the SYSTEMS PROGRAMMER (or a technically competent individual familiar with and having access to the OPERATING SYSTEM) will ultimately have access to these CODES.

Passwords can be checked by the OPERATING SYSTEM, the DATA BASE MANAGEMENT SYSTEM, and other stand-alone APPLICATIONS running in the COMPUTER. INFORMATION transmitted over a COMMUNICATIONS CHANNEL can be SECURED by ENCRYPTION. While precautions can be taken to detect an unauthorized USER, it is extremely difficult to detect the authorized USER performing unauthorized tasks. Effective SECURITY measures are a proper balance of technology and management.

seek

LOCATING A TRACK ON A DISK; A SEEK is the movement of the ACCESS ARM to the requested TRACK on a DISK.

selector channel

HIGH-SPEED CHANNEL WHICH CONNECTS PERIPHERAL DEVICES LIKE DISKS AND TAPES TO THE COMPUTER.

semiconductor

SOLID STATE SUBSTANCE THAT CAN BE ELECTRICALLY ALTERED; Certain elements in nature, like SILICON, when combined chemically with other elements, can perform like SEMICONDUCTORS. A SEMICONDUCTOR is somewhere between a conductor (a material that conducts electricity) and an insulator (a material that resists the flow of electricity). When charged with electricity (or light), it changes its state from conductive to non-conductive, or from non-conductive to conductive. A SEMICONDUCTOR can act like an on/off switch which can be electrically activated (the TRANSISTOR).

sequential access method

ORGANIZATION OF INFORMATION IN A PRESCRIBED ASCENDING OR DESCENDING SEQUENCE; PROGRAMS and INFORMATION stored by this method must be searched for by READING and comparing all the preceding RECORDS to determine when the desired RECORD is found.

serial interface

SINGLE LINE CHANNEL CONNECTION; SERIAL INTERFACES connect single line
CHANNELS together. Most TERMINALS and PRINTERS use SERIAL INTERFACES,
such as the RS-232 standard.

serial printer

PRINTER THAT PRINTS A CHARACTER AT A TIME; See PRINTER.

serial transmission

TRANSMISSION OVER A SINGLE LINE CHANNEL; Most COMMUNICATIONS
NETWORKS employ SERIAL TRANSMISSION between TERMINALS and COMPUTERS.
In SERIAL TRANSMISSION, one BIT follows the other over a single line pathway, such
as a telephone line or COAXIAL CABLE.

service bureau

COMPUTER SERVICES ORGANIZATION; SERVICE BUREAUS offer TIME-SHARING
(HARDWARE) and SOFTWARE services for USERS. Connection is made from
TERMINALS in the USER'S premises by dialing-up an AUTO ANSWER COMPUTER in
the SERVICE BUREAU. USERS LOG-ON to the TIME-SHARING SYSTEM and then can
ACCESS their PROGRAMS and INFORMATION.

SERVICE BUREAUS can offer a wide variety of SOFTWARE PACKAGES as well as
customized PROGRAMMING for their customers. Customers pay for their
PROCESSING, which is calculated from their direct usage of the COMPUTER.
SERVICE BUREAUS also charge a monthly rental for each BYTE of ON-LINE storage
their customers use for their PROGRAMS and DATA.

In addition, SERVICE BUREAUS can offer or specialize in BATCH PROCESSING
services, such as DATA ENTRY or COM PROCESSING.

shadow batch

SIMULATED TRANSACTION PROCESSING; A SHADOW BATCH SYSTEM allows
USERS to interrogate the up-to-date status of a FILE even though it has not been
physically UPDATED by the latest TRANSACTIONS. The MASTER FILE (or DATA
BASE) used is from a previous UPDATE cycle. Any TRANSACTIONS which have come
in (or are coming in) are stored in a FILE on the same COMPUTER SYSTEM.
Subsequent QUERIES interrogate both the MASTER FILE and the TRANSACTION
FILE. Any TRANSACTIONS that are present are PROCESSED in MEMORY to generate
the current status. The USER sees the up-to-date status and makes decisions accordingly.
At the end of the day or period, the TRANSACTIONS are physically BATCH
PROCESSED against the MASTER FILE.

shared logic

THE USE OF A SINGLE COMPUTER BY MULTIPLE USERS CONCURRENTLY; Several USERS at separate TERMINALS share a single CPU for their PROCESSING. SHARED LOGIC implies MULTIPROGRAMMING. See SHARED RESOURCE.

shared resource

COMPUTER RESOURCES SHARED BY SEVERAL USERS; With SHARED RESOURCE SYSTEMS, USERS have their own PROCESSING capability locally and ACCESS DISKS and PRINTERS remotely. WORD PROCESSING SYSTEMS are often SHARED RESOURCE SYSTEMS, whereby the WORD PROCESSING is performed in each USER'S WORKSTATION, and DOCUMENT FILES are transferred between the USER'S COMPUTER and another stand-alone COMPUTER managing the DISKS. OFFICE AUTOMATION NETWORKS may employ a SHARED RESOURCE architecture.

sheet feeder

MECHANICAL DEVICE WHICH FEEDS SINGLE SHEETS OF PAPER INTO A PRINTER.

sign on/sign off

Same as LOG-ON/LOG-OFF.

signal processing

See DIGITAL SIGNAL PROCESSING.

silicon

BASIC MATERIAL FOR FABRICATING MICROELECTRONIC CHIPS; Next to oxygen, SILICON is the most abundant element in nature. It is found in an unpure state in the majority of rocks and sand on the earth. Pure SILICON is obtained through a chemical process at high temperatures. SILICON, in its molten state, is DOPED with other chemicals to alter its electrical nature. SILICON is the primary material used for the fabrication of CHIPS. Its atomic structure and its abundance make it an ideal SEMICONDUCTOR material.

CPU

FILE SERVER

PRINT SERVER

BUS

SHARED RESOURCE

silicon valley

AREA IN CALIFORNIA; SILICON VALLEY is an area south of San Francisco noted for its large numbers of SEMICONDUCTOR and COMPUTER firms.

simplex

ONE-WAY TRANSMISSION.

simulation

(1) EMULATION, (2) SCIENTIFIC MODELING; (1) SIMULATION is performed by a SOFTWARE PROGRAM that translates the MACHINE LANGUAGE of a foreign PROGRAM into the MACHINE LANGUAGE of the COMPUTER being used. See EMULATION. (2) SIMULATION is also a scientific technique for mathematically dealing with the real world. See SCIENTIFIC APPLICATIONS.

single board computer

PROCESSOR AND MEMORY ON A SINGLE PRINTED CIRCUIT BOARD.

single density disk

LOW-CAPACITY FLOPPY DISK.

single sided disk

DISK WHICH IS RECORDED ON ONE SIDE ONLY.

slave

A TERMINAL OR COMPUTER THAT IS CONTROLLED BY ANOTHER COMPUTER; A PRINTER might be located in a remote location and is activated by the central COMPUTER when REPORTS are ready to be printed.

SLSI

SUPER LARGE SCALE INTEGRATION; SLSI refers to ultra-high density CHIPS which contain 1 million or more TRANSISTORS.

Smalltalk

USER-ORIENTED PROGRAMMING ENVIRONMENT; SMALLTALK, developed by Xerox's Palo Alto Research Center, is an integrated OPERATING SYSTEM and PROGRAMMING LANGUAGE. In use, SMALLTALK'S operating environment becomes tailored to individual USER requirements. As an integrated environment, SMALLTALK eliminates the distinction between PROGRAMMING LANGUAGE and OPERATING SYSTEM.

smart card

CREDIT CARD WITH A BUILT-IN COMPUTER; SMART CARDS can be used as identification cards or as financial TRANSACTION cards. The SMART CARD contains a MICROPROCESSOR and MEMORY which, when inserted into a specialized READER, can exchange financial and/or identification DATA about the card holder with a COMPUTER SYSTEM. The SMART CARD is more secure than a MAGNETIC CARD (magnetic strip on the back of a credit card), since it cannot be tampered with. The COMPUTER inside the SMART CARD may be PROGRAMMED to self-destruct if the wrong password is entered too many times. As a financial TRANSACTION card, the SMART CARD can permanently store many TRANSACTIONS and actually maintain a bank balance inside the card.

smart terminal

VIDEO TERMINAL WITH FORMATTING CAPABILITIES; SMART TERMINALS offer a wide variety of features, such as the ability to blink or highlight specific CHARACTERS on the SCREEN and generate reverse VIDEO (dark images on light background), etc. These capabilities allow designers to create a more effective visual image for the USER at the TERMINAL. SMART TERMINALS often contain built-in FUNCTION KEYS and EDITING capabilities which allow for insertion and deletion of CHARACTERS on the SCREEN. They may also feature multiple COMMUNICATIONS PROTOCOLS enabling them to connect to various NETWORKS. SMART TERMINAL sometimes refers to INTELLIGENT TERMINAL. See DUMB TERMINAL and INTELLIGENT TERMINAL.

SMIS

SOCIETY FOR **M**ANAGEMENT **I**NFORMATION **S**YSTEMS; Founded in 1968, the SMIS is an organization of MIS professionals. SMIS members can use the society as an exchange or market-place for technical information. SMIS offers educational and research programs, competitions and awards to their members.

SNA

IBM NETWORK ARCHITECURE; Stands for **S**ystems **N**etwork **A**rchitecture.

SNOBOL

PROGRAMMING LANGUAGE DESIGNED FOR STRING PROCESSING; SNOBOL
was developed by Bell Labs in the early 1960s as a specialized PROGRAMMING
LANGUAGE for the manipulation of large STRINGS. SNOBOL is used in COMPILER
and TEXT EDITOR creation. SNOBOL stands for **S**tri**N**g **O**riented sym**BO**lic **L**anguage.

soft

FLEXIBLE; SOFT, as in SOFTWARE, implies flexibility. The basic concept of a
COMPUTER is its flexibility. It is a general purpose machine made specific by following
INSTRUCTIONS in a SOFTWARE PROGRAM. Contrast with HARDWIRED.

soft copy

INFORMATION IN AUDIO OR VIDEO FORMAT; Contrast with HARD COPY.

soft key

Same as FUNCTION KEY.

soft sectored

SECTOR IDENTIFICATION TECHNIQUE; SOFT SECTORED SECTORS are identified
by numbers WRITTEN on the TRACK itself rather than by fixed location markers. See
HARD SECTORED and MAGNETIC DISK & TAPE.

software

COMPUTER INSTRUCTIONS; Groups of SOFTWARE INSTRUCTIONS make up
SOFTWARE PROGRAMS. There are two major categories of SOFTWARE: (1) SYSTEM
SOFTWARE is control SOFTWARE which performs common functions for all USERS of
the COMPUTER (such as the OPERATING SYSTEM or the DATA BASE MANAGEMENT
SYSTEM) and, (2) APPLICATION SOFTWARE is specific SOFTWARE for particular
USER APPLICATIONS of the COMPUTER (such as payroll, finished goods inventory
and purchasing). See PROGRAM and COMPUTER.

software engineering

SOFTWARE DEVELOPMENT TECHNIQUES AND MANAGEMENT; SOFTWARE
ENGINEERING is the term used to refer to the design and DOCUMENTATION
techniques used throughout the entire SYSTEM DEVELOPMENT CYCLE. See
STRUCTURED PROGRAMMING.

software house

ORGANIZATION WHICH DEVELOPS AND MARKETS SOFTWARE PACKAGES;
Constrast with SYSTEMS HOUSE, which develops customized SOFTWARE for USERS,
as well as TURNKEY SYSTEMS.

software interfaces

See STANDARDS & COMPATIBILITY.

software package

A PROGRAM OR SERIES OF PROGRAMS ALREADY PACKAGED AS A PRODUCT
FOR SALE; SOFTWARE PACKAGES usually come in MACHINE LANGUAGE form,
along with a set of USER DOCUMENTATION which describes their operation.
Sometimes the PROGRAMMING LANGUAGE (SOURCE CODE) is also available so the
USER can make custom modifications to the PROGRAMS. SOFTWARE PACKAGES
written to run under an INTERPRETER, such as BASIC, will always be in SOURCE
LANGUAGE.

software programmer

Same as SYSTEMS PROGRAMMER.

software protection

RESISTANCE TO UNAUTHORIZED COPYING OF SOFTWARE; SOFTWARE
PROTECTION in the MAINFRAME and MINICOMPUTER environment has typically
been an honor system. Since vendor support is usually vital in these environments, there
is often little advantage in obtaining a free copy of SOFTWARE.

The PERSONAL COMPUTER environment is another story. SOFTWARE PROTECTION
is implemented in many PERSONAL COMPUTER products in the following manner: The
copy PROGRAM included with the vendor's OPERATING SYSTEM tests for a special
CODE in a PROGRAM FILE. If the CODE is present, it will not copy the PROGRAM.
However, for every protection CODE created, there is another PROGRAM created to
break the CODE and copy it. SOFTWARE PROTECTION is an important issue in the
home COMPUTER field.

As the PERSONAL COMPUTER market increases, SOFTWARE developers will have a
wider market for their products. Eventually, SOFTWARE may be sold for the price of the
DOCUMENTATION manual. While one BINARY copy of a PROGRAM is as good as any
other, everyone likes a nice clean copy of the DOCUMENTATION.

software publishing

PUBLISHING OF SOFTWARE PACKAGES; Just like book publishing, SOFTWARE PUBLISHERS must discover SOFTWARE that has been written (or contract for the development of new SOFTWARE), analyze its potential viability in the marketplace, develop the DOCUMENTATION for it, and handle the marketing and distribution of the product.

solid state

ELECTRONIC CIRCUITS MADE OF SOLID MATERIALS; CHIPS and BUBBLE MEMORIES are examples of SOLID STATE devices, since electrical and/or magnetic actions take place within the SEMICONDUCTOR and THIN FILM materials. The first SOLID STATE device was the "cat's whisker" of the 1930s, in which a whisker-like wire was moved around on a solid crystal in order to detect a radio signal. SOLID STATE devices for storage of INFORMATION are much faster (and more reliable) than their mechanical DISK and TAPE counterparts. Once INFORMATION is transferred into ELECTRONIC MEMORY, it is PROCESSED at very high speeds. If all INFORMATION were stored in some SOLID STATE form, it could be ACCESSED quickly. However, there is a wide difference in cost between ELECTRONIC MEMORIES (CHIPS, BUBBLE MEMORY) and DISKS and TAPES. Even though SOLID STATE costs continually drop, DISKS and TAPES (and eventually OPTICAL DISKS) continue to improve, as well. It appears there will always be a hierarchy of storage environments, ranging from the very slow MASS STORAGE devices to the fastest SOLID STATE devices.

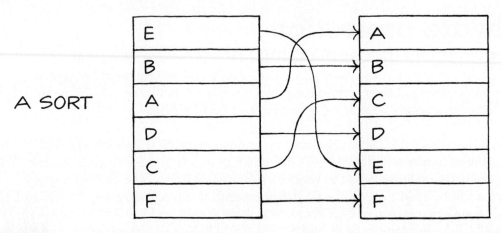

A SORT

sort

REARRANGE INFORMATION INTO A DIFFERENT ORDER; A SORT PROGRAM is a UTILITY PROGRAM that rearranges INFORMATION into a different alphanumeric sequence. SORTING creates a resequenced copy of the original FILE. A SORT can usually be performed on a number of FIELDS in a RECORD at the same time. For example: customer name within department, within region. Customer name, department and region are the SORT FIELDS or SORT KEYS. SORT PROGRAMS may have elaborate selection capabilities, which can be used to extract only certain RECORDS from the FILE for SORTING.

sort keys

FIELDS IN THE RECORD WHICH DICTATE THE SEQUENCE OF THE SORT.

SOS

(1) OPERATING SYSTEM USED ON THE APPLE III, (2) SEMICONDUCTOR FABRICATION TECHNIQUE; (1) SOS stands for **S**ophisticated **O**perating **S**ystem. (2) SOS stands for **S**ilicon **O**n **S**apphire, a technique which incorporates both SILICON and sapphire in a SEMICONDUCTOR CHIP.

source code

INSTRUCTIONS IN THE ORIGINAL PROGRAMMING LANGUAGE; The SOURCE CODE is the set of INSTRUCTIONS written by the PROGRAMMER. The SOURCE CODE is translated into a particular COMPUTER'S MACHINE LANGUAGE by SOFTWARE PROGRAMS called ASSEMBLERS, COMPILERS or INTERPRETERS. The COMPUTER does not EXECUTE (run) SOURCE CODE; it only EXECUTES MACHINE LANGUAGE. In order to make a change in a PROGRAM, the change must be made in the SOURCE CODE, and the PROGRAM is ASSEMBLED or COMPILED again.

source data capture

CAPTURING INFORMATION WHEN IT IS FIRST AVAILABLE; It is more economical to capture the INFORMATION when it originates than afterward. See POINT OF SALE.

source document

THE FORM UPON WHICH THE ORIGINAL TRANSACTION WAS CAPTURED; Order forms, credit card slips, applications, etc., are all forms of SOURCE DOCUMENTS.

source language

Same as SOURCE CODE.

space/time

TERMS USED FOR MEASURING STORAGE CAPACITIES & SPEEDS:

S P A C E = BYTES (or BITS):	T I M E = Fraction of 1 Second:
KILOBYTE (KB) 1,000 (or 1,024)	MILLISECOND (MS) 1/1,000th
MEGABYTE (MB) 1,000,000	MICROSECOND (μS) 1/1,000,000th
GIGABYTE (GB) 1,000,000,000	NANOSECOND (NS) 1/1,000,000,000th
TERABYTE (TB) 1,000,000,000,000	PICOSECOND (PS) 1/1,000,000,000,000th

Storage capacities are usually measured as follows:

DISK, TAPE, MEMORY	BYTES
RAM, FIRMWARE CHIPS	BITS

Transmission speeds are usually measured as follows:

DISK ACCESS TIME	MILLISECONDS
MEMORY ACCESS TIME	MICROSECONDS/NANOSECONDS
MACHINE CYCLE	MICROSECONDS/NANOSECONDS
INSTRUCTION EXECUTION	MICROSECONDS/NANOSECONDS
TRANSISTOR switching	NANOSECONDS/PICOSECONDS

spatial data management

TECHNIQUE ALLOWING USERS ACCESS TO INFORMATION BY POINTING AT
PICTURES; SPATIAL DATA MANAGEMENT simplifies the ACCESSING of DATA
BASES by eliminating the need for typing long requests, or remembering special
CODES or COMMANDS. USERS make direct contact with picture symbols on the
SCREEN that represent DATA BASES or DOCUMENT FILES, or any category of
INFORMATION. The use of LIGHT PENS, JOY STICKS or TOUCH-SENSITIVE
SCREENS are features of the TERMINAL. The USER can directly touch or quickly move
the CURSOR on the SCREEN to the picture of the INFORMATION desired. Special
FUNCTION KEYS that "zoom in" or "display contents" may also be used.

speech synthesis

SYNTHETIC SPEECH; SPEECH SYNTHESIS is the arranging of CODED speech
components into real words and sentences. SPEECH SYNTHESIS methods are used to
construct a random sentence. Straight human voice which is DIGITIZED into words
sounds flat when strung together, and DIGITIZED human voice also requires large
amounts of storage space. SPEECH SYNTHESIS constructs words from PHONEMES
(speech utterances like /k, ch, sh/, etc.). If the COMPUTER can analyze the emphasis of
the message it is composing, then inflection can be added to the spoken synthetic
message. Many varieties of SPEECH SYNTHESIS still sound like machine voice. In time,
the desktop MAINFRAME ought to allow for realistic machine voice responses.

split screen

SPLIT VIDEO SCREEN; SPLIT SCREENS are VIDEO DISPLAY SCREENS that can be
partitioned into two or more areas (called WINDOWS) so that different SCREEN
FORMATS can be viewed by the USER at the same time. For example, the USER could
match DATA from one DATA BASE with DATA from another without having to print one
set and then switch to the other.

spooling

TEMPORARY STORAGE OF BATCH INPUT AND OUTPUT; SPOOLING SOFTWARE stores TRANSACTIONS transmitted from a REMOTE JOB ENTRY TERMINAL on a DISK for eventual PROCESSING by the COMPUTER. PRINTER OUTPUT from a REPORT PROGRAM is stored on a DISK for eventual local printing or transmission back to the RJE SYSTEM. With SPOOLING, several REPORT PROGRAMS can be PROCESSED simultaneously, since the OUTPUT of the PROGRAMS is diverted to DISK. SPOOLING is also used to refer to printing one FILE while EDITING another. Stands for **S**imultaneous **P**eripheral **O**perations **O**n **L**ine.

spreadsheet (simulator)

See ELECTRONIC SPREADSHEET.

SSI

SMALL **S**CALE INTEGRATION; SSI refers to CHIPS fabricated with small numbers of ELECTRONIC components. SSI ranges approximately from 2 to 100 TRANSISTORS on a CHIP.

stack

RESERVED AREA FOR INTERNAL OPERATIONS; A STACK may be used for calculations or for INSTRUCTION EXECUTION. A STACK may be implemented in specially-designed HARDWARE or in MEMORY (controlled by SOFTWARE). STACKS usually work on a last-in-first-out sequence. The last item PUSHED onto the STACK is the first item POPPED from the STACK.

STAIRS

TEXT DOCUMENT MANAGEMENT SYSTEM; STAIRS allows for the creation and interrogation of TEXT DOCUMENT DATA BASES. USERS can retrieve DOCUMENTS based on key words in the TEXT. STAIRS runs on IBM COMPUTERS and stands for **ST**orage **A**nd **I**nformation **R**etrieval **S**ystem.

standards & compatibility

DESIGN OF BASIC HARDWARE/SOFTWARE CODES AND INTERFACES AND THEIR INDUSTRY ADOPTION; STANDARDS provide a framework within which all HARDWARE and SOFTWARE is designed and implemented. Every COMPUTER SYSTEM has STANDARDS; *no* STANDARDS is a misnomer— there's just no **one single** STANDARD adopted by all vendors. When you purchase a COMPUTER SYSTEM, whether it's a VIDEO game COMPUTER or one to run your entire business, the STANDARDS implemented in your COMPUTER will determine the amount of flexibility you will have now and in the future. They will determine how much SOFTWARE will run on your machine and how easy it will be to convert your INFORMATION SYSTEMS to more advanced COMPUTER SYSTEMS later on. Following are the major categories for which STANDARDS exist:

DATA CODES

This is the simplest STANDARD. The DATA CODE is the basic internal DIGITAL CODE (BINARY CODE) which represents a CHARACTER of DATA (and TEXT). The DATA CODE is designed into the COMPUTER and into all the PERIPHERAL devices associated with it. The most widely used CODES are EBCDIC and ASCII. All MICROCOMPUTERS and practically all MINICOMPUTERS are ASCII machines. MAINFRAMES are generally EBCDIC, although some are ASCII and others use their own proprietary CODE.

DATA CONVERSION between EBCDIC and ASCII is a relatively simple SOFTWARE problem, and any desktop ASCII machine can usually manipulate DATA created in an EBCDIC machine.

STORAGE MEDIA

There are several varieties of storage media STANDARDS. The visible STANDARDS are relatively easy to identify. There are several varieties of DISK PACKS, DISK CARTRIDGES, FLOPPY DISKS, reel-to-reel TAPES, TAPE CARTRIDGES and CASSETTES. The visible STANDARDS only ensure the storage medium can be inserted into a particular PERIPHERAL unit. Invisible HARDWARE STANDARDS, determined by the recording characteristics (number of TRACKS, SECTORS, BITS per inch) and invisible SOFTWARE STANDARDS (the physical FORMAT of the RECORDS and INDEXES created by the OPERATING SYSTEM), have established hundreds of storage media STANDARDS.

FLOPPY DISKS used in MICROCOMPUTERS have several dozen HARDWARE STANDARDS, with new ones coming on the market regularly. That means two MICROCOMPUTERS using the same COMPUTER CHIP and the same OPERATING SYSTEM, sitting side by side, often cannot exchange DISKS. FILES are transferred by COMMUNICATIONS in this case, rather than by physically moving the FLOPPY DISKS.

A reasonably common and transportable medium is half-inch MAGNETIC TAPE. There are only a handful of STANDARDS. As a result, a MAGNETIC TAPE DRIVE is generally available for most MAINFRAMES and MINICOMPUTERS (and occasionally MICROCOMPUTERS) which will support a common STANDARD.

MACHINE LANGUAGES

The MACHINE LANGUAGE is the COMPUTER'S NATIVE LANGUAGE designed into the ELECTRONIC CIRCUITS of the PROCESSOR. The MACHINE LANGUAGE defines the INSTRUCTIONS the COMPUTER will EXECUTE. For example: The APPLE II PERSONAL COMPUTER is really a 6502 COMPUTER. Its MICROPROCESSOR is the 6502 and that's all the APPLE II really understands. The BASIC PROGRAMMING LANGUAGE built into the APPLE II (in ROM) turns what you enter into 6502 MACHINE LANGUAGE.

This is the ground-level reason why there is such a lack of COMPATIBILITY in this industry. While there are only a handful of DATA CODES, there are countless numbers of MACHINE LANGUAGES. Many vendors have several families of COMPUTERS, each with different MACHINE LANGUAGES. For example: Although the IBM 370, 3000 and 4000 series COMPUTERS use the same MACHINE LANGUAGE as the older 360 series, the IBM Series 1, System/38 and 8100 series are each different.

PROGRAMS in MACHINE LANGUAGE form will only EXECUTE in a COMPUTER which EXECUTES that exact same MACHINE LANGUAGE. In order to run in a different machine, the PROGRAM must be translated into a different MACHINE LANGUAGE. This may or may not be possible, depending on the type and version of the original PROGRAMMING LANGUAGE.

COMPATIBILITY is achieved at the MACHINE LANGUAGE level in the IBM and MICROCOMPUTER worlds. IBM has spawned imitators who design PLUG COMPATIBLE COMPUTERS which run the exact same MACHINE LANGUAGE. Since the HARDWARE is PLUG COMPATIBLE, all existing SOFTWARE is also PLUG COMPATIBLE. MICROCOMPUTER vendors, for the most part, never designed their own COMPUTER PROCESSOR in the first place. They achieve COMPATIBILITY by selecting a popular CHIP developed by SEMICONDUCTOR companies like Intel, Motorola and Zilog. MICROPROCESSORS like the Z80, 6502, 8086, 8088 and 68000 are used in many different vendors' MICROCOMPUTERS. Some vendors build two or more of the popular CHIPS into the same COMPUTER so that more SOFTWARE options are open to the USER.

The second method for achieving COMPATIBILITY at the MACHINE LANGUAGE level is with an EMULATOR. This is CIRCUITRY which emulates the MACHINE LANGUAGE EXECUTION of another COMPUTER. This method has been primarily used in earlier MAINFRAME conversions. For example, the IBM 360 had a 1401 EMULATOR in it so customers could run their old PROGRAMS in the new machine.

PROGRAMMING LANGUAGES

There are only a dozen or so PROGRAMMING LANGUAGES which have become widely used. FORTRAN, COBOL, BASIC, PL/I, APL, ALGOL, RPG II and LISP are the traditional ones. Languages like PASCAL, C, ADA, FORTH and LOGO are also gaining popularity. The COMPATIBILITY problem lies with the fact that many HARDWARE and SOFTWARE companies implement their own (slightly different) versions of each language. This creates hundreds of dialects, each one able to run on only a limited number of COMPUTERS. COMPATIBILITY is achieved at the PROGRAMMING LANGUAGE level with languages designed for transportability. ANSI COMPATIBLE languages and the UCSD P-SYSTEM are examples of PROGRAMMING LANGUAGES which are transportable to many different COMPUTERS with different MACHINE LANGUAGES.

If PROGRAMS were written in a PROGRAMMING LANGUAGE which was not inherently transportable, they still may be converted into a different dialect. There is no rule of thumb; it may be relatively easy or extremely difficult. Sometimes, SOFTWARE

PROGRAMS can be designed to convert the PROGRAMS automatically. The translation of PROGRAMS into an entirely different SOURCE LANGUAGE is much more difficult than the translation of dialects. Often, it is more economical to rewrite the PROGRAMS from scratch.

HARDWARE INTERFACES

HARDWARE INTERFACES are the physical cables and plugs which provide the connections between HARDWARE components. The HARDWARE INTERFACE specifies the design of the plug, its size, number of wires, etc., and the electrical signals which are transferred over them. There are many STANDARD and proprietary HARDWARE INTERFACES employed by vendors. The design of PLUG COMPATIBLE devices, like DISKS and TAPES, must incorporate these STANDARDS. For COMMUNICATIONS COMPATIBILITY, STANDARDS like the RS-232 are widely used. This type of STANDARD allows for the intermixing of many different vendors' products, like MODEMS, TERMINALS and PRINTERS. Although, HARDWARE INTERFACES generally fall into the domain of the technician, many a USER has plugged an RS-232 cable into the back of their COMPUTER.

SOFTWARE INTERFACES

SYSTEM SOFTWARE is a category of generalized PROGRAMS which act as control PROGRAMS and run in the COMPUTER along with the USER PROGRAMS (APPLICATION PROGRAMS). The major SYSTEM SOFTWARE PROGRAM is the OPERATING SYSTEM, which is the MASTER CONTROL PROGRAM. DATA BASE MANAGEMENT SYSTEMS and COMMUNICATIONS PROGRAMS are also examples. SYSTEM SOFTWARE and USERS' PROGRAMS communicate with each other in the COMPUTER by exchanging messages back and forth. In essence, they "talk" to each other in the COMPUTER'S MEMORY. The messages they exchange make up SOFTWARE INTERFACE STANDARDS. These messages are precisely defined, and all PROGRAMMING LANGUAGES must generate APPLICATION PROGRAMS that "talk" to a particular OPERATING SYSTEM, as well as perhaps a DATA BASE MANAGEMENT SYSTEM.

If it becomes necessary to change vendors, the new COMPUTER may not run the same SYSTEM SOFTWARE as the old COMPUTER. Therefore, even if the APPLICATION PROGRAMS can be transported to the new SYSTEM, they may still require changes. When hundreds of PROGRAMS are involved, this becomes a major operation.

The same problem can occur within the same vendor. If new INFORMATION SYSTEMS or new COMPUTER SYSTEMS require a more advanced operating environment, conversion to a new OPERATING SYSTEM or DATA BASE MANAGEMENT SYSTEM may be required. All the existing PROGRAMS may have to be changed if the new SYSTEM SOFTWARE is not COMPATIBLE with the old PROGRAMS. This may mean the modification of older PROGRAMS just because new PROGRAMS or new COMPUTERS are required. This is often one of the reasons for delaying the development of new INFORMATION SYSTEMS in older COMPUTER SYSTEMS, or for the delay of new COMPUTER SYSTEMS.

SOFTWARE STANDARDS are often the reason for being "locked in" to a particular vendor's HARDWARE series or particular model.

COMMUNICATIONS PROTOCOLS

COMMUNICATIONS PROTOCOLS are the transmission STANDARDS between COMPUTERS and TERMINALS in remote locations. The PROTOCOL defines both the HARDWARE and the SOFTWARE. COMMUNICATIONS between two COMPUTERS of like vintage is relatively straight forward. COMMUNICATIONS between different COMPUTERS may require PROTOCOL conversion. PROTOCOL conversion can be performed by SOFTWARE, BLACK BOXES, DIGITAL PABXs, or via interconnection with VALUE ADDED COMMUNICATION NETWORKS.

ASYNCHRONOUS COMMUNICATIONS, employed in DUMB TERMINALS (called ASCII or TELETYPE PROTOCOLS), provide a common COMMUNICATIONS denominator between almost all COMPUTERS and TERMINALS. These are widely used for connecting TERMINALS to TIME-SHARING services, as well as for the transfer of FILES between PERSONAL COMPUTERS. Connection to a large in-house MAINFRAME or to various COMMUNICATIONS NETWORKS may require a special PROTOCOL in the USER'S TERMINAL or COMPUTER.

COMMUNICATIONS between many different vendors' products in a large organization is a complex task. LOCAL AREA NETWORK planning is the backbone behind a flexible OFFICE AUTOMATION environment for the future.

The International Standards Organization (ISO) has developed a STANDARD for the interconnection of COMPUTERS called the OPEN SYSTEMS INTERCONNECTION (OSI). The ISO/OSI has a defined STANDARD for each layer of COMMUNICATIONS PROTOCOL required to exchange DATA between COMPUTER devices.

STANDARDS ORGANIZATIONS

The primary STANDARDS organizations which are responsible for the adoption of COMPUTER and COMMUNICATIONS STANDARDS are:

ANSI— **A**merican **N**ational **S**tandards **I**nstitute.

CCITT— **C**onsultative **C**ommittee for International **T**elephony & **T**elegraphy.

EIA— **E**lectronic **I**ndustries **A**ssociation (U.S.).

IEEE— Institute of **E**lectrical and **E**lectronics **E**ngineers (U.S.).

ISO— International **S**tandards **O**rganization.

NBS— **N**ational **B**ureau of **S**tandards (U.S.).

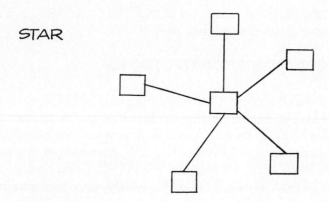

STAR

star network

CENTRAL COMPUTER NETWORK; A STAR NETWORK implies a central COMPUTER
with all TERMINALS and COMPUTERS connected directly to it. The central
COMPUTER acts as the NETWORK controller. A PABX is a STAR NETWORK SYSTEM.

start/stop transmission

See ASYNCHRONOUS COMMUNICATIONS.

static RAM

CATEGORY OF ELECTRONIC MEMORY; STATIC RAMs are MEMORY CHIPS which
require power in order to hold their content. However, unlike DYNAMIC RAMs, they do
not require continuous regeneration of the content. The BINARY content of the storage
cell is maintained by a regular power source. STATIC RAMS are often constructed of
ELECTRONIC components, called FLIP-FLOPS.

statistical multiplexor

COMMUNICATIONS HARDWARE DEVICE; STATISTICAL MULTIPLEXORS combine
several low-speed COMMUNICATIONS CHANNELS into a single high-speed
CHANNEL, and vice versa. A STAT MUX is a COMPUTER which can manage more
COMMUNICATIONS traffic than a standard MULTIPLEXOR by analyzing the traffic and
choosing different transmission patterns.

stat mux

ABBREVIATION FOR **STAT**ISTICAL **MU**LTIPLE**X**OR.

storage media

See STANDARDS & COMPATIBILITY.

store & forward

STORAGE AND SUBSEQUENT TRANSMISSION; STORE & FORWARD refers to the temporary storage of a MESSAGE in a COMPUTER SYSTEM for transmission to its destination at a later time. STORE & FORWARD techniques allow for routing over NETWORKS which are not accessible at all times. MESSAGES headed for different time zones can be STORED & FORWARDED when daytime has arrived at the destination location.

stored program concept

THE EXECUTION OF A PROGRAM IN THE COMPUTER'S INTERNAL MEMORY; See COMPUTER.

streaming tape

CATEGORY OF HIGH-SPEED MAGNETIC TAPE DRIVE; STREAMING TAPES are primarily used as BACKUP devices for DISKS. The STREAMING TAPE DRIVE allows for high-speed copying from the DISK onto TAPE.

stream-oriented file

FILE CONTAINING UNSTRUCTURED DATA; TEXT DOCUMENTS and DIGITAL voice are examples of STREAM-ORIENTED FILES. Contrast with DATA FILE, which implies a fixed (or reasonably rigid) set of structures (FIXED-LENGTH FIELDS within RECORDS, for example).

string

ALPHANUMERIC DATA OR TEXT; A STRING can be a FIELD containing ALPHANUMERIC DATA, or any contiguous set of CHARACTERS that will be treated as a unit. Contrast with numeric DATA. PROGRAMMING LANGUAGES will not allow calculations to be performed upon STRINGS even if numerical DATA is stored in them. In order to be used in calculations, the numbers within the STRING have to be transferred into a FIELD (or VARIABLE) defined as numeric only.

stringy floppy

PERIPHERAL STORAGE DEVICE FOR MICROCOMPUTERS; A STRINGY FLOPPY uses a removable MAGNETIC TAPE CARTRIDGE, called a WAFER. The WAFER is a 1/16" wide, continuous loop of MAGNETIC TAPE. STRINGY FLOPPY is a product of Exatron, Inc.

stroke writer

ANOTHER TERM FOR A VECTOR GRAPHICS TERMINAL.

structured programming

PROGRAM DESIGN AND DOCUMENTATION TECHNIQUES THAT IMPOSE A
UNIFORM STRUCTURE ON ALL PROGRAMS; PROGRAMMING LANGUAGES
themselves impose certain structure by the nature of their design. PASCAL is noted for
its structured approach, whereas languages like ASSEMBLY and BASIC impose very
little structure, and without careful and explicit DOCUMENTATION by the
PROGRAMMER, can be extremely difficult to understand by another PROGRAMMER.

STRUCTURED PROGRAMMING techniques impose their own logic onto the
PROGRAM design so that PROGRAMS can be more readily maintained. They also
require more preparation in the beginning and cannot be developed "on-the-fly."
STRUCTURED PROGRAMMING techniques can be applied from the very beginning of
an INFORMATION SYSTEMS project, from the SYSTEMS ANALYSIS phase, all the way
through to the TESTING and IMPLEMENTATION phases.

stylus

PEN-SHAPED INSTRUMENT USED IN INPUT DEVICES; The STYLUS may be light-
sensitive or may generate some sort of electrical or magnetic field. See DIGITIZER
TABLET and LIGHT PEN.

subroutine

A GROUP OF INSTRUCTIONS IN A PROGRAM THAT PERFORM A SPECIFIC
FUNCTION. Same as PROGRAM MODULE.

subschema

USER'S PARTIAL VIEW OF THE DATA BASE; See DATA BASE MANAGEMENT
SYSTEM.

subscript

(1) LOCATION OF CHARACTERS SLIGHTLY BELOW THE CURRENT LINE, (2)
PROGRAMMING NOTATION FOR LOCATING DATA IN A TABLE;

> (1) SUBSCRIPTS are often used for the alignment of symbols in mathematical
> formulas. Contrast with SUPERSCRIPT, which refers to printing just above the
> line.

> (2) A PROGRAMMING SUBSCRIPT is a method of referencing an internal
> TABLE stored with DATA. The SUBSCRIPT indicates which element in the
> TABLE is referenced. The PROGRAMMING LANGUAGE statement would look
> like this: Display scores (who). Scores refers to the beginning of the TABLE, and
> *who* (the SUBSCRIPT) refers to an INDEX REGISTER (which is keeping track of
> elements in the TABLE). Display scores (who-when) refers to a two-dimensional
> ARRAY of elements. *Who* and *when* refer to two INDEX REGISTERS.

superconductor

ULTRA-FAST ELECTRONIC CIRCUIT; A SUPERCONDUCTOR is a special variety of SEMICONDUCTOR material used to build ELECTRONIC CIRCUITS, having virtually no resistance to the flow of electricity. SUPERCONDUCTORS are used in the JOSEPHSON JUNCTION technology.

supercontroller

See DIGITAL PABX.

super large scale integration

See SLSI

supermini

LARGE-SCALE MINICOMPUTER; SUPERMINIS and small-scale MAINFRAMES overlap in capabilities. See MINICOMPUTER and MAINFRAME.

superscript

SLIGHTLY ABOVE THE CURRENT LINE; Contrast with SUBSCRIPT.

supervisor

ANOTHER NAME FOR OPERATING SYSTEM; See OPERATING SYSTEM.

symbolic language

LANGUAGE WHICH REPRESENTS PHYSICAL MACHINE CODES IN SYMBOLIC FORM; All PROGRAMMING LANGUAGES are SYMBOLIC LANGUAGES. See MNEMONIC and PROGRAMMING LANGUAGE.

synchronous communications

HIGH-SPEED TRANSMISSION; SYNCHRONOUS COMMUNICATIONS is the transmission of contiguous groups of CHARACTERS. Both the sending and receiving devices are set to the same synchronization of pulses (BITS). Contrast with ASYNCHRONOUS TRANSMISSION, whereby each CHARACTER is its own group and can start and stop at random.

syntax error

INVALID EXPRESSION; A SYNTAX ERROR means that the PROGRAM cannot understand the language expression as entered.

sysgen

THE TAILORING OF AN OPERATING SYSTEM; A **sys**tem **gen**eration is the selection of appropriate PROGRAM MODULES that are combined and modified to tailor the OPERATING SYSTEM to a particular COMPUTER SYSTEM environment. The SYSGEN sets up the OPERATING SYSTEM to work in a particular amount of MEMORY and integrates all the PERIPHERAL ACCESS METHODS.

system

A SET OF RELATED COMPONENTS AND EVENTS THAT INTERACT WITH EACH OTHER TO ACCOMPLISH A TASK; See MANAGEMENT SYSTEM, INFORMATION SYSTEM and COMPUTER SYSTEM.

SYSTEM, by itself, often refers to the OPERATING SYSTEM.

system development cycle

THE SEQUENCE OF EVENTS IN THE DEVELOPMENT OF AN INFORMATION SYSTEM; (1) SYSTEMS ANALYSIS & DESIGN (2) USER sign-off (3) PROGRAMMING (4) TESTING and DEBUGGING (5) CONVERSION and IMPLEMENTATION (6) USER acceptance. INFORMATION SYSTEM development is a mutual effort— responsibilities are shared by both USERS and technical staff.

system development methodology

FORMAL APPROACH TO SYSTEM DEVELOPMENT; A SYSTEM DEVELOPMENT METHODOLOGY formalizes and codifies a series of phases for the SYSTEM DEVELOPMENT CYCLE. It defines the precise objectives for each phase and the results required from each phase before the next one can commence. A SYSTEMS DEVELOPMENT METHODOLOGY may provide specialized forms for the preparation of the DOCUMENTATION throughout each phase.

system life cycle

THE USEFUL LIFE OF AN INFORMATION SYSTEM; The length of the SYSTEM LIFE CYCLE depends on the nature and volatility of the business, as well as the SOFTWARE development tools used to generate the DATA BASES and APPLICATION PROGRAMS. Eventually, an INFORMATION SYSTEM that is PATCHED over and over no longer is structurally sound enough to continue to be expanded. Natural changes in business over the years effect the duration of the SYSTEM, no matter how well it is designed. Tools like DATA BASE MANAGEMENT SYSTEMS allow for changes more readily, but increased TRANSACTION volumes can negate the effectiveness of the original selection and design later.

systems

GENERAL TERM FOR THE SYSTEMS DEPARTMENT OR SYSTEMS PERSONNEL; SYSTEMS, or SYSTEMS work, generally refers to SYSTEMS ANALYSIS & DESIGN tasks.

systems analysis & design

SOLVING A USER'S INFORMATION PROBLEM; The SYSTEMS ANALYSIS is the examination of the problem, while the SYSTEMS DESIGN is the creation of the INFORMATION SYSTEM which is the solution to the problem. See SYSTEMS ANALYST, INFORMATION SYSTEM, SYSTEM DEVELOPMENT CYCLE, SYSTEM LIFE CYCLE, PROTOTYPING and DOCUMENTATION.

systems analyst

PERSON RESPONSIBLE FOR THE DEVELOPMENT OF AN INFORMATION SYSTEM; SYSTEMS ANALYSTS design and modify INFORMATION SYSTEMS by turning USER requirements into a set of FUNCTIONAL SPECIFICATIONS. The FUNCTIONAL SPECS are the blueprint of the INFORMATION SYSTEM. They outline the DATA BASE, the people and machine PROCEDURES, and each COMPUTER PROGRAM that must be created. SYSTEMS ANALYSTS are the architects, as well as the project leaders, of an INFORMATION SYSTEM. It is their job to develop INFORMATION SYSTEM solutions to USER'S problems, determine the technical and operational feasibility of their solutions, as well as estimate the costs to develop and implement them. SYSTEMS ANALYSTS require a balanced mix of business and technical knowledge, interviewing and analytical skills, as well as a good understanding of human behavior.

systems engineer

SYSTEMS PROFESSIONAL; SYSTEMS ENGINEER is a title often used by HARDWARE vendors for individuals who perform SYSTEMS ANALYSIS, PROGRAMMING, and/or SYSTEMS PROGRAMMING functions for customers. SYSTEMS ENGINEERS may be responsible for pre-sales activities, as well.

systems house

SYSTEMS CONSULTING FIRM; A SYSTEMS HOUSE usually develops customized INFORMATION SYSTEMS for its customers. It may also be an OEM, whereby it purchases the HARDWARE from a vendor and resells the HARDWARE and SOFTWARE it creates as a complete TURNKEY SYSTEM to the END USER.

systems programmer

SYSTEM SOFTWARE SPECIALIST; SYSTEMS PROGRAMMERS are the technical experts on some or all of the COMPUTER'S SYSTEM SOFTWARE (OPERATING SYSTEM, COMMUNICATIONS,and DATA BASE SOFTWARE). SYSTEMS PROGRAMMERS who work in a USER'S organization (primarily with large MAINFRAMES) often do not write PROGRAMS in the conventional sense. Rather, they understand the interaction between the APPLICATION SOFTWARE and the SYSTEM SOFTWARE in their COMPUTER environment, and act as advisors to SYSTEMS ANALYSTS, APPLICATION PROGRAMMERS, and OPERATIONS personnel. They are responsible for the efficient operation of the organization's COMPUTER SYSTEMS.

The SYSTEMS PROGRAMMER would know what PROCESSING capacity was available in the COMPUTER and would select appropriate SYSTEM SOFTWARE to optimize its performance. In the MAINFRAME environment, there is usually one SYSTEMS PROGRAMMER for every ten or more APPLICATION PROGRAMMERS. In the smaller MINI and MICRO environments, USERS rely on their vendors or CONSULTANTS for SYSTEMS PROGRAMMING assistance.

In a vendor's environment, SYSTEMS PROGRAMMERS design and write SYSTEM SOFTWARE. In this case, they write PROGRAMS often far more complex than the APPLICATION PROGRAMS written in a USER'S environment.

system software

DATA AND PROGRAM MANAGEMENT SOFTWARE; OPERATING SYSTEMS, COMMUNICATIONS control PROGRAMS, and DATA BASE MANAGEMENT SYSTEMS are all SYSTEM SOFTWARE. SYSTEM SOFTWARE interacts with all the APPLICATION PROGRAMS running in the COMPUTER. It also occasionally interacts with the USER; for example, the OPERATING SYSTEM performs the LOG-ON and LOG-OFF function at a TERMINAL. SYSTEM SOFTWARE is rarely written by the USER, since it is much more complex than APPLICATION SOFTWARE. An exception would be a SERVICE BUREAU that writes its own OPERATING SYSTEM to maximize the performance of its COMPUTER SYSTEMS.

SYSTEM 2000 (S2K)

DATA BASE MANAGEMENT SYSTEM WHICH RUNS ON IBM, CDC AND UNIVAC COMPUTERS; SYSTEM 2000 is an example of a HIERARCHICAL DATA BASE and is a product of Intel Systems Corporation.

S-100 bus

MICROCOMPUTER BUS STANDARD; See BUS.

table

AN ORDERED COLLECTION OF DATA; A TABLE in a PROGRAM is a collection of adjacent FIELDS containing DATA. The DATA might be stored permanently in the PROGRAM, or may be entered into the PROGRAM by the USER.

table look-up

SEARCHING FOR DATA IN A TABLE; See SUBSCRIPT.

tablet

See DIGITIZER TABLET.

tape

See MAGNETIC DISK & TAPE.

tape drive

THE PHYSICAL UNIT THAT HOLDS, READS AND WRITES THE MAGNETIC TAPE; See MAGNETIC TAPE & DISK.

tape mark

SPECIAL CODE USED TO INDICATE THE END OF A TAPE FILE.

tariff

SCHEDULE OF RATES FOR COMMON CARRIER SERVICES.

task

INDIVIDUAL RUN UNIT; A TASK refers to the EXECUTION of a PROGRAM or
PROGRAM MODULE as an individual running unit. A TASK can be an entire
PROGRAM or a smaller PROGRAM MODULE which is part of a larger SYSTEM. A
TASK can be run concurrently with other TASKS in the COMPUTER. See
MULTITASKING and MULTIPROGRAMMING.

TCAM

IBM COMMUNICATIONS ACCESS METHOD; Stands for **Tele**Communications **A**ccess
Method.

TDM

TIME **D**IVISION **M**ULTIPLEXING; TDM is a DIGITAL MULTIPLEXING technique which
interweaves several low-speed transmissions into one high-speed transmission. For
example: A, B & C are three DIGITAL transmissions of 1,000 BITS per second each.
They can be interwoven into one higher-speed CHANNEL (3,000 BITS per second) as
follows: AABBCCAABBCCAABBCCAABBCCAABBCC. At the receiving end, the
different transmissions are divided out and merged back together. TDM breaks up the
high-speed CHANNEL into time intervals and alternates BITS from each low-speed
transmission into these intervals.

telecommunications

TRANSFER OF VOICE AND DATA BETWEEN REMOTE LOCATIONS; See
COMMUNICATIONS.

telecommuting

WORKING AT HOME; TELECOMMUTING is working at home with
TELECOMMUNICATIONS between the home and the office.

teleconferencing

CONFERENCING SIMULTANEOUSLY IN TWO OR MORE REMOTE LOCATIONS;
AUDIO TELECONFERENCING connects several telephones together for a verbal
conference. This is performed internally by the customer's PABX and externally by the
telephone companies.

A COMMUNICATIONS NETWORK can connect multiple USERS at TERMINALS
together for COMPUTER TELECONFERENCING.

VIDEO TELECONFERENCING employs VIDEO cameras and MONITORS at two or
more locations. TELECONFERENCING centers are develeped for in-house private use as

well as for public rental. VIDEO signals require large BANDWIDTHS and consequently cannot be transmitted in REAL-TIME over conventional NETWORKS which carry voice and DATA. COAXIAL CABLES, OPTICAL FIBERS and COMMUNICATIONS SATELLITES are required for VIDEO transmission. VIDEO signals are primarily ANALOG signals. DIGITAL VIDEO requires even larger capacity CHANNELS. It will take some time before VIDEO TELECONFERENCING is a universal desktop function.

telecopying

FORMAL TERM FOR FACSIMILE; TELECOPYING means long-distance copying.

Telematics

THE CONVERGENCE OF TELECOMMUNICATIONS AND AUTOMATIC INFORMATION PROCESSING.

Telenet

DOMESTIC COMMUNICATIONS SERVICE PROVIDED BY GTE; TELENET is a VALUE-ADDED, PACKET SWITCHING COMMUNICATIONS NETWORK that enables many varieties of USER TERMINALS and COMPUTERS to exchange INFORMATION.

TELEPRINTER

teleprinter

HARD COPY TERMINAL; Contrast with VIDEO TERMINAL, which is SOFT COPY.

teleprocessing

DATA COMMUNICATIONS AND DATA PROCESSING; See COMMUNICATIONS.

Teletex

INTERNATIONAL COMMUNICATIONS SERVICE; TELETEX is primarily an ELECTRONIC MAIL NETWORK which is also connected to the TELEX NETWORK. TELETEX USERS can exchange correspondence between TELETEX and TELEX USERS.

teletext

INFORMATION SERVICE; TELETEXT provides one-way broadcasting of selected INFORMATION to a USER'S television set, such as news, weather reports, and advertising. TELETEXT INFORMATION is often transmitted in the unused portion of the TV signal called the vertical blanking interval (that's the black line between FRAMES on a TV when the vertical hold is not properly adjusted). Only a small number of FRAMES (around 100) can be transmitted this way; however, TELETEXT can also be broadcast over a dedicated TV CHANNEL, where thousands of FRAMES can be offered to the subscriber.

A special DECODER device which contains a KEYPAD for INTERACTIVE use is necessary for adapting the TELETEXT signal to the USER'S TV. TELETEXT FRAMES are broadcast in a consecutive sequence, this sequence repeating over and over. When the USER selects a FRAME using the KEYPAD, the FRAME is stored in the DECODER and displayed on the TV as soon as it is repeated from the broadcasting station. See VIDEOTEX.

teletypewriter

LOW-SPEED SERIAL TELEPRINTER; Abbreviated TTY.

Telex

DOMESTIC LOW-SPEED COMMUNICATIONS SERVICE PROVIDED BY WESTERN UNION; TELEX primarily uses TELETYPEWRITER TERMINALS. TELEX USERS can send messages worldwide using the international TELEX NETWORK, and can also send messages to TWX USERS.

terminal

USER INTERFACE TO THE COMPUTER; TERMINALS are INPUT/OUTPUT devices which usually have a standard KEYBOARD as INPUT and a VIDEO SCREEN for SOFT COPY OUTPUT and/or a PRINTER for HARD COPY OUTPUT.

test data

INPUT CREATED FOR TESTING and DEBUGGING PROGRAMS; TEST DATA is developed by both USERS and PROGRAMMERS to validate a newly-developed PROGRAM. TEST DATA should contain samples of every possible combination of valid and erroneous conditions that could occur in order to thoroughly test the PROGRAM.

testing

EXECUTION OF A NEWLY-DEVELOPED PROGRAM; TESTING is the running of a newly developed or changed PROGRAM to determine if the PROGRAM PROCESSES properly. PROGRAMMERS DEBUG their PROGRAMS until the TEST DATA PROCESSES correctly.

text

ALPHANUMERIC CHARACTERS; Everything you're reading is TEXT. TEXT is continuous words, sentences and paragraphs. Contrast with DATA, a precisely defined unit according to size, type and limits (such as name, address, city, state, amount due, year-to-date gross pay, etc). However, DATA is regularly intermixed with TEXT. See WORD PROCESSING.

text editing

MANIPULATION OF TEXT; TEXT EDITING is the changing or rearranging of CHARACTERS, words, sentences and paragraphs in TEXT. TEXT EDITING is the EDITING portion of WORD PROCESSING SYSTEMS. TEXT EDITING is used extensively in PROGRAMMING to create the LINES OF CODE in a PROGRAMMING LANGUAGE. Useful TEXT EDITING capabilities are SEARCH & REPLACE, and CUT & PASTE.

text editor

SOFTWARE THAT STORES, RETRIEVES AND EDITS TEXT; TEXT EDITORS are used to create and manipulate SOURCE LANGUAGE PROGRAMS, as well as DATA and TEXT FILES. TEXT EDITORS and WORD PROCESSORS are often the same.

thermal printer

PRINTER THAT USES HEAT SENSITIVE PAPER; See PRINTER TECHNOLOGIES.

thin film

THIN LAYERS OF MATERIAL; THIN FILM technologies refers to thin layers of SEMICONDUCTOR or magnetic materials deposited on a ceramic or metal base. THIN FILM may also refer to the ultra-thin layers of the ELECTRONIC components built into the CHIP.

thrashing

EXCESSIVE PAGING IN A VIRTUAL STORAGE COMPUTER; If PROGRAMS are not written to run in a VIRTUAL STORAGE environment, the OPERATING SYSTEM may spend excessive amounts of time swapping PROGRAM PAGES in and out of the DISK.

throughput

A COMPUTER'S ACTUAL CAPABILITY TO DO WORK; A COMPUTER'S THROUGHPUT is a combination of its PERIPHERAL INPUT and OUTPUT speeds, its internal PROCESSING speed, and the efficiency of its OPERATING SYSTEM and SYSTEM SOFTWARE all working together. Any of these variables will affect a COMPUTER'S total THROUGHPUT.

TI

TEXAS INSTRUMENTS, INC.

tightly coupled

COMPUTERS WHICH ARE DEPENDENT UPON EACH OTHER; TIGHTLY COUPLED PROCESSORS are used in MULTIPROCESSING environments. It implies that they continually monitor each other and/or that one controls the other. Contrast with LOOSELY COUPLED.

time-division multiplexing

See TDM.

time-sharing

COMPUTER SHARED BY SEVERAL USERS; TIME-SHARING most often refers to an external SERVICE BUREAU; however, TIME-SHARING can be implemented on in-house COMPUTER SYSTEMS. TIME-SHARING allows USERS ACCESS to authorized PROGRAMS and DATA BASES from a TERMINAL.

The key to TIME-SHARING is that USERS can initiate the running of their PROGRAMS at any time the COMPUTER is running, as long as they are authorized to do so. Without TIME-SHARING, USERS can only gain ON-LINE ACCESS to PROGRAMS that have been scheduled to run in the COMPUTER at specific times throughout the day. Any changes to this schedule must be entered by the OPERATOR at the OPERATOR'S CONSOLE in the DATACENTER, not by USERS at their own TERMINALS.

token passing

COMMUNICATIONS NETWORK ACCESS METHOD; The TOKEN PASSING method uses a continuously repeating FRAME (the *token*), which is transmitted onto the NETWORK by the COMPUTER controlling the COMMUNICATIONS. When a TERMINAL or COMPUTER wants to send a MESSAGE on the NETWORK, it waits for an empty token. When it finds one, it fills it with some or all of its MESSAGE, as well as the name (ADDRESS) of the destination device. Each device on the NETWORK constantly monitors all the passing tokens to determine if it is the recipient of a MESSAGE from another device. If it is, the device "grabs" the MESSAGE and resets the token to an empty status. TOKEN PASSING may be used in BUS-type and RING-type NETWORKS.

top-down design

STRUCTURED PROGRAMMING TECHNIQUE; TOP DOWN DESIGN imposes a
HIERARCHICAL structure on the design of a PROGRAM. TOP-DOWN DESIGN is both
a DOCUMENTATION and design technique which makes modifications to PROGRAMS
easier at a later time.

TOPS

OPERATING SYSTEM USED ON DEC'S DECSYSTEM SERIES MAINFRAMES.

TOTAL

DATA BASE MANAGEMENT SYSTEM USED ON A WIDE VARIETY OF MAINFRAMES
AND MINICOMPUTERS; TOTAL is an example of a NETWORK DATA BASE and is a
product of Cincom Systems, Inc.

touch-sensitive screen

VIDEO TERMINAL INPUT DEVICE; TOUCH-SENSITIVE SCREENS use a clear panel
overlaid on the SCREEN. The panel is designed as a MATRIX of cells, each cell large
enough (approx. 1/2" square) to receive the end of a person's finger. The PROGRAM
displays options on the SCREEN and the USER'S finger touch selects the option. See
PEOPLE/MACHINE INTERFACE.

TP monitor

TERMINAL/COMMUNICATIONS CONTROL PROGRAM; The TP MONITOR manages
the transfer of INFORMATION between local and remote TERMINALS and the
APPLICATION PROGRAMS that serve them. The TP MONITOR may also include
PROGRAMS which FORMAT the TERMINAL SCREENS and validate the
INFORMATION being entered. Stands for **Tele**Processing **monitor**.

TPI

TRACKS **PER** INCH; TPI measures the TRACK density on a MAGNETIC DISK or
DRUM.

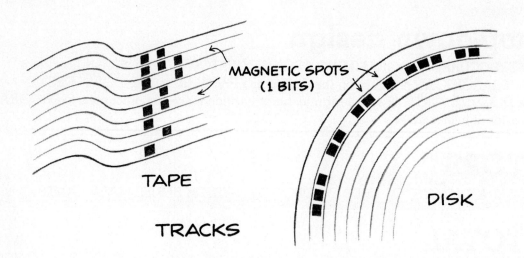

MAGNETIC SPOTS
(1 BITS)

TAPE

TRACKS

DISK

track

A STORAGE CHANNEL ON A DISK OR TAPE; TRACKS are a series of circular channels on DISKS, or a series of parallel channels on TAPE. They are defined by the DISK or TAPE DRIVE that records them. When TRACKS are recorded (WRITTEN) on a particular DISK or TAPE, only that model of DISK or TAPE can READ them. TRACKS are not physical grooves as they are in phonograph records. They are a continuous stream of BITS, one after the other. See MAGNETIC DISK & TAPE.

tractor feed

DEVICE WHICH MOVES PAPER IN A PRINTER; TRACTOR FEED mechanisms use sprocket wheels to move continuous paper forms through a PRINTER. The continuous forms must have sprocket holes prepunched on both the left and right sides. TRACTOR FEEDS provide uniform, high-speed paper movement. SHEET FEEDERS are used for feeding single sheets into a PRINTER.

trailer (label)

TRAILING IDENTIFICATION; A TRAILER RECORD or TRAILER LABEL is an identification RECORD at the end of a FILE. Control totals, such as the number of RECORDS in the FILE or a HASH TOTAL of various FIELDS in the FILE, may be included in the TRAILER. A TRAILER is also a CHARACTER or group of BITS which marks the end of a DATA FRAME for certain COMMUNICATIONS PROTOCOLS. A TRAILER may refer to any CODE which marks the end of a group of DATA.

train printer

LINE PRINTER THAT USES TYPE CHARACTERS WHICH RIDE IN A TRACK AS ITS PRINTER MECHANISM; See PRINTER TECHNOLOGIES.

transaction

ANY BUSINESS ACTIVITY OR REQUEST THAT IS ENTERED INTO THE COMPUTER SYSTEM; A TRANSACTION is the reason for using the COMPUTER. Orders, notifications, changes, QUERIES, etc., are all TRANSACTIONS in an INFORMATION SYSTEM. TRANSACTION volume is one of the major components which determines the basic size of a COMPUTER SYSTEM.

transaction file

COLLECTION OF TRANSACTION RECORDS; A DATA ENTRY PROGRAM allows for the creation of new TRANSACTIONS used to UPDATE a MASTER FILE (or DATA BASE). TRANSACTION FILES are stored either ON-LINE (on DISK) or OFF-LINE (in a DATA LIBRARY) for some extended period of time, to serve as AUDIT TRAILS for the INFORMATION SYSTEM, and as history detail.

transaction processing

PROCESSING AN INDIVIDUAL TRANSACTION AT A TIME; TRANSACTION PROCESSING SYSTEMS are ON-LINE, REAL-TIME SYSTEMS. Contrast with BATCH PROCESSING.

TRANSACTION PROCESSING vs BATCH PROCESSING: If you collect your purchase receipts in a box and add them together at the end of the year for income tax purposes, that's BATCH PROCESSING. If, however, at the moment of purchase you document the purchase in a ledger and add the new TRANSACTION amounts to the previous total accumulations, that's TRANSACTION PROCESSING.

transceiver

TRANSMITTER AND RECEIVER UNIT; TRANSCEIVERS perform both transmitting and receiving of ANALOG or DIGITAL signals. TRANSCEIVERS come in many forms; for example, a TRANSPONDER in a COMMUNICATIONS SATELLITE is a TRANSCEIVER, as is an INTERFACE unit that connects a TERMINAL or COMPUTER to a LOCAL AREA NETWORK.

transfer rate

TRANSMISSION SPEED; The TRANSFER RATE is the number of BITS or BYTES that can be transferred between one HARDWARE device and another within a period of time (usually one second). Same as DATA RATE.

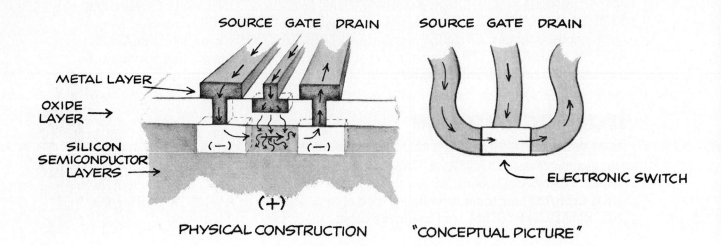

MOSFET TRANSISTOR

SOURCE GATE DRAIN   SOURCE GATE DRAIN

METAL LAYER

OXIDE LAYER →

SILICON SEMICONDUCTOR LAYERS →

(−)   (−)

(+)

ELECTRONIC SWITCH

PHYSICAL CONSTRUCTION   "CONCEPTUAL PICTURE"

A PULSE ON THE GATE TEMPORARILY ALLOWS
CURRENT TO FLOW FROM ONE SIDE TO THE OTHER

transistor

PRIMARY SEMICONDUCTOR ELEMENT; TRANSISTORS are the physical building blocks of LOGIC and MEMORY CIRCUITS. TRANSISTORS are also used to amplify signals; however, in DIGITAL COMPUTERS, the TRANSISTOR acts like an electric switch, similar to a light switch on a lamp. When you toggle the lamp switch, you are connecting one wire with another (bridging the gap) and current flows from the source to the lamp. Now, instead of an actual gap, imagine a hunk of material in the gap that normally resists the flow of current. However, if that hunk of material (SEMICONDUCTOR) is charged from another source, it will allow the current to flow from one side to the other. TRANSISTORS make up LOGIC GATES (along with other components called RESISTORS, CAPACITORS and DIODES). LOGIC GATES make up CIRCUITS, and CIRCUITS make up ELECTRONIC SYSTEMS. See BOOLEAN LOGIC.

transparent

INVISIBLE TO THE USER; Any TRANSPARENT function that is added to the current SYSTEM implies that it will not be visible to the USER, and that there are no changes in PROCEDURE required to use it.

transponder

RECEIVER/TRANSMITTER IN A COMMUNICATIONS SATELLITE; The TRANSPONDER receives a transmitted MICROWAVE signal from earth, amplifies it and retransmits it back to earth (at a different FREQUENCY). There are several TRANSPONDERS on a COMMUNICATIONS SATELLITE.

trapping

SETTING A TRAP FOR A PARTICULAR CONDITION; TRAPPING is used in PROGRAM DEBUGGING to identify why the PROGRAM goes off into an unspecified area. Either through HARDWARE or SOFTWARE (or their combination), a particular DATA CODE or INSTRUCTION CODE can be TRAPPED, causing the COMPUTER to stop, display, or print out the location of the offending CODE.

tree structure

HIERARCHICAL STRUCTURE;
A TREE STRUCTURE is a form of HIERARCHICAL structure with many branches.

TRS-80

SERIES OF MICROCOMPUTERS
AND POCKET COMPUTERS
MANUFACTURED BY
RADIO SHACK.

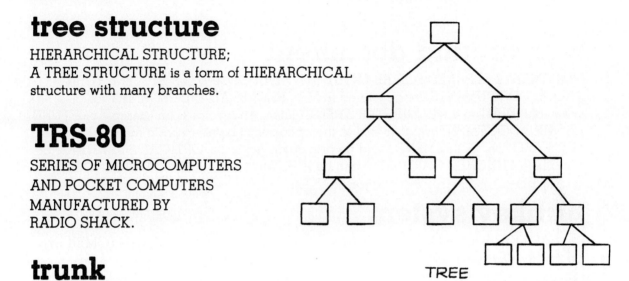

TREE

trunk

COMMUNICATIONS CHANNEL BETWEEN TWO POINTS; A TRUNK implies a primary COMMUNICATIONS link in a NETWORK.

truth table

LOGIC RULES; A TRUTH TABLE defines all the INPUT and OUTPUT conditions for a set of LOGIC GATES. See AND, OR & NOT.

TSO

IBM TIME-SHARING SOFTWARE; Stands for **T**ime **S**haring **O**ption.

TTL

INTEGRATED CIRCUIT DESIGN TECHNIQUE; TTL stands for **T**ransistor **T**ransistor **L**ogic and refers to the design of CIRCUITS which use the TRANSISTOR as its predominant component.

TTY

ABBREVIATION FOR **TELETY**PEWRITER.

TTY protocol

LOW-SPEED ASYNCHRONOUS COMMUNICATIONS PROTOCOL; See
ASYNCHRONOUS COMMUNICATIONS and COMMUNICATIONS PROTOCOL.

tube

See CRT and VACUUM TUBE.

turn around document

DOCUMENT PREPARED FOR RE-ENTRY INTO THE COMPUTER SYSTEM; TURN
AROUND DOCUMENTS are generated in MACHINE READABLE FORMAT for
automatic INPUT to the COMPUTER SYSTEM later. An invoice is an example of a TURN
AROUND DOCUMENT which is sent to the customer to be returned to the vendor. The
TURN AROUND DOCUMENT could be printed on paper for OPTICAL SCANNING, or
could be a PUNCHED CARD which can be INPUT to a PUNCHED CARD READER.

turnkey system

A COMPLETE HARDWARE/SOFTWARE SYSTEM DELIVERED TO A CUSTOMER IN
RUNNING CONDITION; See OEM.

turtle graphics

GRAPHICS LANGUAGE USED IN THE LOGO PROGRAMMING LANGUAGE.

twisted pair

LOW GRADE WIRES; TWISTED PAIRS are small insulated wires used extensively in
ELECTRONICS and telephone interconnections. Contrast with COAXIAL CABLE or
OPTICAL FIBERS, which have greater transmission capacities (BANDWIDTH).

TWX

DOMESTIC LOW-SPEED COMMUNICATIONS SERVICE PROVIDED BY WESTERN
UNION; Stands for **TELETYPEWRITER Ex**change Service and primarily interconnects
TELETYPEWRITER TERMINALS. TWX USERS can send MESSAGES to TELEX USERS.

Tymnet

DOMESTIC COMMUNICATIONS SERVICE PROVIDED BY TYMSHARE; TYMNET is a
VALUE-ADDED, PACKET SWITCHING COMMUNICATIONS NETWORK that enables
many varieties of USER TERMINALS and COMPUTERS to exchange INFORMATION.

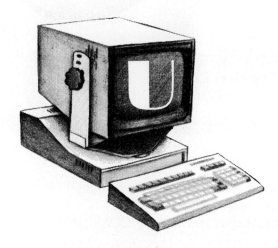

UART

PARALLEL/SERIAL CONVERTER; The UART is an ELECTRONIC device which converts parallel signals to serial signals and vice versa. Inside the COMPUTER, DATA is worked on in parallel (8 or more BITS at a time). Transmission over a COMMUNICATIONS CHANNEL is usually serial (one BIT following the other). The UART is usually used to convert a COMPUTER'S parallel BYTE to a serial BYTE of the COMMUNICATIONS NETWORK. Stands for **U**niversal **A**synchronous **R**eceiver **T**ransmitter.

UCSD p-System

OPERATING SYSTEM AND PROGRAMMING LANGUAGES; PROGRAMS written in the UCSD P-SYSTEM can be run on a variety of different COMPUTERS without change. The PROGRAMS are written in traditional languages like BASIC, FORTRAN and PASCAL, which have been modified to create an interim language called P-CODE, rather than a MACHINE LANGUAGE for a specific COMPUTER. The P-CODE is EXECUTED by P-CODE EMULATORS, each of which having been designed for a different COMPUTER. The UCSD P-SYSTEM stands for **U**niversity of **C**alifornia at **S**an **D**iego **p-System.**

ULA

UNCOMMITTED **L**OGIC **A**RRAY; See LOGIC ARRAY.

unbundled

PRICED SEPARATELY; See BUNDLED/UNBUNDLED.

uninterruptible power supply

See UPS.

unit record equipment

PUNCHED CARD PROCESSING MACHINES; UNIT RECORD machines use PUNCHED CARDS as their unit of storage. Stand-alone devices such as KEYPUNCHES, sorters, collators, reproducers, interpreters and tabulators PROCESS the PUNCHED CARDS. Also called EAM.

UNIX

OPERATING SYSTEM DEVELOPED BY BELL LABS; UNIX was originally designed for the DEC PDP-7 MINICOMPUTER, but was later rewritten in a HIGH-LEVEL PROGRAMMING LANGUAGE (C) and adapted to many other vendors' COMPUTERS.

unpack

See PACK/UNPACK.

UNIVERSAL PRODUCT CODE

UPC (universal product code)

THE BAR CODE USED BY SUPERMARKET PRODUCT MANUFACTURERS AND OTHERS; The UPC identifies the vendor identification number and the particular product number for automatic recognition by OPTICAL SCANNING.

update

MODIFY DATA/INFORMATION IN A FILE OR DATA BASE TO BRING INTO CURRENT STATUS; The steps in a DISK UPDATE are: (1) READING the old INFORMATION (copying it into MEMORY), (2) changing it in the COMPUTER, and (3) WRITING (recording) it back onto the DISK in its changed form (overlaying the original). The steps in a TAPE UPDATE are: (1) READING the old INFORMATION, (2) changing it in the COMPUTER, and (3) WRITING the changed INFORMATION onto a different OUTPUT TAPE.

UPS

UNINTERRUPTIBLE **P**OWER **S**UPPLY; UPS SYSTEMS provide BACKUP power for a COMPUTER SYSTEM. They monitor the incoming power lines and provide continuous electrical current to the COMPUTER in the event of a drop in voltage. The UPS provides a certain amount of battery BACKUP and may also start up an electrical generator that is part of the SYSTEM.

uptime

THE PERIOD OF TIME THAT EQUIPMENT IS WORKING WITHOUT FAILURE; Contrast with DOWNTIME.

upward compatible

COMPATIBLE WITH A LARGER OR NEXT GENERATION MODEL; A COMPUTER that runs PROGRAMS which can also run on the next generation model or on a larger model is UPWARD COMPATIBLE.

USASCII

Same as ASCII.

user

ANYONE USING THE COMPUTER; USER usually refers to the non-technical person providing INPUT to, or receiving OUTPUT from, the COMPUTER.

user-friendly

EASY TO USE; USER-FRIENDLY implies an easy-to-understand dialogue between the USER and the COMPUTER. See PEOPLE/MACHINE INTERFACE.

user group

ORGANIZATION OF USERS OF A PARTICULAR VENDORS PRODUCT; USER GROUPS share experiences and ideas to improve their understanding and utilization of their vendors product. USER GROUPS are often responsible for influencing vendors to change or enhance their products.

utility program

PROGRAM WHICH PERFORMS GENERALIZED FUNCTIONS; SORT PROGRAMS, DISK/TAPE copy PROGRAMS and MEMORY DUMPS are all examples of UTILITY PROGRAMS. UTILITY PROGRAMS are developed by HARDWARE and SOFTWARE vendors and often come as part of the OPERATING SYSTEM or DATA BASE MANAGEMENT SYSTEM.

vacuum tube

ELECTRONIC COMPONENT; VACUUM TUBES were used in 1st-generation
COMPUTERS as on/off switches, eventually being replaced by TRANSISTORS. Today,
the major use of the VACUUM TUBE is the CRT used for VIDEO SCREENS. It too may
eventually be replaced by FLAT SCREEN technologies.

value-added network

COMMUNICATIONS NETWORK THAT PROVIDES ADDITIONAL SERVICES; VALUE-
ADDED NETWORKS provide services in addition to the COMMUNICATIONS
CHANNELS, such as automatic error detection and correction. PROTOCOL
conversions, and STORE & FORWARD message services.

VAN

See **VALUE ADDED NETWORK**.

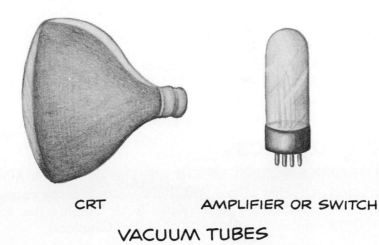

CRT   AMPLIFIER OR SWITCH

VACUUM TUBES

variable

Same as FIELD.

variable length field/record

FIELD AND RECORD STRUCTURES OF VARYING SIZES; A VARIABLE LENGTH FIELD might be used for DATA like name and address since the actual number of CHARACTERS varies. (The total length of the FIELD is stored at the beginning of the FIELD itself.)

A VARIABLE LENGTH RECORD contains VARIABLE LENGTH FIELDS or a varying amount of FIXED or VARIABLE LENGTH FIELDS. While VARIABLE LENGTH FIELDS and RECORDS save storage space on a DISK or TAPE, they require additional PROGRAMMING in the APPLICATION PROGRAMS to compress and restore the DATA. Some COMPUTER SYSTEMS automatically compress all blanks that are WRITTEN to a DISK and restore them when READ back into the COMPUTER.

VAX

MINICOMPUTER SERIES MANUFACTURED BY DIGITAL EQUIPMENT CORPORATION.

VCR

VIDEO CASSETTE RECORDER; VCRs are ANALOG recording and playback devices for VIDEO (TV) signals.

VDT/VDU

VIDEO DISPLAY TERMINAL/VIDEO DISPLAY UNIT; VDT and VDU are alternate terms for the VIDEO TERMINAL.

vector

TABLE OR LINE; When referring to mathematical PROCESSING, a VECTOR is a series of numbers in a TABLE. When referring to COMPUTER GRAPHICS, a VECTOR is a line designated by two x-y coordinates.

vector graphics

COMPUTER GRAPHICS CODING TECHNIQUE; The VECTOR GRAPHICS technique represents an object as a series of lines (VECTORS) starting at one point on an X-Y MATRIX and ending at another x-y point. (Note: Vector Graphic, Inc., is a MICROCOMPUTER vendor.) See GRAPHICS (Vector Graphics).

vertical recording

MAGNETIC RECORDING TECHNIQUE; VERTICAL RECORDING records the BITS on a FLOPPY DISK in a vertical position instead of in a horizontal position. The BITS (which span the thickness of the medium) take up less storage space than the traditional method. The VERTICAL RECORDING technique uses a specialized material for the construction of the DISK.

vertical redundancy checking

See VRC.

very large scale integration

See VLSI.

VHSIC

VERY **H**IGH **S**PEED **I**NTEGRATED **C**IRCUIT; VHSIC refers to ultra-high-speed CHIPS employing LSI and VLSI technologies. Pronounced /vis-ik/.

video

VISUAL RECORDING AND DISPLAY TECHNOLOGY; VIDEO refers to the standard picture recording signals generated by VIDEO (TV-type) cameras and displayed on most VIDEO SCREENS and TERMINALS. See TELECONFERENCING and GRAPHICS.

videodisc

MOVING PICTURES STORED ON A DISC; VIDEODISC is similar to a phonograph record except that VIDEO (moving pictures) signals, as well as AUDIO signals, are encoded into the VIDEODISC. VIDEODISCS are DIRECT ACCESS devices like MAGNETIC DISKS for COMPUTERS. Any picture FRAME on the VIDEODISC can be directly located, just like the tone arm on a phonograph turntable can immediately move to any part of a phonograph record.

COMPUTERS are used in conjunction with VIDEODISCS to provide an INTERACTIVE SYSTEM. The COMPUTER can identify the locations of stored items on the VIDEODISC based on INPUT from the USER, and then direct the VIDEODISC to display them. A customized educational (CAI) lesson can be generated by the COMPUTER and directed to the VIDEODISC.

Like phongraph records, VIDEODISCS are manufactured and cannot be altered. OPTICAL DISK technologies (similar to the LASER-type VIDEODISCS on the market) may provide an alternative to MAGNETIC DISKS for storage. VIDEODISCS can hold a far greater amount of DIGITAL DATA per square inch of surface than MAGNETIC DISKS.

video display terminal/unit

Same as VIDEO TERMINAL.

video teleconferencing

See TELECONFERENCING.

video terminal

TERMINAL WITH VIDEO OUTPUT; Although a VIDEO TERMINAL resembles a television set, the standard VIDEO TERMINAL only displays CHARACTERS, not pictures. The standard CHARACTER display is 24 (or 25) lines by 80 columns (CHARACTERS) across. PERSONAL COMPUTERS may display fewer columns, such as 40, while other VIDEO TERMINALS can display up to 132 columns, equal to the maximum line width of many PRINTERS.

A limited picture capability is available in TERMINALS with CHARACTER GRAPHICS. Full picture capability requires BIT-MAPPED GRAPHICS. See CHARACTER GRAPHICS and GRAPHICS (Raster Graphics).

Like television, VIDEO TERMINALS come in a number of SCREEN sizes (measured diagonally). VIDEO TERMINALS are also available with a wide variety of KEYBOARDS and additional INPUT devices (such as LIGHT PENS and JOY STICKS). See DUMB TERMINAL, SMART TERMINAL and INTELLIGENT TERMINAL.

videotex

INFORMATION AND INTERACTIVE TRANSACTION SERVICE; VIDEOTEX can provide a variety of services to the home and business. VIDEOTEX can provide news, weather reports, and advertising (ELECTRONIC PUBLISHING), as well as shop-at-home and bank-at-home services. Subscribers can leave messages for other subscribers of the service (ELECTRONIC MAIL). VIDEOTEX may also provide a GATEWAY to standard TIME-SHARING services.

VIDEOTEX is delivered over a telephone line (or COAXIAL CABLE or OPTICAL FIBER) to the subscriber's TV set. Subscribers purchase or rent a DECODER which adapts the TV to the VIDEOTEX signal. The DECODER (which includes an AUTO/DIAL MODEM) also contains a KEYBOARD for INTERACTIVE use. PERSONAL COMPUTERS can also be adapted to receive the VIDEOTEX signal.

VIDEOTEX stores and displays INFORMATION using predefined SCREENS, called PAGES or FRAMES. These FRAMES are numbered and can be retrieved directly by number or through MENU selection displayed on the SCREEN. Because of the limited BANDWIDTH of the telephone line, VIDEOTEX cannot deliver fully animated TV-like pictures, but can deliver varieties of billboard GRAPHICS, including limited animation. The DECODER stores the transmitted FRAME in its MEMORY and continuously refreshes the TV SCREEN for viewing from the MEMORY.

Viewdata

BRITISH TERM FOR VIDEOTEX SERVICES; See VIDEOTEX.

virtual

SIMULATED; VIRTUAL methods refer to simulated functions which are not physically present. For example, VIRTUAL STORAGE simulates a larger MEMORY than actually exists. A VIRTUAL PRINTER would allow a REPORT to be PROCESSED even though a PRINTER is not physically present (it would save it on a DISK for later— same as SPOOLING). A VIRTUAL MACHINE simulates different machine environments for different USERS. A VIRTUAL CIRCUIT simulates a point-to-point connection, even though it may physically connect through a multiplicity of routes. VIRTUAL also tends to be a term used to refer to any new method which is an improvement over previous methods. VIRTUAL is often used to mean "virtually" any improvement.

virtual circuit

LOGICAL COMMUNICATIONS CIRCUIT; A VIRTUAL CIRCUIT is the resulting pathway created between two devices communicating with each other in a PACKET SWITCHING NETWORK.

virtual machine

COMPUTER THAT CAN SIMULATE MULTIPLE COMPUTER ENVIRONMENTS; See VM.

virtual memory

Same as VIRTUAL STORAGE.

virtual storage

A TECHNIQUE FOR EXPANDING THE CAPABILITY OF A SINGLE COMPUTER SYSTEM; VIRTUAL STORAGE (VS) eliminates the problem of not having enough MEMORY available in the COMPUTER to run a PROGRAM. VIRTUAL SYSTEMS allow PROGRAMMERS to write a PROGRAM that is larger than the MEMORY size of the COMPUTER.

Rather than copying the entire PROGRAM from the DISK into MEMORY at once, the VIRTUAL STORAGE OPERATING SYSTEM will copy in a small section of the PROGRAM, called a PAGE. When the COMPUTER has EXECUTED all the INSTRUCTIONS in that PAGE, the VS SYSTEM copies in the next PAGE, and so on. VS SYSTEMS are complex because they must keep track of the PROGRAM in MEMORY, as well as on DISK, and may result in additional PROCESSING overhead.

PROGRAMS written to run in a VIRTUAL STORAGE COMPUTER SYSTEM must be specially written to optimize this technique effectively. The PROGRAM LOGIC must be designed so as not to "ramble" all over the PROGRAM. Otherwise there will be an excessive amount of INPUTS and OUTPUTS from the DISK.

VisiCalc

ELECTRONIC SPREADSHEET; VISICALC, developed originally for the APPLE II COMPUTER, popularized the concept of an ELECTRONIC SPREADSHEET. Since VISICALC, there have been dozens of PROGRAMS developed which incorporate the row and column MATRIX approach. VISICALC is a classic example of how a SOFTWARE product can sell a COMPUTER. A large percentage of APPLE IIs were sold, strictly because of VISICALC. That means a $150 SOFTWARE PACKAGE sold a $3,000 COMPUTER. VISICALC is a product of VisiCorp.

VLSI

VERY **L**ARGE **S**CALE INTEGRATION; VLSI refers to the very large number of ELECTRONIC components (TRANSISTORS, etc.) that are built onto a single CHIP. VLSI ranges approximately from 100,000 to 1,000,000 TRANSISTORS on a CHIP.

VM

IBM OPERATING SYSTEM; VM is capable of running multiple OPERATING SYSTEMS, each running their own APPLICATION PROGRAMS within the same COMPUTER SYSTEM. Stands for **V**irtual **M**achine.

VMS

OPERATING SYSTEM USED ON DEC'S VAX SERIES MINICOMPUTERS.

voice/data PABX

See DIGITAL PABX.

voice-grade

COMMUNICATIONS CHANNEL WITH LIMITED BANDWIDTH; VOICE-GRADE CHANNELS are designed for the transmission of voice, which requires a limited BANDWIDTH.

voice recognition

COMPUTER RECOGNITION OF HUMAN VOICE; There are various techniques used for sampling voice and converting it into DIGITAL CODE for storage and retrieval (for example, PULSE CODE MODULATION). However, VOICE RECOGNITION refers to SYSTEMS which analyze the spoken content of a person's voice and convert it into CHARACTERS.

The spoken voice (converted to DIGITAL CODE) is matched against a dictionary of DIGITAL voice prints, either of the person speaking or of a generic voice. When the words match up within a prescribed tolerance, the corresponding TEXT CHARACTERS are generated as OUTPUT.

Although there are VOICE RECOGNITION SYSTEMS today which understand a limited number of words from anybody, most production SYSTEMS require that the USER pre-record a voice sample. Eventually, VOICE RECOGNITION SYSTEMS will understand large vocabularies of non-prerecorded voices.

voice response

VOICE OUTPUT CONTROLLED BY COMPUTER; VOICE RESPONSE units can selectively put together sentences of stored words to create a spoken message for a USER. The stored words that are used for OUTPUT can be real human voice or synthetic voice. For entire messages, human voice can be DIGITIZED and converted back into sound at the appropriate time. Individual words can be spoken and DIGITIZED too, but they sound flat when strung together by the COMPUTER. Synthetic speech is created using a variety of techniques which can generate a spoken phrase with some degree of inflection. See SPEECH SYNTHESIS.

volatile memory

MEMORY THAT DOES NOT RETAIN ITS CONTENT WITHOUT POWER; MAIN MEMORY (RAM) is usually VOLATILE MEMORY. When the COMPUTER is turned off, the BITS lose their charges. Many small hand-held devices employ VOLATILE MEMORY; however, when the machine is turned off, the battery still continues to charge the cells.

volume

PERIPHERAL STORAGE UNIT SUCH AS A DISK PACK OR REEL OF TAPE.

VRC

ERROR CHECKING METHOD; The VRC method uses a PARITY BIT for each CHARACTER. Stands for **V**ertical **R**edundancy **C**hecking.

VRX

OPERATING SYSTEM USED ON NCR'S V8500 AND V8600 MAINFRAMES.

VS

(1) **V**IRTUAL **S**TORAGE, (2) MINICOMPUTER SERIES FEATURING **V**IRTUAL **S**TORAGE MANUFACTURED BY WANG LABORATORIES.

VSAM

IBM DISK ACCESS METHOD; Stands for **V**irtual **S**torage **A**ccess **M**ethod.

VTAM

IBM COMMUNICATIONS ACCESS METHOD; Stands for **V**irtual **T**elecommunications **A**ccess **M**ethod.

VTR

VIDEO **T**APE **R**ECORDER; VTRs are ANALOG recording and playback devices for VIDEO (TV) signals.

V77

SERIES OF MINICOMPUTERS MANUFACTURED BY UNIVAC.

V8500, V8600

MAINFRAME SERIES MANUFACTURED BY NCR.

wafer

(1) SILICON WAFER, (2) MAGNETIC TAPE CARTRIDGE; (1) A thin SILICON WAFER, approximately 4" in diameter, is the base unit upon which hundreds of MICROCHIPS are created through a series of PHOTOMASKING, etching and implantation steps. See CHIP. (2) A MAGNETIC TAPE WAFER is a small, continuous-loop TAPE CARTRIDGE for DIGITAL STORAGE. See STRINGY FLOPPY.

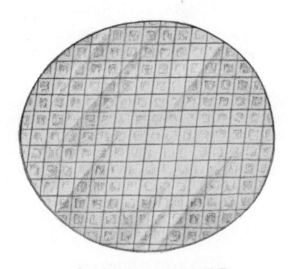

SILICON WAFER

TAPE WAFER

wand

HAND-HELD OPTICAL RECOGNITION DEVICE; A WAND is an INPUT device which is used to recognize OCR FONTS and BAR CODES. The WAND is waved over the CHARACTERS or CODES to be READ in a single pass.

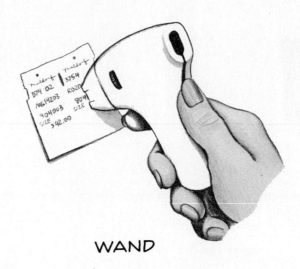

WAND

Wangnet

LOCAL AREA NETWORK DEVELOPED BY WANG LABORATORIES; WANGNET is a BROADBAND COMMUNICATIONS NETWORK.

warm boot

A BOOT THAT IS PERFORMED AFTER THE SYSTEM HAS BEEN RUNNING; See BOOT.

wave

THE SHAPE OF RADIATION; All AUDIO signals, RADIO signals, light, x-rays, and cosmic rays eminate a vibrating energy called electromagnetic radiation. This vibration takes the form of a rippling wave which can be easily visualized. Create an up and down vibration with your hand. While it is vibrating, move your hand slowly in a horizontal motion and focus on the end of your fingers. You can "see" the WAVE. The distance between peaks of a WAVE is called its wavelength.

Winchester disk

A SEALED DISK TECHNOLOGY; The WINCHESTER technique requires that the ACCESS ARM, READ/WRITE HEADS and DISKS are constructed as a sealed unit. By aligning the R/W HEADS to their own set of DISKS, greater storage and ACCESSING speeds are obtainable. The WINCHESTER DISK, although originally a removable DISK MODULE, usually implies a FIXED DISK technology.

window

VIEWING AREA ON A VIDEO SCREEN; The VIDEO SCREEN acts as a WINDOW into the COMPUTER'S MEMORY. PROGRAMS can be developed which allow for multiple WINDOWS to be displayed on the SCREEN at the same time. In this case, separate FILES or DATA BASES can be viewed without having to exit the current PROGRAM, in order to get into another.

WINDOWS

word

COMPUTER'S INTERNAL STORAGE UNIT; A COMPUTER WORD refers to its basic storage structure. The WORD holds a certain number of BITS and determines the overall PROCESSING speed of the COMPUTER. The larger the WORD, the more INSTRUCTIONS or INFORMATION are PROCESSED as a single unit. See 8-BIT/16-BIT/32-BIT COMPUTER.

word processing

TEXT DOCUMENT CREATION AND PROCESSING; WORD PROCESSING (WP) is the creation and manipulation of TEXT DOCUMENTS. WORD PROCESSING replaces all the operations normally associated with a typewriter, as well as the management of the DOCUMENTS that have been created.

WORD PROCESSING is the creation, storage and retrieval of TEXT DOCUMENTS, just as DATA PROCESSING is the creation, storage and retrieval of DATA RECORDS.

WORD PROCESSING allows USERS to create a TEXT DOCUMENT (also called a TEXT FILE) in the COMPUTER, store it permanently on a storage medium like a DISK, and recall it later for further EDITING or printing. A TEXT DOCUMENT is any combination of words and sentences, such as a memo, message, letter, proposal, legal DOCUMENT, REPORT, book or even PROGRAMMING SOURCE CODE. This Glossary is a TEXT DOCUMENT.

WORD PROCESSING can be implemented on almost any of a variety of COMPUTER SYSTEMS, as well as on dedicated SYSTEMS called WORD PROCESSORS. TEXT is usually entered by the USER at a KEYBOARD; however, typed or printed TEXT can be automatically READ into the COMPUTER using OPTICAL SCANNING devices.

A TEXT DOCUMENT is created or changed in the COMPUTER'S MEMORY. For example: An existing TEXT DOCUMENT is copied into MEMORY from the DISK, either in its entirety or a section at a time, depending on the WP SOFTWARE used. Using specific COMMANDS, the USER can rearrange, replicate, delete, or add to the TEXT DOCUMENT in any manner. The USER'S VIDEO SCREEN is a WINDOW into the TEXT DOCUMENT in MEMORY. The changed TEXT DOCUMENT is then stored back on the DISK as an UPDATED version. TEXT can be stored on the DISK to be used to master a copy. For example, a customized DOCUMENT can be created by copying several selected boiler plate paragraphs from the DISK into a newly generated TEXT DOCUMENT (in MEMORY). Customized letters can be created by SOFTWARE that merges names and addresses from a DATA FILE on a DISK into appropriately marked locations in the TEXT DOCUMENT in MEMORY (integration of WP and DP).

After a TEXT DOCUMENT is created, the words can be checked for spelling by SOFTWARE, which matches the words against a dictionary stored on DISK. If a word doesn't match, it is highlighted for USER discretion.

WP SOFTWARE prints the TEXT DOCUMENT according to FORMAT CODES specified by DEFAULTS in the SOFTWARE, and/or FORMAT CODES embedded within the TEXT DOCUMENT itself. These FORMAT CODES specify how the TEXT will print on paper (left and right margins, lines per inch, CHARACTERS per inch, etc.). FORMAT CODES also specify page numbering, page headings, underlines, boldface printing, centering, etc. Usually LETTER QUALITY PRINTERS are used in WORD PROCESSING which print fully-formed CHARACTERS, like a typewriter. These types of PRINTERS usually have PROPORTIONAL SPACING which will print an *I* in less space than a *W*, and also allow for a uniform distribution of CHARACTERS between fixed margins.

TEXT DOCUMENTS can be stored OFF-LINE on FLOPPY DISKS or removable HARD DISKS, or ON-LINE in the COMPUTER SYSTEM'S HARD DISK. WP can be performed in a stand-alone COMPUTER, in a MULTI-USER SYSTEM sharing one central CPU, or as WORKSTATIONS in a NETWORK environment.

Although WORD PROCESSING is a generic APPLICATION for every organization, there are many different features offered in each WP SYSTEM. Creative writers require flexible and easy-to-use TEXT EDITING capabilities, while businesses may require a math package which allows columns of numbers to be calculated within the TEXT DOCUMENT. Organizations may require elaborate INDEXING methods for storing and retrieving TEXT FILES. WORD PROCESSING is a very USER-intensive APPLICATION, and an effective ERGONOMIC design is important. See WORD PROCESSING ERGONOMICS.

WORD PROCESSING is one of the major components of OFFICE AUTOMATION and is often the first approach taken toward OFFICE AUTOMATION.

A significant advantage of ELECTRONIC TEXT creation is the ability to transmit a TEXT DOCUMENT to remote locations for printing, as for example, to a PAGE PRINTER or PHOTOTYPESETTER. Unless the PAGE PRINTER or the PHOTOTYPESETTER equipment comes from the same vendor as the WORD PROCESSING SOFTWARE, the FORMAT CODES will usually not be the same. FORMAT CODES in the TEXT DOCUMENT must be converted to the FORMAT CODES of the PAGE PRINTER or PHOTOTYPESETTER.

The same problem occurs when TEXT DOCUMENTS are transferred between different WORD PROCESSORS. The conversion can usually take place at either end; however, a thorough knowledge of FORMAT CODES is essential. Many SEARCH & REPLACE functions, as well as much manual keystroking, is often required.

Note: WORD PROCESSING FORMAT CODES are printing CODES. If two different WORD PROCESSORS run under OPERATING SYSTEMS from different vendors, then the FORMAT of the PHYSICAL TEXT FILE may require conversion, as well. SOFTWARE and BLACK BOXES can be used to perform the conversion.

word processing ergonomics

WORD PROCESSING USER INTERFACING; WORD PROCESSING is a very USER-intensive operation, often involving long hours at a VIDEO TERMINAL. The design of WORD PROCESSING HARDWARE and SOFTWARE differs widely between vendors.

A WORD PROCESSOR is a COMPUTER that is specialized for WORD PROCESSING. The KEYBOARD contains FUNCTION KEYS assigned to often-used EDITING functions, like insert and delete. PERSONAL COMPUTERS and TERMINALS connected to larger COMPUTERS may or may not have integrated WP FUNCTION KEYS to work with the WP SOFTWARE. Instead of moving the paper, as in a typewriter, the USER moves the CURSOR around on the SCREEN: to next line, to top of SCREEN, to next paragraph, etc. Without KEYBOARD integration, standard EDITING functions like CURSOR movement can be awkward, requiring multiple keystrokes which may not be easily mastered.

In addition, many KEYBOARDS are not standard typewriter KEYBOARDS. The shift and RETURN KEYS are not always in the same place as on a typewriter.

The USER most affected by standard key placement and FUNCTION KEYS is the person who performs many hours of EDITING at one session. For example, a writer may use the COMPUTER as a creative tool. The VIDEO SCREEN becomes a creative work space on which to generate and rearrange words and sentences. FUNCTION KEYS, conveniently placed, let the USER concentrate on the TEXT on the SCREEN, rather than the keys on the KEYBOARD. The non-typist, or the USER who is typing straight TEXT without EDITING, will be less affected by a KEYBOARD not designed for WORD PROCESSING.

Other ERGONOMIC considerations are non-glare SCREENS which can be tilted and swiveled to the USER'S most comfortable viewing position. SCREEN quality is important. Flicker-free, HIGH-RESOLUTION CHARACTER images are easier on the eyes, as is the appropriate use of multiple colors to give the viewer some relief from the monotony of a MONOCHROME SCREEN.

word processing machine

COMPUTER SPCIALIZED FOR WORD PROCESSING; See WORD PROCESSOR.

word processor

WORD PROCESSING HARDWARE AND/OR SOFTWARE; A WORD PROCESSOR may refer to a COMPUTER specialized for WORD PROCESSING, or to a WORD PROCESSING SOFTWARE PACKAGE. WORD PROCESSOR HARDWARE integrates WORD PROCESSING functions into the KEYBOARD FUNCTION KEYS. Functions like insert and delete are single keys which command the SOFTWARE to manipulate the TEXT.

Until the late 1970s, WORD PROCESSORS were dedicated strictly to WP. However, due to competition from MICROCOMPUTERS, which could do WORD PROCESSING and EXECUTE hundreds of other kinds of SOFTWARE PACKAGES, current WORD PROCESSORS usually offer additional SOFTWARE, too. Some WORD PROCESSORS have adopted standard OPERATING SYSTEMS so USERS have many products available to them, while others offer a PROGRAMMING LANGUAGE for customized APPLICATIONS.

WordStar

WORD PROCESSOR FOR MICROCOMPUTERS; WORDSTAR was one of the first full-function WORD PROCESSORS available for MICROCOMPUTERS (running under the CP/M OPERATING SYSTEM). Several MICROCOMPUTER vendors have integrated WORDSTAR functions into their KEYBOARDS. WORDSTAR is a product of MicroPro International Corporation.

word wrap

WORD PROCESSING FORMAT TECHNIQUE; As the USER enters TEXT on a WORD PROCESSOR, the SOFTWARE automatically wraps the words around to the next line when the right margin is exceeded. Unlike typewriter operation, the USER does not press the CARRIAGE RETURN key until the end of a paragraph is desired. WORD WRAP is a feature which usually can be turned off, since certain FILES created on WORD PROCESSORS do not require the WORD WRAP (such as SOURCE LANGUAGE statements and TEST DATA).

workstation

INTELLIGENT TERMINAL; WORKSTATIONS are TERMINALS with sufficient COMPUTER and PERIPHERAL resources to support a particular class of USER. PERIPHERAL devices like PRINTERS and DIGITIZER TABLETS may be included with the WORKSTATION. The term WORKSTATION is also used to refer to any variety of TERMINAL.

WP

ABBREVIATION FOR **W**ORD **P**ROCESSING OR **W**ORD **P**ROCESSOR.

write

RECORD INFORMATION IN A STORAGE DEVICE; Storing INFORMATION on a DISK or TAPE (recording), or into MEMORY, FIRMWARE or BUBBLE MEMORY is called WRITING.

write error

INFORMATION CANNOT BE WRITTEN INTO OR ONTO A STORAGE DEVICE; Dust, dirt, or damaged portions of the magnetic recording surface on DISK or TAPE, or malfunctioning ELECTRONIC components in MEMORY devices will cause the storage locations to be unusable. A WRITE ERROR occurs when attempting to store INFORMATION into or onto the damaged portions.

xon-xoff

COMMUNICATIONS PROTOCOL; XON-XOFF is a simple ASYNCHRONOUS PROTOCOL which keeps the receiving device in synchronization with the sending device. When the BUFFER in the receiving device is full, it sends an XOFF signal (transmit off) to the sending device, telling it to stop transmitting. When the receiving device is ready to accept more, it sends the sending device an XON signal (transmit on) to start again.

x-y matrix

TWO-DIMENSIONAL ARRAY OF ROWS AND COLUMNS; The x-axis defines the points on a horizontal row, and the y-axis defines the points on a vertical column. The X-Y MATRIX is used as a framework to define picture images and is the basis for the design of VIDEO SCREENS (both CHARACTER and GRAPHICS), DIGITIZER TABLETS, PLOTTERS, DOT MATRIX PRINTERS, etc. X-Y MATRICES are also used as references for ARRAYS of numerical elements for mathematical problems.

x-y plotter

GRAPHICS OUTPUT DEVICE; See PLOTTER.

X.21

INTERNATIONAL COMMUNICATIONS PROTOCOL; X.21 defines a CIRCUIT SWITCHING NETWORK.

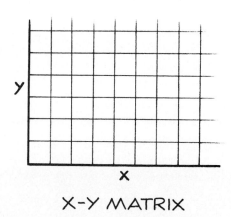

X-Y MATRIX

X.25

INTERNATIONAL COMMUNICATIONS PROTOCOL; X.25 defines a PACKET SWITCHING NETWORK.

Z80, Z8000

MICROPROCESSOR CHIPS DEVELOPED BY ZILOG; The Z80 is an 8-BIT
MICROPROCESSOR which is widely used in desktop, small business and PERSONAL
COMPUTERS. The Z80 was a successor to the Intel 8080 MICROPROCESSOR. The
CP/M OPERATING SYSTEM was originally written for the 8080 (Z80)
MICROPROCESSOR. The Z8000 is a 16-BIT MICROPROCESSOR.

1100 series

UNIVAC MAINFRAME SERIES.

1401

2ND-GENERATION IBM COMPUTER SYSTEM; The IBM 1401 was the most widely used 2nd-generation COMPUTER SYSTEM. Its MAIN MEMORY was CORE MEMORY (16K maximum), and TAPES were the primary storage medium (6 DRIVES maximum). Starting in the mid 1960s, the 1401 gave way to the 3rd-generation 360 series. The 360 contained a 1401 EMULATOR so that 1401 PROGRAMS would run on the new model. PUNCHED CARDS were also a major INPUT source for the 1401.

2780, 3780

IBM COMMUNICATIONS PROTOCOLS FOR BATCH TRANSMISSION.

3270

IBM COMMUNICATIONS PROTOCOL FOR INTERACTIVE TRANSMISSION.

360/370/3000/4300

IBM MAINFRAME FAMILY; IBM introduced the System/360 in 1964 which set a standard COMPUTER ARCHITECTURE and MACHINE LANGUAGE for years to come. The System/360 series was followed by the System/370 series, the 3000 series and the 4000 series. Although there were enhancements to each new series of PROCESSORS, SOFTWARE developed for older SYSTEMS is UPWARD COMPATIBLE to newer models. Switching from one series to another often necessitates PROGRAM changes in order to run under newer OPERATING SYSTEMS.

6502

MICROPROCESSOR CHIP DEVELOPED BY ROCKWELL INTERNATIONAL; The 6502 is an 8-BIT MICROPROCESSOR used in the APPLE II, Atari and Commodore PERSONAL COMPUTERS.

6800, 6801, 68000

MICROPROCESSOR CHIPS DEVELOPED BY MOTOROLA; The 6800 is an 8-BIT MICROPROCESSOR and the 6801 is a COMPUTER ON A CHIP. The 68000 is a 16-BIT MICROPROCESSOR.

7-track/9-track tape

7-BIT/9-BIT MAGNETIC TAPE CODING; The number of TRACKS on a MAGNETIC TAPE indicates the number of BITS recorded in a single CHARACTER column. The TRACKS are the number of rows that are recorded in parallel along the length of the TAPE. 7-TRACK TAPES record a 6-BIT CHARACTER plus PARITY BIT, and 9-TRACK TAPES record an 8-BIT CHARACTER (BYTE) plus PARITY. The physical width of the TAPE is the same.

8-bit/16-bit/32-bit computer

MEASUREMENT OF COMPUTER SIZE AND SPEED; This BIT designation refers to the COMPUTER'S WORD size, which is the number of BITS that are transferred internally at the same time and worked on as a unit. All things being equal, a 16-BIT COMPUTER can PROCESS twice as much INFORMATION in the same time as an 8-BIT COMPUTER. This designation is usually in 8-BIT increments, since a DATA CHARACTER is 8-BITS.

This BIT designation also relates to the amount of MEMORY the COMPUTER can easily work with (which is determined by the size of its ADDRESS REGISTERS). However, the number of BITS in the ADDRESS REGISTERS is usually higher than the number in the designation. For example, 8-BIT COMPUTERS have 16-BIT ADDRESS REGISTERS, 16-BIT COMPUTERS hold 20 or more BITS in their ADDRESS REGISTERS. Each additional BIT in the ADDRESS REGISTER doubles the amount of MEMORY that can be worked on.

MICROPROCESSORS may be designated 16/24 or 16/27 BIT machines (which specifies the WORD size/MEMORY size). Note: Speeds vary considerably within each category of COMPUTER, due to many architectural features.

8080, 8086, 8088

MICROPROCESSOR CHIPS DEVELOPED BY INTEL; The 8080 was one of the first popular 8-BIT COMPUTER CHIPS used. The 8086 and 8088 are compatible 16-BIT (internal) MICROPROCESSORS (the 8088 is used in the IBM PERSONAL COMPUTER). The 8086 uses a 16-BIT DATA BUS, the 8088 uses an 8-BIT DATA BUS.